To Gary,

with my thanks for your
support over the last few years,

Dominic

PICTURING THE CLOSET

DOMINIC JANES

PICTURING THE CLOSET

MALE SECRECY AND HOMOSEXUAL
VISIBILITY IN BRITAIN

OXFORD
UNIVERSITY PRESS

Oxford University Press is a department of the University of
Oxford. It furthers the University's objective of excellence in research,
scholarship, and education by publishing worldwide.

Oxford   New York
Auckland   Cape Town   Dar es Salaam   Hong Kong   Karachi
Kuala Lumpur   Madrid   Melbourne   Mexico City   Nairobi
New Delhi   Shanghai   Taipei   Toronto

With offices in
Argentina   Austria   Brazil   Chile   Czech Republic   France   Greece
Guatemala   Hungary   Italy   Japan   Poland   Portugal   Singapore
South Korea   Switzerland   Thailand   Turkey   Ukraine   Vietnam

Oxford is a registered trademark of Oxford University Press
in the UK and certain other countries.

Published in the United States of America by
Oxford University Press
198 Madison Avenue, New York, NY 10016

Library of Congress Cataloging-in-Publication Data
Janes, Dominic.
Picturing the closet : male secrecy and homosexual visibility in
Britain / Dominic Janes.
pages cm
Includes bibliographical references and index.
ISBN 978–0–19–020563–8
1. Homosexuality and art—Great Britain.   2. Closeted gays—Great
Britain.   3. Gay men in art.   4. Desire in art.   5. Gays in popular culture—
Great Britain.   I. Title.
N72.H64J36 2015
704′.0866420941—dc23
2014028622

1 3 5 7 9 8 6 4 2
Printed in the United States of America
on acid-free paper

CONTENTS

ACKNOWLEDGMENTS

WITH PARTICULAR THANKS to the following libraries, archives, and collections:

Ashmolean Museum, University of Oxford
Berkshire County Record Office, Reading
Birkbeck College Library, University of London
Bodleian Library, University of Oxford
British Board of Film Classification, London
British Film Institute Archive, London
British Library, London
British Museum, London
Cambridge University Library
Clifton College Archives
Dublin City Gallery, The Hugh Lane
John Rylands Library, University of Manchester
Lambeth Palace Library, London
Manchester Metropolitan University Library
National Archives, London
National Art Library, Victoria and Albert Museum, London
National Portrait Gallery, London
Norfolk County Record Office, Norwich
Rare Book and Manuscript Library, Columbia University
Repton School Archives

Sheffield City Council Archives
St. John's College Library, Cambridge
Tate Gallery, London
Tyne and Wear Archives and Museums
William Morris Gallery, London
Winchester College Archives

This book was completed during the tenure of a British Academy Mid-Career Fellowship.

I would like to thank the following individuals who either commented on a draft of this book or provided help or guidance on specific points: Sean Brady, Matt Cook, Julia Douthwaite, Charles Duff, John Dunkley, Charles Knighton, John Lotherington, Les Moran, Michael Pick, Kate Retford, Andrew Rudd, Sebastian Sandys, Paul Stevens, and Jonathan Wright.

My further thanks go to Maney Publishing for permission to include material previously published in "'Eternal Master': Masochism and the Sublime at the National Shrine of the Immaculate Conception, Washington, D.C," *Theology and Sexuality* 15.2 (2009), pp. 161–175 (www.maneyonline.com/tas and www.metapress.com/content/122845); to Oxford University Press for permission to include material from "Unnatural Appetites: Sodomitical Panic in Hogarth's *The Gate of Calais, or O the Roast Beef of Old England*" (1748), *Oxford Art Journal* 35.1 (2012), pp. 19–31; and to Manchester University Press for permission to include material from "Eminent Victorians, Bloomsbury Queerness and John Maynard Keynes' *The Economic Consequences of the Peace* (1919)," *Literature and History* 23.1 (2014), pp. 19–32.

PICTURING THE CLOSET

CHAPTER 1

INTRODUCTION

PICTURING THE CLOSET

THIS IS A book about the ways in which men in Britain have displayed or concealed their sexual tastes for other men since the eighteenth century. It is not a book about "homosexuals" as social or medical types, but rather about the actual or supposed appearances of such men. Because what has been held to be normal, everyday life has long been defined by its very difference from the supposedly strange and exotic lives of others, so being able to spot a queer came to be of great importance and became something of a national pastime. Widespread fear and hostility to the open expression of sexual deviance did not merely problematize the construction of self-identity but also made it harder to meet sympathetic friends and sexual partners. Therefore words and images had to be carefully considered and weighed for significance in order to differentiate a rude stare from the "hard looks" (i.e., cruising), identified by Thomas Newton, who acted as an *agent provocateur* in the 1726 raid on the "sodomites' den" known as Mother Clap's molly house.[1] The effect of describing sodomy as the "unspeakable" vice was to reinforce its place in the world of visual and material signs.[2] By considering the visual history of same-sex desire, I am seeking to further cultural understandings of a subject that has, until recently, most often been treated through historical studies of art made by gays and lesbians,

---

1. Norton (1992), p. 58. Compare Robb (2003), p. 143, on the "delicate art of ambiguous conversation."
2. For connections between legal and cultural unspeakability, see Corber (1990), Bartlett (1998), and Moran (2001a).

and their counterparts in earlier centuries.[3] My aim, indicated by the division of the book into three main sections, is not to provide a continuous narrative of historical events, but to introduce some of the key paradigms at work in the eighteenth, nineteenth, and twentieth centuries, respectively.

Bearing in mind that changes in the visual appearances of same-sex desire were shaped and accompanied by radically evolving terminology, it is difficult, sometimes, to write about terms such as "homosexuality" without immediately putting those words into quotation marks. The term homosexual is employed today to mean men who sexually desire other men. The word was first coined by the Swiss physician Karoly Benkert in 1869 and entered specialist medical usage in English, along with "heterosexual," after the translation in the 1890s of Richard von Krafft-Ebing's *Pyschopathia Sexualis* (first edition, 1886). The usual legal term in England was "sodomite." It is salutary to heed Jonathan Katz's warning, given in his book *The Invention of Heterosexuality* (1995), that people did not even generally think of themselves as being heterosexual before the mid-twentieth century, but labeled and conceptualized what was seen as sexual normality in other ways.[4] It is harder to be sure about the origins of the word "gay" as referring to sexual preferences, save that it appears to have originated in the United States toward the end of the nineteenth century and was in very limited circulation in metropolitan circles in Britain by the 1920s.[5] For these reasons, when studying much earlier periods than this, I have preferred to talk of sodomites and the presence of same-sex desire. There is no single definition of the word "queer" as used in the recent academic discourse that calls itself "queer theory," but I make particular use of this term in order to explore circumstances in which there is some form of overlap between the cultural politics of transgression and the construction of alternatives to normative sexual identities. My stance is to take up what might be termed a position of a qualified cultural constructionism: that same-sex desire is always present, but that its forms and related discourses, both textual and visual, change over time. So to what extent did people think they could identify an "obvious" sodomite before the construction of the homosexual as a type of person during the latter part of the nineteenth century? What role did secrecy and denial play in relation to the visual expression of same-sex desire before the term "the closet" came into widespread use in the latter part of the twentieth century? And what, therefore, did sodomites/homosexuals/gays/queers look like in 1700, 1800, 1900, and 2000? Could they be spotted

3. For instance, compare Cooper (1986), with Saslow (1999), C. Reed (2011), and Lord and Meyer (2013).
4. Before this time, for instance, heterosexuality was sometimes employed to refer to a medical diagnosis of excessive desire for the opposite sex; see Katz (1995), p. 83.
5. Durden (2004).

mincing down the street? Or were such as these just the flamboyant few whose presence conveniently drew attention away from the many others who wanted to appear "normal"?

These issues are not peripheral to the struggle of the last several decades for individual self-determination and self-expression. It was this set of cultural constructions that the pioneering writer Eve Kosofsky Sedgwick (1950–2009) attacked in her book *Epistemology of the Closet* (1990) as representing "the defining structure for gay oppression in this century."[6] As the preface to the second edition of 2008 made clear, Sedgwick was not merely exploring the category of the homosexual *as* a homophobic creation but was doing so at a time when the experience of AIDS had led to a massive political backlash against gay liberation in the United States and around the world.[7] Something that was particularly dangerous about the closet at this time was that its operations could be held to imply that only a small proportion of the population possessed problematic forms of sexual desire.[8] This was a discipline of power that made the pre-modern Christian's fear of the sodomite seem open-minded in comparison, since the sin of the biblical city of Sodom was understood to stand, albeit at the far extremity, in a spectrum of human failings that affected everyone. But whereas the sodomite was understood to be different in moral degree from the ordinary sinner, the homosexual was constructed by doctors and sexologists as being different in kind.[9] Both the sodomite and the homosexual were thought to be aberrant, but it was the supposed intrinsic difference of the latter from heterosexual norms that then furthered the search for characteristic patterns of appearance. Moreover, it was this growing obsession with identifying sexual deviance as visible that led to an accompanying preoccupation with attempts at concealment. Whereas the sin of Sodom would, it was believed, be seen by God, there was no such security that the mark of the homosexual would always be correctly identified by human functionaries. A distinctive "homosexual panic" could then arise not simply from being revealed as a homosexual but, rather, from the very fact of being identified as such, however mistakenly, or even by being the "innocent" object of a homosexual's desires.[10] Yet at the same time, the search for visible markers of same-sex desire gave opportunities—perilous ones though they might be—for people to express their own sexual interests and to claim a new identity.

6. Sedgwick (2008), p. 71.
7. Sedgwick (2008), p. xiv.
8. Sedgwick (2008), p. 246.
9. Sedgwick (2008), p. 184.
10. Sedgwick (2008), p. 186. The term "homosexual panic" was first coined by the psychiatrist Edward J. Kempf in 1920; both it, and the importance of Sedgwick's use of it, are discussed in Chapter 2 of this current book.

In geographic terms, much of the subject matter of this book derives from London and the surrounding areas of southern England. However, I most often use "Britain" to refer to the national context for this study because of that term's predominance in identity discourse from the eighteenth to the twentieth centuries.[11] Although my study is, therefore, concerned with British culture, it is inspired by Sedgwick's work, which explored the literary cultures of Britain, France, and the United States.[12] It is important, therefore, for me to sketch in some elements of contextual background in order to explain her use of certain French depictions as exemplary of the epistemologies of the closet. These, however, were dependent on visual codes that were established in the wake of the trials of Oscar Wilde (1854–1900) in 1895. In the Musée d'Orsay in Paris there hangs a portrait of Marcel Proust (1871–1922) painted in 1892 by Jacques-Émile Blanche (1861–1942) when his subject was twenty-one (Figure 1.1).[13] The description on the Museum's website observes that

Figure 1.1 Jacques-Émile Blanche, *Marcel Proust* (1892), oil on canvas, 73.5 x 60.5 cm, Musée d'Orsay, Paris (RF 1989 4). © RMN-Grand Palais (Musée d'Orsay)/Hervé Lewandowski.

11. On which, see, for example, Colley (1992).
12. On which, see also D. Robinson (2006).
13. A useful summary of Blanche's life and work is available at Tate Gallery, London: http://www.tate.org.uk/art/artists/jacques-emile-blanche-765/text-artist-biography, accessed November 20, 2012.

the young dandy is presented in a front view, in a hieratic pose (the painting was probably originally a full-length portrait). . . . The sharp outlines, the fluid paint, and the delicate strokes bring out a sense of inner feelings. Young Proust with his great dark eyes and sensual mouth is already a little more than a dandy: the perfect oval of his face and the pallor of his complexion give him a grave almost Christ-like look. That probably explains why this portrait has remained the best-known and most accurate representation of the man who was not yet the author of *Remembrance of Things Past*. Proust kept this painting until he died in 1922.[14]

This, then, is a "dandy," a young man who cares deeply about his own fashionable appearance. He is presented full-square, his skin tones almost as pale and bleached as his immaculate shirtfront, his expression as gentle and still as that of a statue of Christ, or perhaps of a mask.[15]

In the fourth volume of his life's great literary work (published in English in two parts as *Cities of the Plain* and *Sodom and Gomorrah*), Proust wrote of the vice of Sodom "flaunting itself, insolent and immune, where its existence is never guessed; numbering its adherents everywhere, among the people, in the army, in the church, in prison, on the throne . . . speaking of the vice as of something alien to it."[16] Sedgwick drew attention to this remarkable statement and argued that it had the effect of highlighting the spectacle of the obviously deviant Baron de Charlus.[17] Thus she identified the early-twentieth-century construction of what she termed "the spectacle of the closet as the truth of the homosexual."[18] The Baron was intended to be seen as a homosexual in the closet, "concealed, with riveting inefficiency, in its supposed interior."[19] This had the effect—notably for those who failed to attend to Proust's comment—of all the more effectively constructing the closet of those who were less obvious than de Charlus.

As this suggests, the spectacle of the open sexual secret was one of great utility to a discreet man of letters. The character of the Baron, for instance, "proved the ideal vehicle for opinions [and interests] the author wanted to express, but for which he did not want to assume responsibility."[20] For instance, just as de Charlus is shown by Proust as following the progress of the Eulenberg affair in Germany from

14. Musée d'Orsay: http://www.musee-orsay.fr, accessed November 12, 2012.
15. For connections between the figure of the dandy, Christianity, and same-sex desire, see J. Adams (1995), on "dandies and desert saints" and Janes (2015), on "queer martyrdom."
16. Proust quoted and discussed in Sedgwick (2008), p. 218.
17. Sedgwick (2008), p. 223.
18. Sedgwick (2008), p. 231; see also Eribon (2004), p. 186.
19. Sedgwick (2008), p. 231.
20. Schmid (1999), p. 974, and see also the interesting study, Michael Lucey, *Never Say I: Sexuality and the First Person in Colette, Gide and Proust* (2006).

Figure 1.2 James McNeill Whistler, *Arrangement in Black and Gold: Comte Robert de Montesquiou-Fezensac* (1891–1892), oil on canvas, 208.6 x 91.8 cm. © The Frick Collection, New York (1914.1.131).

1907 to 1909 that had threatened to implicate the top ranks of German society in homosexual scandal, so, in real life, had Proust.[21] The Baron was also based upon one or more of the writer's close friends. At one point Proust claimed that his inspiration had come from the late Baron Doazan, but it is believed that the primary inspiration was Count Robert de Montesquiou-Fezensac (1855–1921), whom Proust had known since 1893.[22] Close acquaintance with the Count, therefore, may have helped the writer in his transition from a pale imitator of Christ to the documenter of the sins of the modern cities of the plains.

In 1894 James Abbott McNeill Whistler (1834–1903) exhibited his *Arrangement in Black and Gold* (1891–1892) (Figure 1.2). This portrait of the Count was greeted by what the Frick Collection in New York, where the painting now hangs, has described as a "flood of critical reviews, mostly enthusiastic."[23] The work's contemporary significance is such that in 1995–1996 the Frick held an exhibition, *Whistler and Montesquiou: The Butterfly and the Bat*, devoted to this picture and its context. Jonathan Shirland has recently drawn attention to the issue of the spectral in Whistler's "black portraits" of which this is an example. The figures in these portraits possess, or perhaps are possessed by, what he calls a "marginal materiality" in that they appear only partially to emerge out of the surrounding darkness.[24] This may even suggest a touch of the "queer spectrality" identified by Carla Freccero as having visited the *fin de siècle* with gothic suspense.[25] The tonal range in Whistler's painting of de Montesquiou is, of course, essentially the same as that of Blanche's portrait of Proust, and it may be that the resulting creation of mystery was intended to suggest that the subject was merely, in some very general sense, possessed of a tantalizing and fascinating inner life.[26] Bearing in mind that Whistler bestowed this quality on a range of subjects, rather than discovering it in his treatment of de Montesquiou in particular, we might also recall the assertion of the painter Basil Hallward in Oscar

21. Sedgwick (2008), p. 244. On homosexual visibility and the Eulenberg affair, see Steakley (1983) and Bruns (2011).
22. Munhall (1995), p. 53.
23. The Frick Collection: http://collections.frick.org, accessed November 20, 2012.
24. Shirland (2011), pp. 98–99; compare Fletcher (2000) for a literary analysis of "queer spectrality" in the works of Henry James.
25. Freccero (2006), pp. 69–104.
26. Stephenson (2007), p. 99.

Wilde's novel *The Picture of Dorian Gray* (1890–1891), that "every portrait that is painted with feeling is a portrait of the artist, not of the sitter."[27] So all one needs to conclude is that Whistler liked to self-dramatize, which is hardly news.

However, if Whistler's work at this time suggests that a quality of visual ambiguity was in fashion in certain circles in London and Paris in the first half of the 1890s, then the next major portrait of de Montesquiou with which it may be compared emphasizes surfaces and material presence. Stephen Grundle has commented that the work of 1897 by the popular society portraitist Giovanni Boldini (1842–1931) "captures perfectly the precision and vanity of a leading *poseur*. More individual than most of the female portraits, it conveys the effete panache of a man whose self-obsession was notorious. With his white gloves and cane, his perfectly tailored moss-green morning suit, black cravate [*sic*] and coiffured hair, Boldini's de Montesquiou appears almost like a woman in drag." Gender deviance here has been brought forward into an image that relies on "an excess of surface effects to convey style and vanity" (Figure 1.3).[28] De Montesquiou was delighted by the result, which is much closer to the satirical representations of the cartoonist "Sem" (Georges Goursat) than it is to the portrait by Whistler. To Goursat, and to a significant proportion of the public, the significance of the Count was as a source of amusing spectacle (Figure 1.4). In Sem's representations the Count's body twists in an exaggeration of the pose given him by Boldini into attitudes of camp affectation. He was also frequently depicted by Goursat in the close company of his secretary, companion, and—since we know we are in the age of the spectacle of the closet—his presumed lover, Gabriel de Yturri.[29] It was thus that Sedgwick focused, as her key example of closet spectacle in Proust, on what she calls the famous moment "when the narrator, from his place of concealment, witnessed a sudden secret eye-lock between Charlus and Jupien in the

Figure 1.3 Giovanni Boldini, *Count Robert de Montesquiou* (1897), oil on canvas, 116 x 82.5 cm, Musée d'Orsay, Paris (RF 1977 56). © RMN-Grand Palais (Musée d'Orsay)/Hervé Lewandowski.

27. Wilde (2003), p. 9; this text is of the 1891 edition. Robert de Montesquiou is also suggested to have been a model for the character of Jean des Esseintes in the novel *A Rebours* (*Against Nature*) which was first published in 1894 and was admired by Whistler, Wilde, and Dorian Gray; see Huysmans (1998), p. xvii.
28. Grundle (1999), p. 291.
29. Munhall (1995), p. 40.

Figure 1.4 Georges Goursat, *Robert de Montesquiou Delivering a Lecture* (undated), print, 34.3 x 51.4 cm. © The Frick Collection, New York (1993.12.16).

courtyard." The two then line up into a series of poses so that the reader knows of the similarity and physical connections: "[Jupien] had—in perfect symmetry with the Baron—thrown back his head, giving a becoming tilt to his body, placed his hand with grotesque effrontery on his hip, stuck out his behind, struck poses with the coquetry that the orchid might have adopted on the providential arrival of the bee."[30]

In an article of 1901, the Count expressed the view that the art of the portrait lay in blending the personalities of the painter and of the model—and that the greatest works of genius showed both the true character of the subject and the opinion of the artist.[31] After the trials of Oscar Wilde in 1895, it might have been thought that the affected pose would have gone out of style—but quite the contrary. The fame of Wilde's posing appears to have reinforced such behavior as representing the fascinating spectacle of the closet; and it did so, not in the sense that it enabled others to read the degree to which de Montesquiou was, or was not, in denial about his own sexual tastes, but as the increasingly important repository for signs of sexual deviance. This did not mean that the open avowal of such deviance could be tolerated, but

30. Note the white orchid in Proust's buttonhole in Figure 1.1. See Proust, quoted and discussed in Sedgwick (2008), p. 228.
31. Bertrand (1996), 1, p. 398.

its elaborate and obvious concealment could be, because it enabled the average person to seem normal and unremarkable. Wilde's mistake was not to pose, or to think that he was fooling people with his posing, but to think that he could justify such behavior in a court of law that would, however reluctantly and by its very nature, force the parties concerned to confront the truth in *words*.[32] The role of the visual spectacle of the closet was, by contrast, that it allowed for great subtlety in the degree to which sexual truths could appear to be perceived.

But de Montsquiou/de Charlus was now, in a sense, trapped. In order to establish his deviant subjectivity, he had to perform himself in the expected manner and appreciate that his performance would be greeted with a peculiar mixture of hatred and delight. It is this spectacle that Allan Hollinghurst evoked in his novel *The Swimming Pool Library* (1988) by recounting a screening of an imaginary film clip of the "precious" British author Ronald Firbank (1886–1926). To William Beckwith, the central protagonist of the novel, Firbank appears to be a "bona fide queen." The dead writer is conjured into motion, jostled by children in an Italian street, yet

> as they mobbed him they seemed somehow to be celebrating him. He became perhaps for a moment, what he must have always wanted to be, an entertainer. The children's expressions showed that profoundly true, unthinking mixture of cruelty and affection. There was fear in their mockery, yet the figure at the heart of their charivi took on the likeness not only of a clown, but of a patron saint.[33]

At the time when the film is shot, Firbank is dying of tuberculosis. His performance is thus even more contingent than it might at first appear to be since the path he has to follow in order to be acceptable as spectacle depends on his death. It is only as a scapegoat, the bearer out of normal society of the supposed sins of sexual perversion, that the homosexual was allowed to be seen by the public.[34] The spectacle of the closet, therefore, required an impossible figure—one that failed to cast a shadow, in which a sparkling but dead parody of life and love was to be played out over and over again. The secret of power behind this, the real disciplinary force of the spectacle of the closet, lay precisely in the realization that this production was a fake and that the alternative to putting up in private was to be sacrificed in public.

32. On same-sex desire as "unspeakable" in the nineteenth century, see Corber (1990) and Cocks (2006a).
33. Hollinghurst (1988), pp. 185 and 186–187. This scene appears to be inspired by the death of Sebastian, a homosexual, whom we see fatally mobbed by children in the film version of Tennessee Williams's play *Suddenly, Last Summer*, dir. Joseph Mankiewicz (1959), on which see Ohi (1999).
34. Scapegoating is considered in detail in Chapter 5 of the current book.

However, certain forms of self-conscious camp could facilitate the reclamation of such abject spectacles in projects of queer self-empowerment.[35] It was in this manner that the performances of Quentin Crisp (1908–1999) horrified or amused habitués of central London for decades before the TV film of his autobiography, *The Naked Civil Servant* (1968), made him, for better or worse, the face of the English homosexual in 1975.[36] Andy Medhurst recalled in his article "One Queen and his Screen" (2009) the experience, as a sixteen-year-old, of seeing the program one evening when his parents just happened to be out of the house:

> Dazed by this ridiculous stroke of luck, and conscious that they might return at any minute, I sat about six inches from the screen with one finger on the "off" button, drinking in every second as if my life depended on it . . . its celebration of Quentin Crisp's unrepentant queenliness filled me with an elated, vertiginous sense of identification, belonging and defiant pride . . . I had seen the future—and it minced.[37]

It had taken the scriptwriter, Philip Mackie, three years of hard advocacy, backed up by the director Jack Gold and the actor John Hurt, to get anyone interested in the project, before it was finally produced by Thames Television. The result saw Hurt acclaimed as best actor at the British Academy Awards, while Gold was given a Desmond Davis award for contributions to television. From having long occupied an abject position in society, Crisp and his style of transgression were recuperated as a source of popular entertainment that fitted the culturally liberalizing sensibilities of the times.[38] Moreover, so overt was his camp that his presence might have reassured the masses that if *that* was a homosexual, then there must be very few of them. He might, thus, have been filed under the same heading of "drag" that was served up to delighted—and unthreatened—audiences by Danny La Rue (as by Liberace in the US). In other words, Crisp might, at first glance, be understood to be acting out a spectacle for straights that could be read as evidence of inner shame. However, he never presented himself as an un-ironic spectacle of artificial glamour.[39] He did write of his being "disfigured" by being effeminate, but rather than trying in vain to hide this, he became not just self-confessed but "self-evident." His new guise of spectacular effeminacy was his "uniform."[40] His example should remind us that lives of queer spectacle provided room for a range

---

35. For introductions to camp, see Bergman (1993) and Cleto (1999).
36. Crisp (1977), p. 61.
37. Medhurst (2009), p. 82. On Crisp in general, see also N. Kelly (2011).
38. Hotz-Davis (2010), p. 179.
39. Berrett (2000).
40. Crisp (1977), p. 7.

Figure 1.5 Mr. Crisp is politely requested to leave a queer club. *The Naked Civil Servant,* dir. Jack Gould (1975).

of creative self-expression. Thus what appeared on screen in the TV film of 1975 was not the spectacle of a closet that contained a simple homosexual "truth" because it revealed that he was outstanding for *not* feeling secret shame—as, for instance, in a scene where he is required to leave a queer drinking club because he is not dressed like a "normal" man (Figure 1.5).

Quentin Crisp did not, therefore, fit the model of the disempowered effeminate that the phobic model of the spectacle of the closet was designed to produce. His defiant and deliberate stance gave him the pleasure of self-expression but also laid him open to verbal and physical attack. Yet his attitudes also did not fit with gay liberation stances of claiming the right to happiness but were evocative of an ascetic project of forming the self through a rigorous practice of self-discipline. This appears to have been much more important to him than sex, as his comment on cruising in the dark at movie houses during World War II suggests: "I had always shunned these homosexual playgrounds; less from purity than vanity. I did not want a liaison in conditions which might tend to obliterate my individuality."[41] Sexual liberation did not, to him, go to the essence of individual freedom. He was most certainly visible in the sense of unabashedly giving off the signs expected of the sexual pervert, but was that the same thing as being "out" in terms of positive self-identity?[42] And it what sense was he "out of the closet," if

41. Crisp (1977), p. 156.
42. Armstrong (2012), p. 52, accepts the notion that Crisp was never in the closet. See also Armstrong (2011) and Bendall (2008).

what he was claiming was the right to be of effeminate appearance, as opposed to the right to have sex with men? I have focused on the complex phenomenon that was Quentin Crisp in order to emphasize that the boundaries of the closet and its attendant spectacle were never fixed but represented zones of contestation between societal, institutional, and individual imperatives. There were, potentially, as many forms of sexual secret and closeted life as there were varieties of personal identity and desire.[43] The current study acknowledges that important fact by focusing on the major issues that have shaped the evolution not only of the homosexual closet, but of its various precursors since the eighteenth century, as sites not just of oppression but also, at times, of creative opportunity. The result was less the creation of a single entity that can be called "the closet" but of a set of variations within a theme, and this is why I wish to avoid attempting to giving the word, and phenomenon, a single and precise definition.

Sedgwick was a literary scholar, and by focusing her discussion on Melville, James, Nietzsche, Proust, and Wilde, she located the creation of the closet in the literary, high culture of the *fin de siècle*. The purpose of my current book is to explore some of the ways in which it is possible to write a more extensive, and visual, history of the closet and of its spectacle. In order to do justice to the complexity of this phenomenon, I have explored a range of approaches and sets of source material through the medium of case studies in the history of art (as in the chapter on Hogarth), in the history of ideas (as in the chapter on Burke), in social and cultural history (as in the chapter on expulsions from public schools), and so forth. I chose this approach in order to make clear the possibility of engagement with the closet from a wide range of disciplinary perspectives. It has been my aim to attempt a balance between the appreciation of cultural phenomena as chronologically and spatially located, as well as being comprehensible within a broader sweep of cultural history rooted in the concept of the *longue durée* (i.e., that some ideas and cultural forms persist, with variations of course, over long periods of time). But all of these chapters and approaches return to the opposition between states of invisibility and of being conspicuous, and the subtle median positions between these two extremes. They thus develop the interrogation of the notion of the "open secret" whose focus as a textual problem in the works of D. A. Miller directly inspired Eve Sedgwick's work.[44]

In this introduction I now wish, first, to ask whether the homosexual closet had a predecessor—some sort, perhaps, of sodomitical closet—attended with its own form of sodomitical panic. Second, I want to explore the issue of the closet and its visibility not merely as a visual

43. Note the revealing comment of Lord (2013), p. 29, on Susan Sontag's reluctance to clarify her sexual identity, that she "never found a closet that suited her."
44. D. Miller (1985) and (1988), pp. 192–220.

metaphor within textual culture, but also as an aspect of visual culture, and of cultural history in general. Third, I wish to raise the issue of the significance of the date of Sedgwick's own work. Not only was she writing in the context of AIDS, as I have already noted, but she was doing so in order to make a self-conscious contribution to the progress of gay liberation that had, arguably, only made substantial progress in the United States since the Stonewall riots of 1969. Open reference to the closet as a place of a homosexual secret, and the visual metaphor of "coming out" of the closet, only came into use in the 1950s. Should we then talk with impunity of the cultural construction of the homosexual closet for periods before there was such a usage of the word "closet"? This is a matter of particular importance in relation to Sedgwick because she followed the interpretation popularized by the social theorist and philosopher Michel Foucault (1926–1984) that homosexuality was formed out of discourse and that there were no homosexuals before the coining of the term. Finally, the question remains of the effect on the closet of gay liberation. If, as some critics have argued, we are now emerging into a post-gay or even a post-queer world, then will the history of the closet come to an end? The chapters of this book present a series of examples. I do not pretend to be able to address all of these matters in detail, but I do aim to begin to sketch out what exploration of these diverse terrains might begin to reveal.

Since the first edition of Sedgwick's study, and often inspired by it, writers from a range of disciplines have begun to elaborate and explore a history of the closet that begins in the early modern period and continues to the present day.[45] The closet, a room purposely designed for discussion of secret matters, appeared in houses during the sixteenth century. Along with it, there developed the office of the "secretary," a man whose job it was to look after the private papers of the head of the household. Alan Stewart, notably in a chapter on the "epistemologies of the early modern closet" in *Close Readers: Humanism and Sodomy in Early Modern England* (1997), has discovered homoerotic effects in the closet related to the fact that this was the one area of aristocratic life where men were expected to meet to review intimate secrets, away from the rest of the household: "I suggest that the closet is not designed to function as a place of individual withdrawal, but as a secret non-public transactive space between two men behind a locked door."[46]

Yet when Allen Frantzen surveyed attitudes toward same-sex acts in Anglo-Saxon England, he concluded that the early Middle Ages must be considered to be "before the closet," not simply because the word was not in use, but also because he considered that to be an age before the development of modern identity politics.[47] There is, however, no

45. Girouard (1980), p. 56.
46. Stewart (1995), p. 171, and (1997).
47. Frantzen (1998), pp. 3–4.

universally agreed date at which same-sex desire first established patterns that were comparable to those of the present day. While there are those who seek to tie identities to the prevalence of particular terms such as "sodomite" or "homosexual," one of the most influential positions on this subject has been set out by Randolph Trumbach. Thus, in *A Gay History of Britain* (2007), edited by Matt Cook, Trumbach provides separate chapters for "Renaissance Sodomy, 1500–1700" and "Modern Sodomy: The Origins of Homosexuality, 1700–1800."[48] He sees the former as focused on forms of pederastic desire that were not then seen as necessarily incompatible with normative manhood. Yet this assertion has itself been challenged, for instance by Joseph Cody, who has argued for the existence of a category of "masculine love" between adult men in the Renaissance that witnesses what he terms a "definite awareness and language for a distinct homosexuality."[49]

However, recent scholarship has developed an increasingly nuanced understanding of some of the ways in which forms of pederastic desire could have operated as norms within, for instance, early modern aristocratic society. Notably, Thomas King has developed a sophisticated reading of seventeenth- and eighteenth-century male sexual politics in which a social model of younger men courting richer and older men and women for promotion is replaced by a new ideal of the autonomous male participant in public life whose status depends not upon his superior social connections but on the maintenance of his own patriarchal household.[50] Those who, in the course of the eighteenth century, appeared to maintain outdated modes of slavish adulation of male superiors could be condemned not just for personal dependency but for effeminacy. The multiplication of types of effeminate characters on the stage, such as mollies, fops, and fribbles, points to a growing social stereotyping of gender deviance.[51] Not only that, but these phobic creations can be seen as participating in the origins of an attempt emphatically to separate male friendships from erotic desire. Thus Hutson commented on the revival in 1749 by the famous actor manager David Garrick of Ben Jonson's *Every Man in His Humour* (1598) that "in Garrick's hands, the process Jonson had begun—the process of predicating the entitlements of intimate male friendships on their very mastery of tacitly understood, unexpressed homoeroticism—was taken to that extreme of complete disavowal, the consequences of which have been analysed by Sedgwick in *Epistemology of the Closet*."[52]

This current book begins in the eighteenth century, therefore, because it was then that the image of the flamboyant, effeminate man

48. Trumbach (2007b).
49. Cady (1992), p. 12.
50. King (2008), pp. xix–xxii, provides an overview of this.
51. King (2008), p. 11.
52. Hutson (2004), p. 1086.

first became established as a lightning rod for the deflection of sodomitical suspicion from the body of the normative, self-disciplined male.[53] At the same time, rakishness was decreasingly viewed as admirable since idealized manliness had begun to incorporate an enhanced element of self-discipline.[54] This meant that the suppression of masculine desires became part of what it was to be truly manly. Religious reformers played a considerable role in campaigns for a more subdued and compassionate form of manhood. The connection between the closet where one went to pray in solitude as a place of secrets, including sexual secrets, and of that as the location of the truths of the self emerged in the course of the seventeenth century, as charted by Richard Rambuss in *Closet Devotions* (1998). He points out that Protestant devotional poetry was often strongly erotic. In his chapter on "Christ's Ganymede"—that is, on the believer who dreams of being swept up by Christ, much as Jupiter supposedly had literally swept the boy Ganymede off his feet— Rambuss "traces some of the circuits of male desire, vectored to and through Christ's body, that continue to magnetize the Christian prayer closet with a homoerotic penumbra."[55] In other words, the encounter between man and deity was potentially homoerotic because man, being made in the image of God, was encountering a greater reflection of himself. Rambuss argues that it was the Protestant Reformation—with its emphasis on intimate and unmediated connection between God and man—that reinforced the need for a devotional closet as a conceptual space for personal contact with God.[56]

Gary Fergusson, in *Queer (Re)readings in the French Renaissance* (2008), pointed out that a similar shift to private and interiorized, as opposed to public and socially mediated, confession of sins happened in Roman Catholic countries in the early modern period, but here the relations were based on the questioning of sins by a priest rather than their admission, privately, to God.[57] This, famously, was posited by Foucault as the origin of sexual subjectivity through inscription into discourse and was intended to be one of the central themes of the projected fourth volume of his *History of Sexuality*, provisionally titled *The Confessions of the Flesh*. Moreover, it is important to note that Foucault intended this as an analysis of early Christianity, a putative focus that has attracted some degree of criticism from those who advocate the adoption of detailed historical contextualization.[58] A particular problem with the confessional

---

53. As discussed in Trumbach (2012), pp. 540–541.
54. M. Cohen (2005), p. 313.
55. Rambuss (1998), p. 13.
56. Rambuss (1998), p. 123.
57. Fergusson (2008), pp. 294–298 and 332–324; Baughman (1967) and Tambling (1990), pp. 88–102, on "Protestant confession," but also pp. 103–133 on "romantic confession."
58. Clark (1988), p. 621. This article concludes that "the Christian desert city of late antiquity shares slightly more with ancient Athens, but slightly less with

model of the origins of sexology is that it fails to connect with the diversity of confessional traditions among Protestant and Roman Catholic countries. The cultural historian Sean Brady, in particular, has recently directed some particularly strong criticism toward the application in Britain of models based upon the influence of German sexology since this was, in his view, little known in the United Kingdom before the mid-twentieth century.[59]

It is not the business of the current book to interrogate the connections between the confessional and sexology, but it is pertinent to observe that it is the Protestant distinction between private truths confided only to God and public effects displayed to the community that bears some plausible connection to the two states of the closet (as a state of subjective secrecy and as the spectacle of the closet), that are reliant on the public scrutiny of appearances. The metaphor of coming out bears no clear resemblance to Roman Catholic/sexological/psychoanalytical modes of institutional inscription of the self, since one does not come *out* to confess in this tradition, but rather goes *in* in order to do so. It was only in the Protestant tradition that one might come out from the closet to admit secrets to the household or congregation. There was, moreover, a specifically Protestant and, indeed, anti-Catholic use of the term from the Reformation, which was derived from Revelation 18.4 (King James version): "And I heard another voice from heaven, saying, Come out of her, my people, that ye be not partakers of her sins, and that ye receive not of her plagues." Babylon was identified by Protestants with Rome. Thus Peter Lake, in his article on "The Significance of the Elizabethan Identification of the Pope as Antichrist" (1980), has described how, writing in 1588–1589, a group of London puritan ministers argued that "as the first absolute kingdom to 'come out of Babylon,' England should take the lead against Rome."[60] The theme of coming out from a state of sin repeatedly surfaced in Protestant discourse. It played a vital role, for instance, in Charles Fitch's sermon, *Come Out of Her my People* (1843), which was one of the founding tracts of the Seventh-day Adventists and which condemned as inhabitants of Babylon all Protestants who did not attend to the Second Coming of Christ as being imminent.

A detailed examination of the emergence of the term "to come out the closet" has yet to be written. A camp allusion to coming out of a state of secret sin seems likely to have been combined with a reference to a young girl's coming out into society. This was identified in

fin de siècle Vienna, than Foucault himself imagined," p. 637. On Foucault and religion, see Foucault (1999) and Bernauer and Carrette (2004).

59. Brady (2005), p. 18, is criticizing Foucault, not Sedgwick; however, it is important to note that those researchers whose methods are rooted in social history (and, possibly, have class-based approaches) may not approve of reading everyday sexual behavior from the canons of "high" art or literature; note the comments of T. Edwards (1998), p. 476.

60. Lake (1980), p. 164, n. 15.

the pioneering research of Evelyn Hooker, which began with a grant in 1953 from the (American) National Institute of Mental Health.[61] Speaking as an anthropologist might once have done of a "newly discovered" tribe, she was nevertheless exceptional at this time in recognizing that "every deviant group has a special culture, with its own norms, standards, mythology and goals." She noted in 1956 that "we know little" about the homosexual group "except from impressionistic accounts by a few of its members. . . . Several years ago I asked a sociologist to give me some help in locating sociological material on male homosexuality. His reply was that there was none and that any sociologist who dared to try to obtain it would be suspect."[62] She introduced the term "come out" to an academic audience, noting that this was about the process by which a person came to identify himself as homosexual and acted so as to join a group of his peers. Such a person might be "described as being the debutante at a ball," but such a process may have been precipitated in all manner of far from glamorous ways, for example as a result of having being thrown into the "'queer' tank" in a gaol. Hooker observed that "whatever its variation, there is a mixture, for most, of disgust, shame, hatred, with pleasure and relief in finding that one is not alone."[63] Coming out was, therefore, in the first place an act of witness before the homosexual community, and it was only with the advent of gay liberation in the 1970s that it was re-inscribed as an act of avowal aimed at a straight audience.[64]

The term "to come out" was thus employed by members of the gay liberation movement of the early 1970s to indicate an instrumental act of the erasure of shame. A prominent example of this is Laud Humphreys, *Out of the Closets: The Sociology of Homosexual Liberation* (1972), which quickly (on page 5) establishes the Stonewall riots of June 27–28, 1969, as a foundational act of coming out of private rooms as closets onto the public streets. The association of being "in" with oppression became a central tenet of gay faith and formed the basis of such studies of social progress as Steven Seidman's *Beyond the Closet: The Transformation of Gay and Lesbian Life* (2002), in which it is argued that the closet is "about social oppression"; those in the closet conceal "who they are from those who matter most"; and although some "manage somewhat satisfying work and intimate lives, even under strained circumstances," the closet is a place of "systematic harm" enforced by *"heterosexual domination"* [original emphasis].[65]

In essence, I think this is correct, but I do think it is notable that the situation is depicted with such intense emphasis as a state of error

61. Hooker (1993).
62. Hooker (1956), p. 220.
63. Hooker (1956), p. 221.
64. Chauncey (1994), p. 8.
65. Seidman (2002), pp. 30–31.

versus truth, of oppression versus liberation, of, shall we say, and *just to be Devil's advocate*, Babylon versus Jerusalem. There has been a strand in gay liberation thinking that has been strongly hostile to male displays of femininity. Insofar as the spectacle of the closet was structured around what was held to be "effeminate" display, it is possible to say that a degree of misogyny may be contained in positions of hostility to the likes of Robert de Montesquiou as bearers of the projected shame of all those in the closet. Moreover, if we are to follow an instrumental view of the power of language, then Seidman, like Sedgwick, was also not simply commenting on but also contributing to the construction of the closet, at least the closet of the time at which he was writing, as a place of oppression. It is possible to imagine other narratives, such as one in which the closet was a device that enabled many people to develop their sexual lives in private, in a process that Jeffrey Weeks has referred to as "comfortable 'ghettoization.' "[66] This was, after all, one of the key purposes of the Sexual Offences Act (1967), which specifically decriminalized same-sex acts taking place between two men aged over twenty-one in private in England and Wales. As Stephen Jeffery-Poulter has written with heavy irony in *Peers, Queers and Commons: The Struggle for Gay Law Reform* (1991), "although this sinful and distasteful behaviour [i.e., homosexuality] was to be permitted in the sphere of private relations, it was essential to ensure that it was entirely banished from the public area once and for all."[67] By the 1960s, the spectacle of the closet appears to have become decreasingly effective as a convenient mirage and the Act can be interpreted not as an attempt to stop homosexual promiscuity (since that was prosecuted in the same manner as before) but to end what had become an ineffective floor show. This putative alternative history would be one in which the spectacle of the closet was seen as, perhaps, the only possible form that queer visibility could have taken in the earlier twentieth century and one which, moreover, did give some individuals scope to express their sexual and cultural deviance, albeit in coded forms.

The challenge to representation offered by the concept of the closet could also, in itself, have been an important spur to artistic creativity since, as Jason Edwards has argued, "silence and secrecy [in themselves can] become manifest as a possible homosexual secret."[68] If, as he argues, "textual silences can signify any number of possibilities . . . [such] as a pause, break, cut, opacity, turbidity, shade, darkness, murkiness, blur, tear, hesitation, hole or breathing space," then so might important traditions of blurring and abstraction in modern art, as I will suggest in Chapter 8.[69] Henry Urbach has argued for the physical role

66. Weeks (2011), p. 27.
67. Jeffery-Poulter (1991), p. 81.
68. J. Edwards (2009), p. 58.
69. J. Edwards (2009), pp. 57–58.

of the walk-in wardrobe (aka closet) in the postwar American home as a vital space that enabled a desire for mass purchase and consumption of clothes and other objects of the self to be decorously accommodated within a modernist aesthetic of clean lines and plain surfaces.[70] Queer creative absences may, therefore, have much to tell us about the development and accommodation of mass-market consumerism. And finally, parading about as a camp spectacle of the closet could be seen as a prefiguration of the parodic practices of postmodernity.[71]

It is only recently that the spatial materiality of the closet has begun to be addressed in any detail. For instance, a recent discussion of Sedgwick's work on the closet in relation to geography included the comment of one scholar that "I was frustrated by all the metaphorical, nonmaterial and relentlessly textual dimensions of the book (Sedgwick was, after all, an English professor). . . . I read the exclusive focus on the text as the exclusive space of the closet as potentially blinding us to the materiality of the closet."[72] If the limitations (or, one might better say, the disciplinary boundaries) of Sedgwick's work have irritated some scholars outside her field, then her high standing in the academic community as a whole has been demonstrated by the range of testimonies to her achievements that emerged in the months after her death in 2009.[73] What Sedgwick did or did not decide to focus on is, in itself, an illuminating artifact of the relations between her interests and her times. I am not a literary theorist, and I am not intending this book to represent a critique, even an implicit one, of her methodologies. What I must attest, however, is that I have been inspired by her work to develop my own readings in cultural history and visual culture.

As will be clear by now, the current book takes a broad and introductory approach, but I have imposed some important limitations on its scope. Sedgwick's book focused much of its attention on male experience and I have followed on from that. This does not mean that important work is not waiting to be done in relation to women, visuality, and the closet. Further work could also be done that could bring close attention to bear on the class-based aspects of these cultural structures. I also follow Sedgwick in locating my center of operations in

70. Urbach (1996).
71. C. Reed (1996), p. 68, says of camp that "definitions, though notoriously vague, stress the reclamation (often through nostalgia) of what has been devalued in a way that exposes (often through exaggeration and incongruity) the structure of assumptions undergirding normative values." Thus the camp spectacle of the closet could still be, at some level, subversive.
72. Brown, Browne, and Brown (2011), p. 124. Other readings of the closet as queer space include C. Reed (1996), Betsky (1997), and M. Brown (2000), p. 2, which "attempts to reorient a tendency in queer theory to conceptualise the closet as an aspatial force."
73. Sedgwick's work is contextualized in the field of sexuality studies by Bristow (2011), pp. 185–188. J. Edwards (2009) is an excellent introduction to Sedgwick's work. More detailed appraisals can be found in Barber and Clark (2002).

Anglo-American culture with, as has been seen, excursions to France. My primary theater of operations is Britain and, within that country, London (the British city with the most developed same-sex subcultures over the last several centuries). Because gay liberation was, to a substantial degree, a product of American civil rights culture and because Sedgwick was an American scholar, Chapter 9 incorporates transatlantic perspectives. Again, this focus is not meant to imply that other parts of the world were not in their own ways decorated and afflicted by the closet and its spectacle. I have already identified that it is not meaningful to try to excavate a pre-history of the closet prior to the early modern period and, therefore, this book is about the history of modern culture understood as beginning in the mid-eighteenth century in the context of the age of the Enlightenment. The following chapters proceed chronologically, but they do not attempt to provide a decade-by-decade coverage of events and materials. Rather, they focus on a series of case studies, the aim of which is to shed light on the state of cultural formations during key periods of change.

Part One explores cultural changes taking place during the eighteenth century, which is the first period when a subculture of "effeminate" men can be clearly identified in Britain. This implies the origins of new perceptions of sexual deviance as being associated with particular types of person. This took place as part of a process of rising recognition of same-sex desire and a concomitant concern for social restraints and punishments. As older patterns of the establishment of status by reference to rank began to break down, gender became an increasingly important component of identity. This led to what I term "sodomitical panic"—that is, a fear of being viewed as a sodomite. This form of panic is explored through a reading, in Chapter 2, of William Hogarth's (1697–1764) *The Gate of Calais*, also known as *O, the Roast Beef of Old England* (1748). I argue that Hogarth's experience as a prisoner in France aroused in him a sodomitical panic that can be seen as the precursor of the homosexual panic studied by Eve Kosofsky Sedgwick as an aspect of male anxiety at the end of the nineteenth century. Edmund Burke's (1729–1797) *Philosophical Enquiry into the Origin of Our Ideas of the Sublime and Beautiful* (1757) is interpreted, in Chapter 3, as an attempt to manage masculine desires in a period when traditional modes of homosocial association were coming under suspicion of concealing within them the evidence of sodomitical desires. Burke overtly associates love and lust with the realm of the beautiful, which, according to him, is emphatically feminine. The realm of the sublime, by contrast, is a place of masculine endurance and transcendent experience, which is superior in intensity to that derivable from the contemplation of beauty. In this way Burke created a space for the private, invisible experience of intense same-sex encounters, which was modeled both on the Protestant prayer closet and the contemplation of the works of God as seen in nature. This is not to say that Burke was a sodomite, but simply to emphasize that he was attempting to find ways of accommodating male care for and submission to other men at a time when emotional homosocial bonds were beginning to fall under suspicion of containing sexual content.

For men who did feel same-sex desire, such as many of those in the circle of friends of Horace Walpole (1717–1797), the world of sublime homosociality was both alluring and threatening, as I go on to discuss in Chapter 4. On the one hand, it might appeal to their erotic desires, but on the other hand, the expression of those desires might prove fatal to their lives and reputations. The spectacle of the closet, as elaborated by Sedgwick, is discussed as having been prefigured in Walpole's house, Strawberry Hill, in Twickenham, west of London, as well as in his novel, *The Castle of Otranto* (1764). This last work is viewed as a fantasy space of desire in which Walpole could express his dread of and desire for rampant manhood. This chapter then concludes by examining the case of William Beckford (1760–1844), who was "outed" as a sodomite in the English press in 1784. His life, literature, and building works are understood as attempts to express a sexual identity that was at once sodomitical and flamboyant, but which refused the contemptuous ascription of his tastes to personal effeminacy. Through these case studies, the long eighteenth century can be seen as a period during which the confessional closet was evolving into a place associated with contestations of homosociality as being implicit in, or free from, sodomitical desire. At the same time, characteristic modes of visible behavior were beginning to be developed that enabled the transparently veiled expression of same-sex desire, so prefiguring the spectacle of the closet as identified by Sedgwick in the literary culture of the early twentieth century.

The nineteenth century saw the continuation of a number of important trends that had originated over the previous decades. On the one hand, penalties for same-sex offenses were made less severe, but on the other, the number of prosecutions rose. Fear of blackmail was still widespread, despite the passing in 1825 of the Threatening Letters Act, which made it easier for men of property to face down their accusers.[74] The rise of the culture of respectability meant that satirical representations of the corruptions of society had become even more carefully encoded than before. Nevertheless, it is clear from reading Thackeray's *Vanity Fair* (1848), which was set around 1810–1820, that the problem of excessive and aberrant male desires had not gone away.

> Jos's former shyness and blundering blushing timidity had given way to a more candid and courageous self-assertion of worth. "I don't care about owning it," Waterloo Sedley would say to his friends, "I am a dressy man"; and though rather uneasy if the ladies looked at him

74. Upchurch (2009), pp. 94–100.

at the Government House balls, and though he blushed and turned away alarmed under their glances, it was chiefly from a dread lest they should make love to him that he avoided them, being averse to marriage altogether. But there was no such swell in Calcutta as Waterloo Sedley, I have heard say, and he had the handsomest turn-out, gave the best bachelor dinners and had the best plate in the whole place.[75]

Jos(eph Sedley), who falsely claimed when settled in India to have been a hero of the battle of Waterloo, is shown here coming out as a man who cares greatly for his own pleasures of dress, food, and male company, but not for the ladies.

Social life for men such as Jos depended heavily on institutions such as schools, Parliament, the army, and the Church, where men could gather with members of their own sex. Part Two of this book is focused on exploration of the particular importance for the formation of the closet of the regulation of homosocial lives by such institutions in the course of the long nineteenth century. Chapter 5 argues for the continuing importance of Christian notions of the connections between universal sin and sodomy through the exploration of a case study of the paintings that William Holman Hunt (1827–1910) completed in the Holy Land in the mid-1850s. I then propose that the attempts of Charles Kingsley (1819–1875) to disassociate Christianity from effeminacy can be read as having the effect of developing the Church as one of a series of institutions responsible for fostering and developing the closet in Victorian society.[76] The hypocrisy inherent in this situation was one of the subjects of *Eminent Victorians* (1918) by Giles Lytton Strachey (1880–1932), a prominent member of the Bloomsbury Group and the focus of Chapter 6. Writing in the aftermath of the trials of Oscar Wilde, which had established the homosexual type as effeminate in the public mind, Strachey was able to express himself from his own position of queer spectacle by not simply acting as an object of the gaze, but also by turning his own eye upon the contents of the Victorian closet and discovering there all manner of titillating detail that was, nevertheless, unthreatening to the interwar status quo. The comfortable aspects of the collusion between the closet and those spectacularized in relation to it is then shown, in Chapter 7, to have been most seriously threatened by revelations resulting from disciplinary action. Paradoxical as it might at first seem, institutional authorities, in this case public schools (one of the categories studied by Strachey), did *not* want to divert great energy to the "discovery" of homosexuals. An important reason for this was that those who were caught for committing homosexual transgressions rarely seemed to fit the expectations of effeminacy and ornamentality

75. Thackeray (1848), p. 284, with the important analysis of Sarah Cole (2006).
76. On the rules of institutions referred to as "total organizations," see Goffman (1961).

expected of the sexually deviant male, and thus became, in themselves, a visible threat to the fictions of normative masculinity.

In Chapter 8, the first section of Part Three of this book, the disciplinary gaze of London's Metropolitan Police is shown, through discussion of a series of raids on clubs during the interwar period, to have been fixed upon the persons of effeminate homosexuals. Such men were regularly arrested—often because such displays were interpreted by the police as acts signaling availability as male prostitutes—while those frequenting the same clubs who were dressed "normally" were often ignored. The effect of this was to perpetuate the cultural construction of the flamboyant few who were to be both stared at and disciplined should they show signs of attempting to satisfy their perverted lusts. It should also be noted that although the stereotype of effeminates was of weaklings, the scale of the energy that was directed to pursing and repressing effeminacy implies that its employment was a socially significant strategy. This may be related to the intense and supposedly contagious seductiveness of same-sex desire.[77] Those who were arrested for sexual offenses were treated, conceptually, as dirty and disordered beings. Nevertheless, as evidenced by the art of Francis Bacon (1909–1992), creative opportunities could be enjoyed even in these criminalized circumstances. Bacon is shown as creatively, and masochistically, eroticizing these very conditions of abjection in an echo of Burke's accommodation of the structures of power. But crucially, Bacon was also intent on depicting what he felt to be the ecstatically destructive experience of the closet. By plunging himself into the sublime, Bacon attempted to separate himself from the beautifully decorative world of courtiers of royalty, such as the photographer Cecil Beaton (1904–1980), as I discuss in Chapter 9. Yet the works of both Bacon and Beaton were open to circulation in the cultural economy of postwar Britain and, in the case of the latter, even encompassed iconic images of British patriotism, such as the series of coronation photographs of Queen Elizabeth II. This suggests some of the ways in which artists could generate aesthetic, erotic, or humorous pleasures from conditions that might otherwise seem to be simply ones of phobic oppression.

I, thus, look at the way in which the closet—both as a place of intense darkness and mystery and its spectacle as a sight of ornamental superficiality—in fact offered opportunities for a wide variety of forms of self-fulfilment and expression. Artists and writers contested the strict and disciplinary delineation of these two realms by expounding both the subjective depths of the spectacularized surface and the ornamental attractions of the hidden depths. This work often took place in collusion with the structures of the closet, but it ultimately was one of the features that led to its instability as a cultural formation. Whereas

77. Greene (2003), p. 225.

conventional narratives of gay rights, notably those from the United States, have focused on the Stonewall riots of 1969, the work of creative artists in exploring the troubling complexities of the closet as a structure that contained far more than a simple secret of homosexual desire also needs to be celebrated as having played a role in the advent of a society that was more tolerant of sexual diversity and individuality. Reconceptualization and rejection of the closet via gay liberation was, thus, not the only positive and creative course of action at the time, as I argue in relation, for instance, to Benjamin Britten.

In the final chapter of this book, I explore one of the ironies that has arisen in connection with greater public acceptance of sexual deviance, one that becomes apparent on examination of the posthumous erasure of many of the values of Derek Jarman (1942–1994). Certain aspects of Jarman's cultural legacy, notably his garden in Kent, have inspired popular enthusiasm and imitation. In the process, Dungeness has become a fashionable and expensive residential location, and the figure of Jarman the radical, queer bricoleur with a taste for perverse asceticism has been replaced by his re-presentation as a pioneer of decorative self-expression. Jarman referenced ascetic traditions partly derived from medieval and Reformation Christianity as sources for creating ironic pastiches of contemporary religious bigotry and also as a basis for explorations of the erotics of suffering. However, his legacy has been appropriated by commerce through a focus on aesthetic appreciation of aspects of his style. This has resulted in the post-queer disappearance of many of his cherished countercultural values as the landscape of Dungeness has evolved into a new place of economically enforced conformity. This suggests that "coming out" as gay or queer as a normative process may not, in fact, spell the end of a cultural structure that seeks to separate ornamental spectacle from inner truth. It may be that homosexuality as the secret of the twentieth-century closet was simply a phase in the ongoing life of a more deeply rooted cultural construction.

At a press conference on February 12, 2002, Donald Rumsfeld, United States Secretary of Defense, said, in relation to supposed links between the government of Iraq and terrorism, that "there are known knowns; there are things we know that we know. There are known unknowns; that is to say there are things that we now know we don't know. But there are also unknown unknowns—there are things we do not know we don't know." The cultural critic Slavoj Žižek has criticized this statement by arguing that, in his opinion, "the main dangers lie in the 'unknown knowns'—the disavowed beliefs, suppositions and obscene practices we pretend not to know about, even though they form the background of our public values."[78] This study is about the

78. Žižek (2004).

closet as the location of such "unknown knowns." Certain forms of gender performance, notably those associated with male "effeminacy" were, from the eighteenth century onward, publically spectacularized as representing locales of same-sex desire in supposed contradistinction to the norms of homosocial interaction. At the same time, the prayer closet came to be transformed into a place of private, masculine truth. Different strands of Christian opinion contested such Enlightenment attempts to rationalize male fear of submission to scopic authority. Some of those who were, themselves, marginalized as effeminate attempted to use their artistic and literary creativity both to express their personal subjectivity and to bring amusing or arousing aspects of the contents of the closet to light. Meanwhile, regimes of institutional and state discipline attempted to police the boundaries of the closet, without, in the process, revealing the full extent of perverse desire. The theorization of the closet and its spectacle was the result of the gay liberation movement. But just as these cultural constructions had a complex history stretching back over the previous centuries, so the significant successes of gay liberation have not necessarily destroyed the closet and its attendant spectacle so much as laid the groundwork for their reconfiguration in the twenty-first century.

PART ONE

QUEERNESS IS NOT just for queers, as Eve Sedgwick argued when she wrote at the beginning of *Epistemology of the Closet* that "an understanding of virtually any aspect of modern western culture must be, not merely incomplete, but damaged in its central substance to the degree that it does not incorporate a critical analysis of modern homo/heterosexual definition."[1] Likewise, queer affect in early modern Europe was anything but confined to a small subgroup of minor significance. For instance, it has been argued that the verb "to camp" finds its origins in the faked battles held on "the fields" (*les champs*) at the court of Versailles. Philippe de France (1640–1701), or "Monsieur" as he was known—the brother of Louis XIV (1638–1715), the Sun King—enjoyed attending such events dressed as a woman. His extraordinary hobby, or at least the fact that he was able to indulge it quite openly was, in effect, an indication of the legitimating power of rank at the French court in allowing the display of what otherwise would have been denigrated as a disgrace.[2]

Unfettered aristocratic power and the moral license that sometimes accompanied it in France appalled many Britons; nevertheless, it is fair to say that the mood in their country was less restrained after the return of Charles II from exile than it had been earlier in the century, when sodomy had often been taken very seriously indeed and was viewed as an aspect of devilry and witchcraft. A brand of libertinage made its appearance,which gave a degree of free reign to the likes of John Wilmot, Second Earl of Rochester (1647–1680) to whom the obscene drama *Sodom; or, the Quintessence of Debauchery* (first published in 1684) has been attributed. In this play, Bolloxinion, King of Sodom, prescribes sodomy as the sole acceptable sexual practice. This simple pornographic joke serves as the starting point for a burlesque satire on the interrelations of power and pleasure at the court of Charles II.[3] *Sodom* is perhaps an extreme example of its type, but there were many

1. Sedgwick (2008), p. 1.
2. Zoberman (2008). Compare R. Jones (1997).
3. Elias (1978).

other writings produced at this time in which political critique was coupled, so to speak, with erotic fantasy.

James Turner has explored the "libertine sublime" of Restoration England in general and of Rochester in particular as being based on an erotic heroism that expresses a "rage against its own inadequacies, and an incessant (and obsessive) attack upon dullness. It aims not to celebrate but to control and transcend the parameters of life."[4] Such libertinism was, however, to come under powerful attack after the Glorious Revolution of 1688. Not merely aristocratic license but the emergent urban subculture of the molly house was quickly challenged by an increasing frequency of raids and sodomy prosecutions. The result was that as public awareness of sodomites increased, so did the care with which sodomitical desires were expressed in the forms of textual and visual codes. In this part of the book, I look at the way in which rising anxieties over suspicions of sodomy led to a reformulation of homosocial space and the production of private repositories of personal queerness. In this process, strenuous attempts were made to distinguish regimes of public expression from those of private subjectivity. In the age of the Enlightenment, the prayer closet was beginning to be reformulated as a place of human self-scrutiny. The precursors of the modern closet can be traced to this rising culture of male discretion, politeness, and sensibility.[5]

4. Turner (1989), p. 106.
5. Key works on these topics include Barker-Benfield (1992), Klein (1994), Langford (2002), and Goring (2005).

CHAPTER 2

HOGARTH'S PANIC

BY THE END of the eighteenth century a few men, at least, appear to have become sufficiently enlightened about their sexual tastes that they could begin to take steps rationally to address the problems of authentic self-presentation in the context of a hostile society. The English had been laughing for decades at effete and effeminate men. The audience for Restoration comedies of the late seventeenth century thought that it knew well, after all, that Frenchified foppish behavior was hardly the way to an Englishwoman's heart and would only be embarked upon by men who were as enfeebled in mind as they were in body. However, by the mid-eighteenth century, male effeminates had begun to be taken much more seriously because these exotic creatures seemed now to be seeking each other's company, as in this naval scene from Tobias Smollett's (1721–1771) picaresque novel *The Adventures of Roderick Random* (1748): "Whiffle, for that was his name, took possession of the ship, surrounded with a crowd of attendants, all of whom, in their different degrees, seemed to be of their patron's disposition; and the air was so impregnated with perfumes, that one may venture to affirm the clime of Arabia Foelix was not half so sweet-scented."[1]

Rictor Norton's study *Mother Clap's Molly House: The Gay Subculture in England, 1700–1830* (1992) drew attention to the appearance during this period of men who were not merely "scented," but who were also associated with cross-dressing and with playing the passive role in sodomy.[2] This meant that those who moved in high society had to take extra care when flirting with what were increasingly being regarded

---

1. The "overdetermination" of the longer description of which this is part is discussed, with quotation, in Haggerty (2012), p. 318.
2. Norton (1992); see also Trumbach (1998), esp. p. 7, and (2007b), and compare, Richlin (1992), pp. 220–226.

as the exclusive sartorial prerogatives of the female sex. Thus when the twenty-five-year-old Horace Walpole (1717–1797), the youngest son of the great Whig politician Robert Walpole, attended a masquerade in 1742 in drag, he had himself done up as an *old* woman, as he wrote to his bachelor friend Horace Mann.[3] By so doing, he avoided the possibility that the guests might think that he was trying to solicit the erotic attentions of other men, and he safely cultivated his reputation as a lover of enjoyable but harmless burlesque. Nevertheless, he was, by so doing, publicly flirting with transgressive gender performance at a time when it was becoming increasingly dangerous to do so. As Terry Castle has argued, even in "supposedly 'decent' or non-pornographic accounts, the masquerade is an acknowledged setting for acts of real or ostensible homoerotic flirtation."[4] Therefore, even if Walpole had no such interests, he was, at the very least, parodying the possibility not simply of transgressions of gender, but also of sexual desire.

In a similar fashion it can be suggested that some of those men who were alleged to have been mollies may, in fact, have been doing little more than indulging themselves in a spot of misogynistic parody of women who were a little past their prime.[5] Besides, the mollies were neither, it seems, numerous, nor was their culture widespread.[6] Yet even if sodomitical mollies were few, and Walpole not of their number, it is quite clear that the first half of the eighteenth century saw a notable rise in popular concern over a supposed increase in a seemingly novel combination of effeminacy and sodomitical activity. A wave of persecution in the Netherlands during the 1730s, which led to nearly 300 executions, was extensively reported in Britain.[7] This was but one element that fed into what has perhaps been an under-recognized trend toward moral and social reform at the mid-century.[8] The Jacobite rebellion of 1745–1746 was followed by a crime wave associated with military demobilization in 1748. Sections on crime became a regular feature of newspapers. Then, in 1750, an earthquake struck London, and moralists were quick to draw the comparison between the sins of the modern metropolis and those that had resulted in the destruction of the biblical city of Sodom.[9] Meanwhile, an uneasy peace with Catholic France left the country in a state of simmering fear in which concerns for the vigor of British manhood mingled unpleasantly with religious

3. Walpole (1937–1983), 17, p. 359. References to Horace Walpole's letters are to the Yale edition of the correspondence, which is available in digitized form at http://images.library.yale.edu/hwcorrespondence. See Castle (1995), p. 88.
4. Castle (1995), p. 95.
5. Stephen (2005), p. 111.
6. Phillips and Reay (2011), p. 82.
7. Bentman (1992), p. 210.
8. B. Harris (2002), p. 281.
9. B. Harris (2002), p. 290.

and moral prejudice. Terror over the twin possibilities of execution and the pillory was accompanied by fear of blackmail.[10]

This paranoid landscape provided the inspiration for the art of Britain's most famous painter of social satires, William Hogarth (1697–1764).[11] In 1748 Hogarth painted what has been referred to as "the best known anti-Catholic picture of the period" (Figure 2.1).[12] *The Gate of Calais*, or *O, the Roast Beef of Old England*, became most widely known in the form of a print produced from an engraving that was completed in part by Charles Mosley. This was published on March 6, 1749, priced at five shillings, and advertised as "A print design'd and engrav'd by MR HOGARTH, representing a PRODIGY which lately appear'd before the Gate of CALAIS. O the Roast-beef of Old England, &c." This work was Hogarth's response to the days he had just spent in Calais, during which time he had been arrested on suspicion of spying while sketching the fortifications of the town. His revenge took the form of a dramatic visual satire on the connections between consumption and morality. "The Roast Beef of Old England" was a verse written by Henry Fielding for *The Grub-Street Opera* (1731) and was sung by the cook-maid Susan,

Figure 2.1 William Hogarth, *The Gate of Calais*, or *O the Roast Beef of Old England* (1748), oil on canvas, 78.8 x 94.5 cm. © Tate Gallery, London (2014) (N01464).

10. Trumbach (2007a) and Greene (2003).
11. The following section is an abbreviated version of Janes (2012c).
12. Haydon (1993), p. 47.

lamenting the meanness of her mistress. However, it was soon appropriated as a straightforwardly patriotic piece.[13] Hogarth sang the song regularly, since this was the custom at the Saturday meetings in Covent Garden of the Sublime Society of Beefsteaks, of which he had been a founding member in 1735.[14]

> When mighty Roast Beef was the Englishman's Food
> It enobled our Hearts, and enriched our Blood . . .
> Then, Britons from all nice Dainties refrain
> Which effeminate Italy, France and Spain;
> And mighty roast beef shall command on the Main.[15]

The denunciation of foreign "made dishes" involved the suspicion that sauces were simply attempts to disguise second-rate ingredients. The exaltation of manly British meat appears to have inspired the first short-lived Beefsteak Club, which had been established in 1705. The virtue of native beef was also the subject of a widely discussed article in *The Tatler* in 1710 that is generally attributed to Joseph Addison.[16] Good meat was, supposedly, not to be had in France, not simply because of the sharp practices of cooks, but also because of poverty and, during Lent, because of Catholic dietary practices. All this meant, as explained visually by Hogarth, that a fine joint of beef had to be shipped to the British Inn in Calais from his native land, much to the wonder and amazement of the locals.[17]

It is obvious that this picture is about bodily appetites and the way in which these were supposedly well managed in Britain but not in France; however, the precise nature of those appetites could bear a little more scrutiny. Bernd Krysmanski has recently pointed to a trend for readings of Hogarth that place less emphasis on moralism and more on constructions of gender and sexuality. His recent book, *Hogarth's Hidden Parts* (2010), presents Hogarth's art as being saturated with sexual imagery. He advances what he refers to as "for the first time, a claim to a thoroughly 'bawdy' Hogarth."[18] It is notable, however, that references to sodomy are presented by this artist via (comparatively) subtle modes of allusion. Thus the corruptions of *Marriage à-la-Mode IV, The Toilette* (ca. 1743, National Gallery, London) present a swirl of implied links between money, immorality, and illicit sex, but sodomitical desire is merely hinted at through devices such as the presence of paintings in

---

13. Baldwin and Wilson (1985), pp. 203–204.
14. Baldwin and Wilson (1985), p. 205; Paulson (1992), p. 62, and Broglio (2007), p. 42.
15. Simon (2007), p. 12.
16. Discussed by Volke-Birke (2010), p. 170.
17. This is not to say that Hogarth had to have been in Calais during Lent because he could simply have been exploiting widespread prejudice on the issue.
18. Krysmanski (2010), p. 10.

the background that show the story of Lot and his daughters and the rape of the boy Ganymede by Zeus.[19] The latter detail also appears in *The Marriage Contract* (early 1730s), now in the Ashmolean Museum in Oxford.[20] A mode of oblique allusion, therefore, as opposed to a simple lack of awareness, appears to pervade Hogarth's approach to male same-sex desire, as has also been suggested in relation to the juxtaposition between a statue of Antinous (the young lover of the Roman Emperor Hadrian) and a dancing master in one of the illustrations of Hogarth's book *The Analysis of Beauty* (1753).[21]

Hogarth, of course, was no prude. He had been involved in rakish circles, such as those centered on Sir Francis Dashwood and the Society of Dilettanti. His *Sir Francis Dashwood at His Devotions* (1757) hung behind a private curtain before it gained notoriety as a result of Dashwood's decision to have it engraved for a wider audience.[22] In this picture, Hogarth showed his patron dressed as a Franciscan, but one who was engaged in contemplating the body of a naked woman in place of a crucifix. The greedy cleric as fornicator was a cliché of British anticlericalism. Moreover, as Peter Wagner has argued, "stereotypes of Catholic clerics as lechers and fornicators had an essential . . . place in anti-Catholic erotica during the Age of Enlightenment."[23] Friars, monks, and nuns were, in particular, fantasized as being at the mercy of peculiarly intense and perverse sexual desires. Bawdy houses were jocularly referred to as nunneries.[24]

That the friar at the center of *The Gate of Calais* may be in the grip of lust has been hinted at by various writers, who have described him as "fondling, or perhaps blessing the joint," or who have tried to make out a ring, symbolic of lechery, on the friar's hand.[25] But a much more obvious point can be made: hunger for food was widely employed as a metaphor for lust in the eighteenth century. For example, in John Cleland's (1710–1789) *Memoirs of a Woman of Pleasure* (1748–1749), when Fanny Hill arrived in London from the country she was spotted by the predatory brothel madam, Pheobe, who "look'd as though she would devour me with her eyes." The madam then initiates Fanny into sex, following which she only has experiences with men, after having first caught sight of a penis, which immediately led her to pine for "more solid food" than another woman could give her.[26] Henry Fielding's appetite for beef has already made itself more than apparent, but he can

19. Nussbaum (2003), pp. 14–16.
20. Santesso (1999), p. 514.
21. King (2008), p. 70, fig. 17, and pp. 74–77.
22. J. Kelly (2006), p. 779.
23. Wagner (2005), p. 86.
24. Wagner (2005), p. 81.
25. B. Rogers (2003), p. 100, and Wagner (2005), p. 73.
26. Cleland (1999) [1st ed., 1748–1749], p. 34, and Binhammer (2010), p. 2.

be found expatiating in his satirical novel *The Life and Death of Jonathan Wild* (1743) on sexual gluttony, which

> the Gentlemen of this Age agree to call LOVE, and which is indeed no other than that friendship which, after the Exercise of the Domincal Day is over, a lusty Divine is apt to conceive for the well-drest Sirloin, or handsome buttock . . . which so violent is his Love, he is desirous to devour. Not less ardent was the hungry passion of our Hero, who from the moment he cast his Eyes on that charming Dish, cast about in his Mind by what Method he might come at it.[27]

Wild wonders how he might convey "his Dish, to continue our metaphor . . . to one of those Eating-Houses in Covent-Garden, where female flesh is deliciously drest, and served up."[28] The "Dish" is one Mrs. Heartfree, and this imagery may have been particularly inspired by the practice of serving up women in brothels on pewter plates—a practice that Claude Rawson has suggested may be hinted at in *The Rake's Progress 3*.[29]

Though Fielding's rake was after a woman, his divine was, in similar fashion, intent upon a "well-drest Sirloin, or handsome buttock." Theodosius Forrest, the son of one of Hogarth's friends, published a cantata, headed by a reduced copy of Hogarth's print that had inspired it:

> A meagre Frenchman, *madame Gransire's Cook,*
> As home he steer'd his Carcase, that Way took,
> Bending beneath the Weight of fam'd Sir-Loin,
> On whom he often wish'd in vain to dine.
> Good Father *Dominick* by Chance came by,
> With rosy Gills, round Paunch, and greedy Eye,
> Who, when he first beheld the greasy Load,
> His Benediction on it he bestow'd [original emphases].[30]

"Sirloin" comes from "above the loin" in Old French, but there is a spurious etymology relating Sirloin to "Sir Loin," as repeated by Jonathan Swift in his *A Treatise on Polite Conversation* (1738): "*Miss*. But, pray, why is it call'd a Sir-loyn? *Ld. Sparkish*. Why, you must know, that our King James the First, who lov'd good Eating, being invited to Dinner by one of his Nobles, and seeing a large Loyn of Beef at his Table, he drew out his Sword and in a Frolic knighted it."[31] The form "Sir-Loin" brought with it a considerable quantity of queer cultural baggage, bearing in

27. Fielding (1743), pp. 155–156.
28. Fielding (1743), p. 157.
29. Rawson (2009), p. 95.
30. Forrest (ca. 1750–1759) [2nd ed., 1759].
31. Swift (1738), p. 121.

mind that the loins were known "as the seat of physical strength and of generative power," that "beef" vulgarly referred to the male genitals, and that James has long been implicated in homoerotic desire.[32] In Smollett's *Roderick Random* (1748) a young man finds out concerning Lord Strutwell that "it was a common thing for him to amuse strangers whom his jack-calls run down, with such assurances and caresses as he had bestowed on me, until he had stript them of their cash and every thing valuable about them;—very often of their chastity, and then leave them a prey to want and infamy."[33] The implication was that rakish sodomitical behavior, including the kind supposed by Protestants to be popular among unmarried Catholic clergy, could be motivated by greed for food, money, and sex.

The Sublime Society of Beafsteaks was one of a number of such groups that were, in Peter Wagner's words, founded by "men with rakish interests" and only later became "honoured societies."[34] Hogarth's obsession with manliness can be seen from what has been called his "almost mystical insistence on the eating of beef as a means of acquiring the virility and virtues of the sturdy, freeborn Englishman."[35] Hogarth was, therefore, working very hard to be hearty and to locate himself in a homosocial space of manly friendships that avoided both the feminizing culture of excessive emotionality and the dangers of excessive male carnality.[36] Yet, as Krysmanski points out,

> Hogarth had close connections with the young Lord Charlemont who in Rome had patronised the homosexual Thomas Patch. Most of the men to whom he dedicated his *Election* series—Henry Fox, Sir Charles Hanbury Williams, Sir Edward Walpole, and George Hay— had homoerotic attitudes. Hogarth was also in touch with the homosexual circle around Lord Hervey, who he had painted together with his male friends, and he was on friendly terms with the gay comedian, Samuel Foote.[37]

Hogarth was, thus, well aware of the possibilities of same-sex desire and of its presence as a threat to the homosocial environments in which

---

32. "Loin, n.," Oxford English Dictionary, 2nd ed. (Oxford: Oxford University Press, 1989); online version (2010): http://www.oed.com/, accessed March 9, 2011. See also G. Williams (1994), p. 92, and Bergeron (1999).

33. Smollett, quoted and discussed in Norton (2003), who further points out that the utilitarian philosopher Jeremy Bentham, in his manuscript essay on the subject written in 1785, includes this passage as one of the key testaments to anti-sodomitical prejudice in the literature of the age.

34. Wagner (1990), p. 58.

35. Jarrett (1976), p. 22. Compare with Kirschstein (1998), p. 160, on masculinity and William Morris as an eater of beef.

36. K. Harvey (2004), p. 74.

37. Krysmanski (2010), p. 147. Note, however, the somewhat indiscriminate use of terms to refer to sexual desires in this passage.

he could indulge (some, at least) of his bodily appetites together with other men.

It was perilous to be suspected of being a sodomite in early Georgian Britain, but why was Hogarth in a particular panic about same-sex desire in 1748? It would appear that his heterosexual desires had not found satisfaction in the appearance of the women of Calais. Rather than the rosy cheeks of a native *Shrimp Girl* (1745), all he had found around the docks were fisherwomen with faces of "absolute leather."[38] Further information was obtained by John Nichols from an eminent British engraver, possibly John Pine, who happened to be there at the time, and who, much to his displeasure, was the model for the friar. He gave Nichols a picture of Hogarth as being spectacularly rude about everything French, of being taken into custody and told he would have been hanged had the Peace of Aix-la-Chapelle not just been signed, and then, finally, being expelled from the country.[39] Another version of these events comes to us from the hand of Horace Walpole in a letter he wrote to his friend Horace Mann on December 15, 1748:

> Hogarth has run a great risk since the peace; he went to France, and was so imprudent as to be taking a sketch of the drawbridge at Calais. He was seized and carried to the governor, where he was forced to prove his vocation by producing several caricatures of the French; particularly a scene of the shore, with an immense piece of beef landing for the Lion-d'argent, the English inn at Calais, and several hungry friars following it. They were much diverted with his drawings, and dismissed him.[40]

Walpole was a scholar and an aesthete and was certainly not a foreigner-baiting, beef-eating hearty.[41] This was even more true of his correspondent, the recipient of almost 1,800 letters from Walpole, who lived a life of determined effeminacy and affectation in Florence.[42] George Rousseau has commented that "the activities of English homosexuals abroad—Walpole, Gray, and their circle—have caused confusion and falsification in the standard biographies and cultural histories in which these figures appear."[43] The issue of Walpole's sexual preferences will be discussed in more detail in Chapter 4, but it does not take a huge stretch of the imagination to see these two sophisticates sharing a chuckle over the "manly" artist's bravery in popping across the Channel. They may also have had a notion as to why Hogarth was so particularly jumpy in France, as may Tobias Smollett, who used the

38. Crown (2001), p. 237, and Hogarth, quoted in J. B. Nichols (1833), p. 63.
39. J. Nichols (1782), pp. 43–44.
40. Walpole (1937–1983), 20, p. 13.
41. P. Rogers (1996), p. 33; Haggerty (2001), p. 242, and (2006c), p. 544.
42. Belsey (2009).
43. Rousseau (1991), p. 176.

The Gate of Calais as inspiration for his novel *The Adventures of Peregrine Pickle* (1751). In this work, Pallet, a painter, comments, while explaining how the animals in France are badly fed, that "for my own part, I am none of your tit-bits, one would think, but yet there's a freshness to the English complexion, a *ginseekeye*, I think you call it, so inviting to a hungry Frenchman, that I have caught several in the very act of viewing me with an eye of extreme appetite as I passed."[44] If we accept Paulson's argument that the character of Pallet is substantially modeled on Hogarth, we can understand Pallet/Hogarth as expressing fear that he would be lusted after by Continental sodomites.[45] Hogarth painted himself in *The Gate of Calais* being approached from behind by a French soldier with a large weapon who is about to take him off into captivity. Smollett's burlesque version of these events, meanwhile, sees Pallet, "conscious of his own attractions" and "alarmed for his person," flee a drunken dinner party at which two men are groping each other.[46] Subsequently, Pallet is persuaded to attend a masquerade in drag but, according to George Haggerty, the comic effect in these passages of "the homosocial is precisely intended to cancel the force of the homo-erotic . . . we would call this relation homophobia, and this is one of its richest articulations in the century."[47] Fear of same-sex desire was, thus, both evoked and exorcised through burlesque.

"Homosexual panic" was a term first employed by the psychiatrist Edward Kempf in 1920 to describe a temporary state of paranoid psychosis on the part of a man who was, or who thought himself, subject to unwanted homosexual advances. Notoriously, it became accepted in the United States as a criminal defense for those accused of attacks on gay men. Eve Sedgwick produced a powerful application of such notions to the origins and development of gothic literature in *Between Men: English Literature and Male Homosexual Desire* (1985), in which she argued that "the gothic novel crystallized for English audiences the terms of a dialectic between male homosexuality and homophobia, in which homophobia appeared thematically in paranoid plots. Not until the late Victorian Gothic did a comparable body of homosexual thematic appear clearly. In earlier Gothic fiction, the associations with male homosexuality were grounded most visibly in the lives of a few authors, and only rather sketchily in their works."[48] Hogarth's *The Gate of Calais* can be considered to lie in this sketchily paranoid tradition, save that, since the notion of homosexuality as such was unknown in the eighteenth century, it is better to regard the artist as having suffered from "sodomitical panic," a malady that Matthew Kuefler has explored

44. Smollett (1751), 2, pp. 69–70.
45. Paulson (1964) with the discussion of Cantrell (1995), pp. 84 and 88, n. 44.
46. Smollet (1751), 2, p. 89.
47. Haggerty (2003), p. 179.
48. Sedgwick (1985), p. 92. On queer gothic in general, see Haggerty (2006b) and Hanson (2007).

as having developed ultimately from the formulation of sodomy by medieval theologians as a range of sinful sexual practices outside the sanctioned social space of marriage.[49] Therefore, just as "mollies," those male effeminates who had sex with men, were condemned as "revers-ers of nature" (for instance, in a broadsheet of 1763, "This is not the THING: or, MOLLY EXALTED"), so Hogarth may have feared for his manhood in Calais, where the women disgusted him and "nor are the priests less opposite to those of Dover, than the two coasts."[50] The roots of this panic lay in the strain of having continually to demon-strate manliness and the related fear that, in failing to do so, one might appear to be a molly and thus might be subject to assaults composed either of sexual aggression or of phobic hatred.

A proto-homophobe he may have been, but Tobias Smollett's novels are instructive insofar as they show that an interesting distinction was beginning to emerge between effeminate Whiffles, who were constitu-tionally effeminate and visually obvious, and unscrupulous rakes who could only be differentiated from other men by the perverse nature of the acts they were willing to commit in the pursuit of money or other forms of gratification.[51] Both types were popularly understood to become physically degraded, whatever their motivation, as a result of their abominable practices.[52] Attempts to depict male sexual deviance in the mid-eighteenth century, therefore, began to establish themselves into something of a pattern. The worry that masculine men might har-bor rakish sodomitical desires was the foundation on which the closet was to be built, since ordinary men would be eager to single themselves out both from those who were obviously in the grip of monstrous lusts, such as the corpulent friar, and from those who were weakly prone to womanly pleasures and whose vaporings prefigured the spectacle of the closet as sketched by Sedgwick.

The paradox of this repressive cultural formation was that the more that visible effeminacy in men was demonized as expressive of sexual deviance, the more effectively it could function as a signal of openness to exactly that. A focus on a spectacularized effeminate "type" that functioned as, among other things, a smoke screen for the secret sexual desires of more ordinary men on the street, thus began to develop dur-ing the late eighteenth century. That stereotype was less threatening, and easier to mock, than that of the aggressive sodomite. This under-lies aspects of the popular mockery of "macaronis," who supposedly founded a rival club to the Beefsteaks where they could eat Italian delicacies, the first mention of which comes from the pen of Horace

49. Kuefler (2003), p. 173, n. 7. See also Jordan (1997).
50. Anon., "This is not the THING," quoted in R. Meyer (2001), p. 163, and Hogarth, quoted in J. B. Nichols (1833), p. 63.
51. Haggerty (2012), p. 323.
52. Upchurch (2009), p. 191.

HOW D'YE LIKE ME.

Printed for Carington Bowles, Map & Printseller, N° 69 in S¹ Pauls Church Yard, London. Published as the Act directs.

Figure 2.2 *How d'Ye Like Me*, published by Carington Bowles (1772), hand-colored mezzotint, 35.3 x 25.1 cm (trimmed). © Trustees of the British Museum, Department of Prints and Drawings (1935,0522.1.119).

Walpole in 1764.[53] They soon became such a byword for effeminacy that "the Macaronis' painted, patched, amazingly coiffed heads and slender, delicate, beribboned bodies filled the print-shop windows."[54] In the broadest terms, a "macaroni" was simply a person, and it need not be a man, who exceeded the normal bounds of fashion.[55] But by doing so, "macaronis" drew attention not only to dress and deportment as an artificial performance but also to similarities between fashions for men and women. This, in turn, allowed space for what might be termed a degree of gender confusion.[56]

53. McNeil (2000), p. 377. The implication behind the word "club" here is of a circle of friends and associates, rather than a formally constituted organization.
54. Shapiro (1988), p. 409.
55. Rauser (2004), p. 101.
56. McNeil (2000), p. 397, and Rauser (2004), pp. 103 and 106.

Peter McNeill has argued that such deliberately mannered and excessive self-presentation could, in some instances, encode not simply effeminacy but also sexual preference: "by the 1760s when the macaroni emerged, such attention to fashion was [sometimes] read as evidence of a *lack of interest* [emphasis original] in women, or as potentially unattractive to women."[57] It was in this mode that the London publisher Carington Bowles (1724–1793) brought out *How d'ye Like Me* in 1772 (Figure 2.2).[58] Exaggerated French fashions in dress and furnishings here signaled the comforting fiction that a same-sex come-on was foreign, clearly identifiable, and unthreatening. The classical discourse of the hermaphrodite was called upon by depicting the simpering figure with but a vestigial sword and a prominent vulva-like crease where his penis ought to be.[59] The viewer was thus being educated away from the fear that anyone was capable of experiencing perverse desires into thinking that this was the special property of a narrow group of contemptible persons. Conversely, those who wished to explore sexual experimentation may have increasingly found themselves having to adopt styles that evoked androgyny in order to signal their interest to others of like mind. In those circumstances the cultivation of the androgynous self could have started to become a strategy toward not simply sexual opportunities but also personal self-expression. Moreover, the assumption of effeminate manners could also function as a way of signaling that one was not, in fact, a sexual threat to ordinary men. The sodomite effeminate thus began to hide in plain view, risking ridicule with the aim of avoiding anything worse; for how could a frail hermaphrodite possibly threaten the vigorous manhood of England with sexual violence?

57. McNeil (1999), p. 418. Compare Norton (2005).
58. McNeil (1999), pp. 424–425; on print culture and the figure of the "macaroni," see West (2001).
59. Donoghue (1993) and McClive (2009).

CHAPTER 3

BURKE'S SOLUTION

SODOMY WAS MADE fearful by law in early modern Britain. Buggery as a sign of "extreme violence"—not just to the person, but to the symbolic order of the nation—had been inscribed within the English law by its removal from ecclesiastical jurisdiction and its temporary appearance in royal statute in 1533–1534 prior to enactment in perpetuity in 1562.[1] What were regarded as the most severe cases were punished by hanging, but the more usual penalty was the pillory, concerning which the real deterrent lay not in the threat of being chained up in public for a period of time, but in the behavior of those who came along to watch. As the level of panic rose in society over the issue of sodomy, so those in the pillory were increasingly scapegoated by mobs who used the occasion to assert their normality and moral probity through displays not only of scorn, but of physical violence. Peter Bartlett has argued that "rather than merely reflecting social attitudes, the reports of the aggressive usage by the crowds were a part of the symbolic erection of sodomy in the eighteenth century."[2] In effect, the image of the convicted sodomite was deliberately constructed as a site of horror. George Haggerty has given a chilling description and analysis of the extremes to which this process had progressed at the time of the pillorying of the "Vere Street club" in 1810. Such was the quantity of "dung, guts and blood" with which those convicted were pelted as they were transported to the pillory that they lost all visible semblance of humanity and were reduced to bleeding, broken heaps of refuse.[3] Such terrible scenes projected the sodomite, stripped of his layers of concealment,

1. Moran (2001b), pp. 81–82.
2. Bartlett (1997), p. 570.
3. Haggerty (2006a).

as a disgusting species of monster.[4] The culture of the male macaronis, with its obsession with elegance and sophistication, attempted to place itself at as great a distance as possible from such states of visible bodily abjection. All this left people unclear as to whether they should fear male monstrosity or effeminate delicacy as the most likely sign of sodomitical desire.

Only one figure of any significance made clear public objection to this state of affairs. On April 13, 1780, the conservative writer and statesman Edmund Burke stood up in Parliament to denounce the suffering and death of a pair of sodomites who had been put in the pillory the previous day.[5] In this chapter I will seek to explain why Burke rapidly, and extraordinarily, appears to have noticed the plight of such men whom society had decided to put on display in a manner that, however, simply fed the suspicion that yet more sodomites remained to be uncovered. Burke, like Hogarth, feared for the traditional bonds of manly solidarity, but, unlike the painter and the mobs, he offered a solution that helped to advance the formation of the closet through figuring masculine secrecy as sublime.

The cult of the sublime, which was to become such a marked feature of eighteenth-century sensibilities, drew its original inspiration from the thought of the Greek philosopher Epicurus, as mediated via the writings of Longinus. His concern was to expatiate upon the power of rhetoric to move the listener, above all when the grandness of high style was matched to the description of power. Bearing in mind that the deities of ancient Greece and Rome had long been eclipsed in European thought by the Christian God, it was hardly surprising that early modern theorists of the sublime connected it with their own religious beliefs. The appearance of a deist understanding of a remote deity who stood back from everyday affairs led to a tendency to praise God not in relation to acts of active intervention in daily life but in terms of His evidences as laid out in the form of nature. This meant that while the plains of Italy were the destination for many young men whose classical education was understood to find completion in contemplation of the monuments of the south, those of an emotional frame of mind became prone to find the crossing of the Alps to be almost, if not more, affecting. To some of such mind, the jutting heights of nature suddenly appeared more alluring than the thought of pursuing Venus on the horizontal plains below.

Thomas Burnet (ca. 1635–1715), who was to become famous for writing *Telluris Theoria Sacra* (*The Sacred Theory of the Earth*) (1681–1690), a pioneering work of natural philosophy, crossed the Alps by the Simplon Pass. He was acting as tutor to the young Earl of Wiltshire at the time

4. Greene (2003). For connections with gothic literature, see Corber (1990), p. 101, and the discussion in Fludernik (2001).
5. Munt (2007), pp. 31–53.

and was suddenly struck by how much more intense the Alpine experience was than that of seeing the Catholic churches and towns of France. Looking for evidences of the Creator, he found them both in the spires and towers of the mountains, but also in the ruins of pagan Rome, which he thought, just like Sodom and Gomorrah, had been consigned to oblivion due to the sins of its masters and inhabitants. Landscape read as a moral tract was to form the basis of his geological writings, which were, in themselves, influenced by the literary sublime. Trangressive sexual desire was of particular importance to his theories. As Harry Cocks has argued, "Sodom and Gomorrah, rather than the more obviously punitive fires of hell, were central to Burnet's theory, because, unlike hell flames, the cursed cities allowed him to combine a vision of God's power with naturalistic and geological explanation."[6] In other words, if anyone complained that the ancient Roman temples had fallen due to earthquakes rather than due to the actions of angels descending from heaven, Burnet could retort that the terrifying power of an earthquake could only have been caused by God. All of this meant that to contemplate the works of God was equally to tremble before the actions of an irresistible force.

Another unmarried man of intense sensibility, John Dennis (1658–1734), recorded his experience of vertigo in the Alps as being one in which terror was combined with exhilaration.[7] In 1704 he expressed his feelings in ways which, for Catherine Maxwell, put a "homoerotic penetration of the male subject" as the essence of the sublime.[8] Dennis wrote that "the sublime does not so properly persuade us, as it ravishes and transports us . . . it gives a noble vigour to a discourse, an invisible force, which commits a pleasing rape upon the very soul of the reader; that whenever it breaks out where it ought to do, like the artillery of Jove, it thunders, blazes, and strikes at once, and shows all the united force of a writer."[9] But it is important to note that he qualified the power of sublime rhetoric by arguing that "no passion is attended with greater joy than enthusiastic terror, which proceeds from reflecting that we are out of danger at the very time that we see it before us."[10] In other words, pleasure does not come from being in danger, but from imagining what it is like really to be in peril. This means that an intensity of sublime horror is to be obtained from, say, imagining that one is about to be struck down by God as a sodomite but knowing that, in reality, it is not going to happen.

God, for Dennis, was the epitome of sublime puissance, and as such he argued that "this enthusiastic terror is chiefly to be derived from

6. Cocks (2010), p. 5.
7. Nicolson (1997), p. 281.
8. Maxwell (2001), p. 8.
9. Dennis (1704), p. 79, and Cocks (2010), p. 6.
10. Ashfield and de Bolla (1996), pp. 37–38.

religious ideas."[11] This point was accepted by John Baillie in his *Essay on the Sublime* (1747), in which he expressed his belief that "it is in the Almighty that the sublime is completed."[12] Yet he also maintained that it was not merely the actions of the just deity that inspired sublime affect:

> The hero who insults mankind, and ravages the earth merely for power and fame, is but an immense monster, and as such ought only to be gazed at [and not idolized]. . . . Yet such is the force of the sublime, that even these men, who in one light can be esteemed no other than the butchers of the human race, yet when considered as braving dangers, conquering kingdoms, and spreading the terror of their name to the most distant nations, tower over the rest of mankind and become almost the objects of worship.[13]

Baillie, thus, argued that the power of the sublime might emanate from the workings of evil among humans. The implication of this is that one might thrill not only at the sight of those upon whom divine judgment was being enacted, but also at the sight of those who might impose their evil will upon the onlooker.

It will be clear from all this that when Edmund Burke (1729–1797) came to write his *Philosophical Enquiry into the Origin of Our Ideas of the Sublime and Beautiful* (1757), he was elaborating a set of ideas that had been in development for several decades.[14] He agreed with the preceding writers in emphasizing the connections between the sublime, pleasure, and horror. He also emphasized the importance of affective responses to material objects, including landscapes, and he stressed the importance of the subjection of the self in the course of such experiences. His most significant innovation was to propose a parallel realm, which he referred to as "the beautiful," and to associate that with all the soft, gentle qualities that were driven out by the sublime. Moreover, he posits the beautiful as being the locale of aesthetic experience, whereas the effect of the masculine sublime was almost to obliterate the senses:

> Whilst we [metaphorically] contemplate so vast an object, under the arm, as it were, of almighty power, and invested on every side with omnipresence, we shrink into the minuteness of our own nature, and are, in a manner, annihilated before him. And though a consideration of his other attributes may relieve, in some measure, our apprehensions; yet no conviction of the justice with which it is exercised, nor the mercy with which it is tempered, can wholly remove

11. Ashfield and de Bolla (1996), p. 38.
12. Ashfield and de Bolla (1996), p. 93.
13. Baillie (1953), pp. 27–28.
14. Burke (1990).

the terror that naturally arises from a force which nothing can withstand.[15]

The point is that for Burke the sublime is not simply a show that leaves us gasping, having imagined the thought of our own violation; for when he writes that "we are, in a manner, annihilated before him," what he is saying is that we are changed by this encounter in our very essence. Because Burke emphatically genders the sublime as male and the beautiful as female, it becomes clear that we have moved from the notion of a "pleasing rape" to something which transfigures and transforms the self, breaking through all our defenses in an experience of ecstatic terror.

Edmund Burke was the son of an Irish Protestant father and a Catholic mother, whose political and literary career in London was shaped by contemporary conflict between conservative desires for stability and radical dreams of revolutionary change. His work on the sublime has been read as representing evidence for the development of conceptual linkages between the emerging middle class as a focus for manliness, truth, and hard work, on the one hand, and the aristocracy as a focus for effeminacy, idleness, deception, and leisure, on the other. It is clearly, also, influenced, by powerful ambiguities of religious identity and relationships to gender roles. Isaac Kramnick attempted to explain Burke's *A Philosophical Enquiry* in relation to "sexual ambivalence" in his study *The Rage of Edmund Burke: Portrait of an Ambivalent Conservative* (1977). Kramnick deployed notions of sexual identity that did not exist in the eighteenth century and, as such, provided what was, in some ways, a problematic set of explanations. Nevertheless, the vehemence with which Kramnick's ideas were rejected, at least in certain quarters, arguably owes something to the contemporary cultural politics of the 1970s in which conservatives, for whom Burke was a hero, were fighting a rear-guard action against civil-rights activism. To take just one example, when Frederick S. Troy reviewed the book in the *Massachusetts Review*, he said that Kramnick

> is not reluctant to insinuate anything he chooses in his speculation about Burke's so-called sexual ambivalence . . . [in weaving] this strange web of fancy about Burke . . . his general handling of the subject must appear embarrassingly inept to professionals and his tone is smarmy . . . there is simply no evidence for the thesis that governs this book and that is stated with damnable iteration throughout.[16]

The general consensus was that the scholarship of the book was unsound, but it did garner some favorable reviews. Nannerl Keohane,

15. Burke (1998), p. 63.
16. Troy (1981), pp. 98–99.

for instance, writing in the *Journal of Interdisciplinary History*, noted that the study does have a "tendency to rely heavily on some tenuous pieces of evidence about Burke's psyche . . . but it is surely more worth having than another eulogy of this Tory saint."[17]

What Kramnick did to warrant such critical outrage was to posit his subject as, in modern terms, a bisexual, who was most passionately attracted to men. Kramnick situates this in the context of Burke's marriage to Jane Nugent in 1756 and his ongoing (merely homosocial, it is assumed) relationship with William Burke, a friend, with whom he had been living since 1750 and who did not move out six years later. For Kramnick, *A Philosophical Enquiry* was, among other things, an evolution of Burke's musings over whether he should "be the assertive male and thus a fit suitor for Jane, or . . . the passive idle female drawn to and dependent on Will's masculinity?"[18] This is further linked into Burke's parentage and religious heritage, such that Kramnick argues that "Will provided Edmund [with] the mirror of his father (Protestant, masculine, and assertive) and Jane his mother (Catholic, feminine, and passive)."[19] Arguments for the implication of Burke in forms of same-sex desire have found more defenders among literary scholars than among historians.[20] As mentioned previously, Burke was just about the only figure of his time to protest that punishments for sodomites were unduly cruel—not simply in relation to the above-mentioned speech in Parliament in 1780 (an act which generated such negative publicity that he fought a libel case in 1784 against *The Public Advertiser* on the grounds that it had called him a sodomite), but also in 1772, when Robert Jones was due to be convicted of sodomy on the evidence of a thirteen-year-old boy and Burke argued for a stay of execution on the grounds that the boy was too young to give reliable evidence on a capital charge. F. P. Lock, a leading academic historian and biographer of Burke, assures us that Burke had not "condoned sodomy. . . . His willingness to speak on their behalf implies no sympathy for their sexual orientation. Rather, it testifies to the nobler side of his self-righteousness."[21] Kramnick's book is dismissed by Lock in a footnote: "I find Kramnick's argument unpersuasive, based as it is on the application of Freudian dogma to a biographical vacuum."[22]

The most substantial evidence for Burke's experience of same-sex desire comes from a series of intense letters that he wrote to Richard Shackleton (1728–1792). Most scholars argue that the emotionality of these communications does not reflect erotic desire but merely passionate friendship and that to suggest otherwise risks reading modern sexual

17. Keohane (1978), p. 332.
18. Kramnick (1977), p. 79.
19. Kramnick (1977), p. 80.
20. Kramnick (1977), p. 68.
21. Lock (1998), 1, p. 464.
22. Lock (1998), 1, p. 464, n. 65.

understandings into the very different conditions of the eighteenth century (which is, *inter alia*, the essence of the case against Kramnick). However, this is a question that demands careful weighing of the evidence. Simply because friendships *could* be emotional does not mean that they were incapable of also possessing an erotic dimension. In the view of Katherine O'Donnell, Burke's feelings were a species of "passionate love that was silenced by Shackleton's marriage." Burke sent a copy of *A Philosophical Inquiry* to Shackleton and inscribed it thus: "may it be a testament to a long love."[23] O'Donnell concludes that it makes no sense to see this as an "unerotic" or "Platonic" friendship:

> whatever label we might wish to apply to Burke's love, the letters to 'Dear Dicky', 'Dear Dick', 'Dear Friend', and 'Dear Shackleton' remain a testimony to the young Burke's remarkably perverse reaction to heterosexual intercourse and marriage and give a moving record of his passion for Shackleton, a passion whose delight, intensity, heartbreak, anxiety, jealousy, and masochism, exceeded the decorum of friendship as it was understood in eighteenth-century British culture.[24]

Moreover, O'Donnell also talks of the "lifelong partnership" with Will, a man whom Edmund, in his own words, "tenderly loved, highly valued and continually lived with, in a *union not to be expressed* [my emphasis], quite since our boyish years."[25] Max Fincher has recently argued that "queer readers of literary history need to worry less about whether or not writers had physical relationships and to focus [instead] on how queerness gets expressed, silenced and buried."[26] In that spirit it may be legitimate to put to one side the issue of who Burke may have slept with, or may have wanted to sleep with, as being essentially unprovable and to replace it with a different question: Might consideration of the role of sodomitical desire in eighteenth-century culture advance our understanding of *A Philosophical Enquiry*?

One problem with the dogmatic position of writers such as Lock is that it does not pay quite enough attention to how extraordinary Burke's interventions on behalf of sodomites were. Even Jeremy Bentham did not dare to publish his utilitarian rationalizations of same-sex eroticism.[27] What if, for the sake of argument, we assume that Burke had been passionately fond of Shackleton in a "purely Platonic" way? Might he not, in the climate of rising animosity toward sodomites, have feared that his emotionality would be read as sodomitical? His actions in Parliament suggested that he was, at least at a later date, unusually

23. O'Donnell (2006), p. 635.
24. O'Donnell (2006), p. 638.
25. Burke, quoted and discussed in O'Donnell (2006), p. 619.
26. Fincher (2007), p. 163.
27. Hobson (2000), p. 19.

sensitive to the issue of the maltreatment of sodomites. Moreover, as has been explained, the tradition of the sublime that he not only reiterated, but also developed, was predicated upon placing the self in positions of imaginary violation by a vastly superior masculine force. Thus Sally Munt has argued that Burke was primed to empathize with what she refers to as the "sublime shame" of the sodomite displayed "under the arm, as it were, of almighty power."[28] Such a spectacle could be understood as a manifestation of the Burkean sublime.

It is important to note that Burke had argued of sublime experiences that "when danger or pain press too nearly, they are incapable of giving any delight, and are simply terrible; but at certain distances, and with certain modifications, they may be, and they are, delightful."[29] Could it be suggested, therefore, that Burke intervened because this was a situation in which danger pressed "too nearly" since he could only too acutely imagine himself dragged to the pillory (if only by mistake) because of his youthful indiscretions? One of the important characteristics of the sublime for Burke was darkness and obscurity. Might he have thought of this darkness as being partly composed of the willed desire not to see or to recognize the truth of desires of the self? The effort of seeing into darkness stirred in Burke the thoughts of the painful opening of the body since he argued that the "circular ring of the iris be in some sense a sphincter, which may possibly be dilated by a simple relaxation, but in fact it does not relax so easily . . . since it is furnished with antagonist muscles" that pull against each other, with the result that one set is "forcibly drawn back."[30] This description implies an act of physical transgression. As Suzannah Biernoff has commented, "the feeling of the sublime occurs at precisely those thresholds, between self and other, subject and object, human and non-human. The sublime is fundamentally about frontiers" that are threatened with breach.[31] The Burkean sublime is thus, in some degree, about pleasure associated with violent same-sex contact.

It is interesting to compare the case of Burke with that of the greatest Continental theorist of the sublime, Immanuel Kant (1724–1804), who demanded a "deathbed kiss from his male friend Pastor Wasiansky" and who has been discussed as a "crucial, indeed pivotal, figure in the prehistory of homosexual lifestyle."[32] As Santanu Das reminds us, death-bed kisses were being given as late as World War I without this indicating homoerotic desire, but that hardly indicates that the presence of intense male-male emotionality can be used as clear evidence for the absence of same-sex desire.[33] One cannot say that Kant, or Burke, was

28. Munt (2007), pp. 40–53.
29. Burke (1998), p. 36.
30. Burke (1998), p. 132.
31. Biernoff (2001–2002), p. 72.
32. O'Rourke and Collings (2004–2005), para. 13.
33. Das (2002).

PICTURING THE CLOSET

in the closet, in the way that, say, Wilde was for part of his life, for two reasons: first, because the imputation of same-sex desire on the part of Burke remains unproven, and second, because the closet as a structure focused on denial of *homosexuality* had not yet been formed. However, something looking suspiciously like a closet, something perhaps proto-typical of the homosexual closet, begins to appear if we think analo-gously to the prefiguration of homosexual panic in sodomitical panic. In an atmosphere of rising fear and scrutiny, might not the repeated pillorying of sodomites have been instrumental in developing a specta-cle of a closet that contained the shameful secret of sodomitical desire, if not yet of homosexual identity?

For this idea to have purchase in the case of Burke, one need not even posit that he felt sexual attraction to other men, but merely sug-gest that he eroticized power, since it is clear that for the Burke of the *Philosophical Inquiry* "the [masculine] sublime is clearly the greater, the more important, the more fascinating quality" than the [feminine] beautiful.[34] The Burkean experience of ecstatic thrall bears some rela-tion, even if it is not identical, to what was going to be identified as mas-ochism by nineteenth-century sexology—named with reference to the novel *Venus im Pelz* (*Venus in Furs*) (1870) by Leopold von Sacher-Masoch (1836–1895).[35] The terms "masochism" and "sadism," as they are com-monly employed today, have developed through the medicalized dis-course of the late nineteenth century, which powerfully gendered the concepts such that masochism was understood (within limits) as a nat-ural state of female subjection, appearing as a perversion in the male, and sadism (again, up to a point) as a natural state of male dominance, manifesting as a perversion in the female. Freud's interpretations were crucial in ensuring the wide dissemination of these categories.[36] This is, of course, not to say that erotic power-play was invented at this time. Such practices as the spanking of males by women were widespread in early modern pornography, but the significance of such acts was changed by an increasingly rigid separation of gender roles. This meant that sexual desires came to be carefully categorized, but also that the very imposition of regimes of regulation offered new opportunities to develop complex relationships between power and pleasure.[37] The sig-nificance of this is that, although masochism is often regarded as an act of failure and as being little more than abject submission to that which should be resisted, it can be argued to the contrary that "masochism is not the love of submissiveness. It is not the pursuit of unpleasure or humiliation. It is a complex set of practices for transforming sub-missiveness, pain, and unpleasure, into sexual pleasure. But over and

---

34. Kramnick (1977), p. 97.
35. The following section is derived from part of Janes (2009a).
36. Noyes (1997), p. 6, and Moore (2009), pp. 139–140.
37. Noyes (1997), p. 87.

above this, it is the appropriation of the technologies that our culture uses in order to perpetuate submissiveness."[38]

One of the premier exponents of this viewpoint was Michel Foucault, who advanced "S/M" as a space for the working out of ideas and practices of resistance. It is important to emphasize that he wished to distinguish "S/M" from sadism and masochism, or "so-called sadomasochism," which represent erotic power play only as viewed through medical and psychoanalytic understandings of deviance.[39] As one commentator put it, the aim was that "the genealogist of 'suffering pleasure' might even be able to imagine *new* combinations of impulses and phantasms, *new* relationships of power, a *new* 'style' of life—perhaps even a new 'game' of truth."[40] However, Leo Bersani, writing in his influential book *Homos* (1995), is critical insofar as he argues that the subculture of S/M is "profoundly conservative in that its imagination of pleasure is almost entirely defined by the dominant culture to which it thinks of itself as giving 'a stinging slap in the face.'"[41] And he argues that although "far from enjoying pain, masochists have developed techniques to bypass pain . . . [yet] pain is the organism's protection against self-dissolution."[42] The prominent American novelist Edmund White commented, shortly after Foucault's death, that he "was a man deeply attracted to power in its most totalitarian forms, politically and sexually. Throughout his life he struggled against this attraction. That is what I admired most about him."[43] One way in which masochism can be positively re-evaluated, however, is by distinguishing it from sadism (and from "S/M," which includes a sadistic component) because it involves delight in the renouncing of self to power, rather than delight in power relationships themselves. This was the line take by Bersani in his article "Is the Rectum a Grave?" (1987), written at the height of the AIDS crisis. This piece argues that sex is fundamentally masochistic since its aim is the annihilation of the self in the orgasm. He wished to agree with certain feminist writers that personal relationships carried the freight of oppressive patriarchal power structures but, unlike them, he saw the answer not in avoiding sex, but in having as much as possible so as to avoid relationships via the multiplication of random sexual encounters.[44]

Just as the fops, Whiffles, and their ilk were condemned for their visible excesses, so the Burkean sublime can be understood as a method of experiencing sensational excesses in secret that involved imagining states of constraint before power. Both masochism and the Burkean sublime are concerned with the experience of just the right degree of

38. Noyes (1997), p. 12.
39. Discussed by K. Robinson (2003), p. 129.
40. J. Miller (1993), pp. 277 and 279.
41. Bersani (1995), p. 87.
42. Bersani (1995), pp. 93–94.
43. Edmund White, interview, March 12, 1990, quoted in J. Miller (1993), p. 281.
44. Bersani (1987), p. 218.

horror and pain. Such experiences could involve erotic delight, but their essence is likely to have been closer to that of the ego-enhancing masochism that John Kucich has identified as a self-justificatory mechanism in the British imperial project.[45] He argued that the aestheticized suffering of imperial functionaries was used to justify their position in an organization whose operations were based on political suppression. Such a stance would make sense for an Irish subaltern, such as Burke, who was making his way up the ranks of power in England, since, as Peter Cosgrove has argued, "instead of freeing the subject . . . the sublime inducts us into a stricter identification with the humiliating power . . . the self is annihilated by a greater power only to be reconstituted as its functionary."[46] The quest for the sublime can be seen as inherently destructive and related perhaps to the death drive, but this is emphatically not how Burke saw it.[47] He modeled his vision of sublime masculine encounters on those with God in the prayer closet and understood them to be both terrible and exalting experiences of subjection. He sought a mode of invisible subjection that was constituted as the antithesis of the beautiful as the true threat to the self since it was that latter quality that weakened and dissolved manhood in "the feminine sphere of companionable dissolution."[48] The beautiful world of surfaces that he distrusted was not simply that of women, of course, but also of Whiffles. He, therefore, sought to reinforce what might be termed the "proto-closet" as a space where perverse pleasure and pain could be mingled without resulting in public implication in sodomitical effeminacy. This necessitated opposition to the threat to that emerging closet space posed by the sodomy laws, which, when enforced, revealed the sodomite to the world.[49]

The sublime was thus to be approached almost like a gym workout:

> Melancholy, dejection, despair, and often self-murder, is the consequence of the gloomy view we take of things in the relaxed state of body. The best remedy for all these evils is exercise or *labour*; and labour is a surmounting of *difficulties*, [original emphases] an exertion of the contracting power of the muscles; and as such resembles pain, which consists in tension and contraction, in every thing [sic] but degree. . . . [A]s due exercise is necessary to the coarse muscular parts of the constitution . . . the very same rule holds with regard to those finer parts we have mentioned; to have them in proper order, they must be shaken and worked.[50]

45. Kucich (2007).
46. Cosgrove (1999), p. 427.
47. Mishra (1994), p. 255.
48. Shaw (2006), p. 63; see also Furniss (1993), p. 38.
49. Note that Greene (2003), p. 215, argues that the pillory played a role in moving public attention from sodomitical acts to the perception of sodomitical persons.
50. Burke (1998), p. 122.

Burke, therefore, advocated the periodic encounter with pain as a tonic that could counteract the debilitating effects of the experience of enervating pleasure. But it is important to emphasize that this salutary pleasure is carefully screened off from lust, which is positioned as produced by contact with the beautiful. This is why, in the view of another commentator, the Burkean sublime represents a form of "masochism indulged in bad faith, since it works to disavow the sexual component of the pleasure it enjoys."[51] Thus the contents of Burke's "proto-closet" may also have contained the secret that the pleasure of the sublime *was*, at least potentially, erotic. Being subjected to sodomy, therefore, would not be erotic because it was about sex with another man, but because it represented an act of the violation of the self. It is in this manner that we can understand the sexual thrill felt by the narrator of Sacher-Masoch's *Venus in Furs* (*Venus im Pelz*, 1870) when his mistress gives her furs and whip to another man, Alexis Papadopolis: "a cold shudder ran down my back, when my rival stepped from the bed in his riding boots, his tight-fitting white breeches, and his short velvet jacket, and I saw his athletic limbs."[52] The script of violation is what renders this male-male encounter erotic. The Burkean sublime is, however, carefully positioned as a space of obscurity where the precise nature of male-male contact is never clearly defined. It represents a homosocial space that contains the invisible secret, not to be divulged, of deviant desire. Those desires may be associated with eroticism within male groupings, or formations associated with power-relations, or both. Its action is to operate as the unseen counterpart of a spectacle of effeminate sexuality that is projected as safely outside the masculine self. The shaping of same-sex desire as *the* secret of the closet was, thus, not Burke's doing, but his striking ideas of the 1750s provide important clues to what was to happen next.

51. R. Gross (1995), p. 233.
52. Sacher-Masoch (1991), p. 266.

CHAPTER 4

THE DECORATIVE
AND THE DAMNED

IT WAS LATE in the year and the weather correspondingly bad when Horace Walpole (1717–1797) and Thomas Gray (1716–1771) crossed the Alps in 1739 on their way to Italy on their Grand Tour.[1] Walpole wrote home from Turin to another close friend, Richard West, on November 11 to lament the death of his lapdog, Tory, who had been eaten by a wolf in one of the high passes: "such uncouth rocks and such uncomely inhabitants! my dear West, I hope I shall never see them again!"[2] The tone of Gray's letter to West was very different. He describes the journey to the Grand Chartreuse in France before depicting the passage of the Alps:

> . . . I do not remember to have gone ten paces without an exclamation, that there was no restraining: Not a precipice, not a torrent, not a cliff, but is pregnant with religion and poetry. There are certain scenes that would awe an atheist into belief . . . you have Death perpetually before your eyes, only so far removed. . . . Mont Cenis, I confess, carries the permission mountains have of being frightful rather too far; and its horrors were accompanied with too much danger to give one time to reflect upon their beauties.[3]

It was such a sensibility as this that had informed Burke. These landscapes were only sublime and exalting insofar as they did not, in

1. Nicolson (1997), pp. 356–358.
2. Walpole (1937–1983), 13, p. 189.
3. Gray (1971), 1, pp. 128–129.

reality, become personally dangerous. Gray, like Burke, also gendered his view of mountain landscapes, which appeared as up-thrust and male in comparison with the supine fertility of the plains spread out below. Thus he had written to West of the confluence of two rivers at Lyon that

> the lady [Rhone] comes gliding along through the fruitful plains of Burgundy . . . the gentleman [Saône] runs all rough and roaring down from the mountains of Switzerland to meet her and with all her soft airs she likes him never the worse. She goes through the middle of the city in state and he passes incog. without the walls but waits for her a little below.[4]

Not simply the gendering but also the eroticization of landscape was a feature of certain works of eighteenth-century erotica.[5] As a matter merely for comparison, since it is rather later in date, there is a synopsis and collection of research notes preserved among the papers of James Emerson Tennent (1804–1869) in the Public Record Office of Northern Ireland for a study into the depiction of hills and mountains as phallic.[6] Nevertheless, such later preoccupations emerged from a tradition of interest among a number of eighteenth-century antiquarians into aspects of male fertility worship as evidenced, so they imagined, by things perpendicular (such as the towers that, as we shall see at the end of this chapter, preoccupied William Beckford). Both Gray and Walpole have been strongly associated with aspects of same-sex desire and, therefore, it might be tempting to associate Gray's engagement with his masculine mountains as having an erotic component. But why then do we hear none of this from Walpole? I have argued, in relation to Burke, that what might be termed "the sodomite as proto-homosexual subject" was slowly coming into formation at this time, and with it the fear of being labeled and exposed. This means that the closet was evolving from a place in which to transact private household business or for the confession of spiritual unworthiness to God to a place in which to conceal the shame of problematic aspects of relations with other men. Gray's responses appear to place him closer to Burke, but I will go on to argue that Walpole was also a person of remarkable cultural creativity and a pioneer in the cultural work of creating the closet and its beautiful spectacle as a place that held secrets that were ever more significantly homoerotic. It was, thus, absolutely in character that he took in the view of the mountains but affected not to have been impressed.

4. Gray (1971), 1, p. 118.
5. Janes (2012c), p. 27.
6. My thanks are due to Jonathan Wright for this information. For the wider context of the ensuing nineteenth-century interest in these topics, see Janes (2008).

If Burke had been passionately devoted to Richard Shackleton as a friend, it seems clear that Gray had been deeply in love with Richard West. His death in 1742 plunged Gray into years of deep depression, yet critics still have to work hard to refute the arguments of those who insist on the presence of nothing more than homosociality "innocent" of erotic desire. [7] Raymond Bentman, for instance, feels it is necessary to take considerable care to explain that those in homosocial friendships did not "speak of dreaming of the other, did not mention physical contact . . . did not attempt to compare their friendship to that of famous lovers; and did not use language like 'half my soul.' They did not use the rhetoric of romantic love."[8] The central problem for Gray was that, as has already been noted above, society was becoming more "antisodomitical." As a result, his frustrated "sexuality, bound by the particular constraints of eighteenth-century England, was to influence some of his most important poems, enriching their profound commentary on human suffering and helping to create their haunting, elusive flavor."[9] Gray remained, as far as we know, celibate, and he aestheticized his isolation, purging the shame of illicit physical desire with the tortures of refined sensibility. It was part of the reasoning of this conceptual space to create a separation between sodomitical brute force and spiritualized love—which does not mean, of course, that the former might not threaten to break through in a dark moment of ecstasy and terror.[10]

The men I have been discussing were haunted by monsters that were objects both of terror and of fascination. Burke wrote that

> the large and the gigantic, though very compatible with the sublime is contrary to the beautiful. It is impossible to suppose a giant the object of love. When we let our imagination loose in romance, then the qualities we naturally annex to that size are those of tyranny, cruelty, injustice and everything horrible and abominable. We paint the giant ravaging the country, plundering the innocent traveller, and afterwards gorged with his half-living flesh.[11]

A perverse fascination with giants was, in fact, a widespread eighteenth-century enthusiasm based upon travelers' tales of savages of extraordinary proportion.[12] Such accounts inspired satires, the most famous of which is Jonathan Swift's *Gulliver's Travels* (1726, amended 1735).[13] A key point of such satire was to instill various notions of

---

7. Bentman (1992), p. 217.
8. Bentman (1992), p. 205.
9. Bentman (1992), p. 203.
10. Haggerty (1996).
11. Burke (1998), p. 143.
12. Fausett (1994), pp. 152 and 191.
13. Its full, relishable, title is *Travels into Several Remote Nations of the World, in Four Parts. By Lemuel Gulliver, First a Surgeon, and then a Captain of Several Ships, in which Gulliver is himself a Giant in Lilliput, but a Pigmy in Brobdignag.*

relativism, not only between Europeans and others, but also between men and women. Thus Laura Brown has argued that "Gulliver actually does take the place of the female figure at more than one prominent point in the *Travels*. In the relativist comparison between Gulliver's own form as a giant in Lilliput and his encounter with the giants of Brobdignag, he repeatedly occupies the position of a woman. . . . To say that Gulliver occupies the place of the woman at recurrent moments in the *Travels* is not to say that Gulliver is the same as a woman, but to suggest a systematic pattern of implication, which moves from the various forms of interchangeability."[14] In other words, if we understand sexual orientation to have been based at this stage upon power relations (male = control; female = acquiescence), then to be a pigmy in a land of giants was to be reduced to the sexual status of a woman, a thought that, as I have suggested for Burke, may have been masochistically alluring.

Dennis Todd has stated in *Imagining Monsters: Miscreations of the Self in Eighteenth-Century England* (1995) that "turning Gulliver into a diversion [that is a spectacle] is a way of neutralizing the threat of his monstrous difference, a way of managing the radically alien so that it does not disrupt the comforting assurances of the usual."[15] As Shearer West has argued, "before the eighteenth century, people laughed at the scatological manifestations of the body's inner workings: during the course of the eighteenth-century, people came to laugh at external signs in which physiognomy and singularity were privileged over the universality of the body's functions."[16] This is what Walpole may have had in mind when he satirized the Patagonian reports of John Byron (1723–1786) in *An Account of the Giants Lately Discovered* (1766):

> If they are not *Jews*, but idolators, the statues of their Divinities, their sacrificing Instruments, or whatever are the Trinkets of their Devotion, will be great Rarities, and worthy of a place in any Museum [original emphasis].
>
> Their Poetry will be another Object of Inquiry, and if their Minds are at all in proportion to their Bodies, must abound in the most lofty Images, in the true Sublime. Oh! If we could come at an Heroic Poem penned by a Giant! We should see other Images than our puny Writers of Romance have conceived; and a little different from the Cold Tale of a late notable author who did not know what to do with his Giant than to make him grow till he shook his own castle about his own ears.[17]

14. L. Brown (1990), p. 435.
15. Todd (1995), p. 162.
16. West (2001), p. 175.
17. Byron (2000), p. 47; and see Walpole (1766), pp. 29–30.

Westerners such as Byron encountered giants "simply as enormous bodies" because they could not speak the same language.[18] Walpole laughs at the notion that such monsters could be creatures of sensibility, but in so doing emphasizes their dangerous, exciting, and even revolutionary corporality; as he says, "bless us, if like that Pigmy old *Oliver* [Cromwell, original emphasis], they should come to think the Speaker's Mace a Bawble!"[19] Bearing in mind Lord Rochester's satirical comment on Charles II in 1674, that "his sceptre and his prick are of a length," these are creatures of phallic potency and thus of the Burkean sublime, to be scrutinized by the connoisseur from a safe distance.[20]

The "notable author" that Walpole is referring to is himself, and the castle that of his pioneering gothic novel *The Castle of Otranto* (1764). In this story the gigantic ghost of Alfonso the Good, last legitimate ruler of Otranto, destroys the castle that has been usurped by the tyrannous Manfred (inspired by Manfred, King of Sicily, an excommunicate and usurper who lived from 1232 to 1266) and, thereby, brings order to the kingdom. Walpole wrote on March 9, 1765, to William Cole with an explanation of the genesis of the tale:

> I waked one morning in the beginning of late June from a dream, of which all I could recover was, that I thought myself in an ancient castle (a very natural dream for a head filled like mine with Gothic story) and that on the uppermost bannister of a great staircase I saw a gigantic hand in armour. In the evening I sat down and began to write, without knowing in the least what I intended to say or relate. The work grew on my hands, and I grew fond of it.[21]

This fantasy had its counterpart in material reality: Strawberry Hill, a villa to the west of London that Walpole had been busily remodeling in ways that did not fuse the gothic style with classical architectural plans but deployed it in order to create a play of visual effects that mingled delight and unease. Thus when he positioned his "armoury," that is to say an assemblage of armor and weapons, evocative of course of masculine violence, on his own staircase, it was as if he was inviting the fantasy that they might come uncannily to life. Among this assemblage was a curious padlock in the shape of a hand. The item is now lost, but it can be seen depicted by John Carter among various key-like weapons in a page bound into an "extra-illustrated" edition of *A Description of*

---

18. J. Campbell (1998), p. 256.
19. Walpole (1766), p. 17.
20. Bruce (1994), p. 309.
21. Walpole (1937–1983), 1, p. 88, quoted and discussed in Mowl (1996), pp. 182–183, and Haggerty (2011), p. 91.

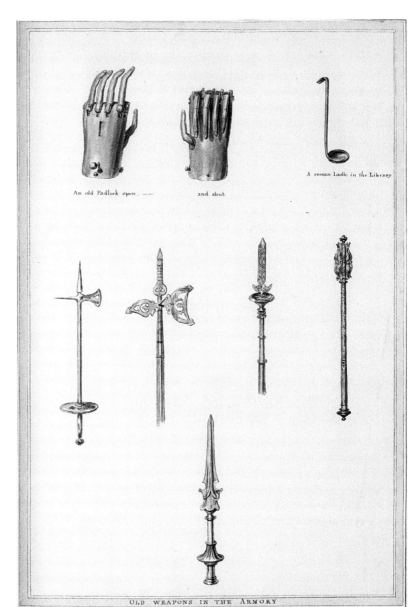

An old Padlock open ——   and shut.   A roman ladle in the Library

OLD WEAPONS IN THE ARMORY

Figure 4.1 John Carter, *Old Weapons in the Armoury* (undated), Lewis Walpole library, laid in Richard Bull's extra illustrated edition of *A Description of the Villa of Horace Walpole* (1784). Courtesy of The Lewis Walpole Library, Yale University (Strawberry Hill ID: sh-000374).

the Villa of Mr. Horace Walpole Strawberry Hill (London: Kirkgate, 1784), once owned by the MP Richard Bull (Figure 4.1).[22] What this strange lock implies, perhaps, is the potential for something to be hidden inside Walpole's armor.

Manfred's son is killed early on in the novel: "he beheld his child dashed to pieces, and almost buried under an enormous helmet, a hundred times more large than any casque ever made for a human

22. Ashmolean Museum (2005).

being, and shaded with a proportionable quantity of black feathers."[23] The giant is then first seen by servants: "No, no, said Diego, and his hair stood on end—it is a giant, I believe, he is all clad in armour, for I saw his foot and part of his leg, and they are as large as the helmet below in the court."[24] So what might this "giant helmet and grotesquely engorged armoured limbs" indicate?[25] Was Walpole fetishing huge, male body parts? In her introduction in her series *The British Novelists*, the critic Anna Barbauld suggested a story by Anthony Hamilton (1644/1645?–1719), an unmarried Catholic Irish nobleman who spent most of his life in exile in France, as a source for Walpole's giant and his monstrous limbs.[26] Hamilton's writings combined flippancy, an interest in the fantastical and same-sex eroticism (he is noted for discussing relations between women at the Stuart court and for an interest in hermaphrodites).[27] Walpole was sufficiently a fan that he produced an edition of Hamilton's memoirs at his own press at Strawberry Hill in 1772 and preserved a copy in his "glass closet" of important books.[28] In *Le Bélier* (*The Ram*), written circa 1705, but first published in 1730, we encounter a giant who fancies that he will sire an heir even larger than he:

> At the bare rumour of this freak
> All blanch'd was many a beauty's cheek,
> For what was fitter to appal them,
> Than to reflect that such a lot
> Might, by some accident befall them.[29]

This is from the first English translation. Another of Hamilton's stories had been translated at an earlier date, and by none other than Matthew Lewis, author of *The Monk* (1796), a gothic novel that was also notable for its exploration of aspects of secrecy and same-sex desire.[30]

---

23. Walpole (1998), p. 19.
24. Walpole (1998), p. 35.
25. Gentile (2009), p. 16.
26. Barbauld (1810), 22, p. ii; see also C. Johnson (2001) for a discussion of *The British Novelists* as an editorial project.
27. Bobker (2011).
28. Anthony Hamilton, *Memoires du Comte de Grammont* (1772), Horace Walpole's Strawberry Hill Collection, The Lewis Walpole Library, Yale University: http://lwlimages.library.yale.edu/strawberryhill, accessed February 10, 2013; see G. Avery (2002), p. 154, n. 5.
29. Hamilton (1849), p. 447.
30. Norton (2008), p. 97, argues that "same-sex eroticism is central to the plot of Matthew Lewis's *The Monk*." There is a wide range of literature on this, for which a useful lead is provided by Tuite (1997). It should also be noted that, like Beckford, as discussed below, Lewis was the owner of slave plantations in Jamaica and, moreover, he took over the rotten borough parliamentary seat of Hindon in Wiltshire when Beckford vacated it in 1796, on which see Harkin (2002).

In Walpole's skit "The Judgment of Solomon" (1753)—parodying 1 Kings 3—a wife and a mistress ask the king to choose between their rival claims to a young man in general and to his penis in particular:

> By nature's undeceitful clue
> The Monarch to unravel knew
> The closet web, the strongest line
> That art could weave or Women twine. . . .
>
> It was—what was it not?—a Prize
> Of that majestic goodly size,
> Of compass such, as Solomon
> In all his glory ne'er had known.[31]

Banter about giant phalluses might be dismissed as no more than libertine braggadocio were it not for the fact that both Hamilton and Walpole approach the penis, so to speak, from the point of view of a woman's emotions—not to mention that Solomon appears to be a diviner of the deepest secrets of both closets and of women. Beyond all this, when one bears in mind that Walpole's "glass closet" of literary treasures came to include not merely Richard Payne Knight's *A Discourse on the Worship of Priapus* (1786), but also the memoirs of the cross-dressing Chevalier d'Éon, the poems of Thomas Gray, and Anthony Hamilton's gossipy memoirs, you have something that begins to look like a reference collection of forms of sexual deviance.[32] Of course these materials were but part of the contents of the closet and yet, as the notably un-progressive Walpole collector and editor Wilmarth Sheldon Lewis commented, this was "the most intimate and personal section of the library."[33]

In his article "'It stood as an object of terror and delight': Sublime Masculinity and the Aesthetics of Disproportion in John Cleland's *Memoirs of a Woman of Pleasure*," Mark Blackwell described how Fanny Hill viewed the penis of her lover as being a giant thing, so large that it would give her pleasure and pain at the same time in a way that "anticipates Burke's aesthetic vocabulary."[34] And Elizabeth Kubek has discussed the action of the penis in this erotic novel as being like "a man machine"—that is, a terrifying masculine implement endowed with uncanny life.[35] It is only, with great suspense, at the very end of Walpole's gothic tale that we see the full giant form rising up before us to devastating effect:

> The moment Theodore appeared, the walls of the castle behind Manfred were thrown down with a mighty force, and the form of

31. Walpole, quoted in Haggerty (2001), pp. 244–245.
32. Haggerty (2001), p. 242.
33. W. Lewis (1958), p. 16
34. Blackwell (2003), p. 49.
35. Kubek (2003), p. 49.

Alfonso, dilated to an immense magnitude, appeared in the centre of the ruins. Behold in Theodore, the true heir of Alfonso! Said the vision: and having pronounced these words, accompanied by a clap of thunder, it ascended solemnly toward heaven, where the clouds parting asunder, the form of St. Nicholas was seen; and receiving Alfonso's shade, they were soon wrapt from mortal eyes in a blaze of glory. The beholders fell prostrate on their faces, acknowledging the divine will.[36]

Just as the ideal form of Burke's sublime was in the form of a transcendent encounter with God, so here we see a vision inspired by the occasion when Jesus Christ ascended to heaven: "now when He had spoken these things, while they watched, He was taken up, and a cloud received Him out of their sight" (Acts 1:9). But where Burke shrouds his divinity in patriarchal obscurity, Walpole invites us to visualize the male form in its full scale and inflated magnificence.

There is no same-sex fulfillment in *Otranto*, but perhaps, in the embrace of Jesus it might be looked for in Heaven? This was the sentiment expressed by Thomas Gray in his "Elegy Written in a Country Churchyard" of 1750.

> He gave to Misery all he had, a tear,
> He gained from Heaven ('twas all he wished) a friend.
>
> No farther seek his merits to disclose,
> Or draw his frailties from their dread abode,
> (There they alike in trembling hope repose)
> The bosom of his Father and his God.[37]

Gray's wish for a love in heaven that could not be found on this earth is now widely understood to have been derived from the death of the aforementioned Richard West in 1742. George Haggerty has seen the extent of Gray's grief as evidence not so much of clinical illness but of a queer refusal to accept the consolations offered by family and the prospects of marriage.[38] Yet he also saw the real subject of the poem not as being death, but as being the "fond breast" and "the bosom of his Father," which sexualizes heaven.[39] The English grave was, for Gray, a sort of closet, which should not be disturbed. Where Gray used his literary talents in order (at least obliquely) to be able to express his fears and desires, so did Walpole. In *Otranto* giant bodies—and those haunting bodies are male—transgress the boundaries of past and present, earth

36. Walpole (1998), pp. 112–113.
37. Gray (2012), lines 122–128.
38. Haggerty (2004), p. 390; but see also Haggerty (1999), pp. 113–135, and Sacks (1985), pp. 8–9.
39. Haggerty (1999), pp. 132–135.

and heaven, that limit erotic possibility.[40] Writing in the midst of what he referred to as the beautiful, miniature world of Strawberry Hill and his circle of friends, Walpole invented the gothic novel as a place in which to evoke the sublime as a site—and sight—of pleasurable danger and fantasies of fulfillment.[41]

The role of agent provocateur played by Kramnick in the case of Burke is taken by Timothy Mowl in his book *Horace Walpole: The Great Outsider* (1996). The counterpart of the set of letters to Richard Shackleton by Burke is that addressed by Walpole to Lord Lincoln from 1739 to 1744. These appear to show Walpole scheming, successfully, to get the two of them together on the Grand Tour. Mowl presents the two as having been lovers and reproduces the portraits from 1741 by Rosalba Carriera (1675–1757) of the two men wearing the same coat as evidencing the spectacle of a closet of same-sex desire. Pat Roger's review of Mowl's work enshrines a more nuanced approach than that which Lock applied to Kramnick's views of Burke, and this probably represents the position that many would take regarding the issue of the precise nature of Walpole's sexual desires. Rogers comments that "it is altogether plausible that Walpole was exclusively homosexual, and he may have had a physical relationship with Lincoln—the letters leave that a real possibility, but no more."[42]

George Haggerty has worked through the evidence for Walpole and sex in perhaps more detail than anyone else, and he is concerned that Mowl's interpretation is anachronistic. Moreover, Haggerty has expressed impatience with the entire notion of trying to position Walpole into a sexual category at all, arguing that

> what the letters reveal is a bitchy, playful, arrogant, self-satisfied, intriguing, acquisitive, loving and devoted friend who loved deeply and long and devotes himself to his house and his collections with the same kind of energy he puts into friends and (sometimes) politics. This is the person who emerges so vividly and richly in the letters that he himself preserved for posterity: isn't it enough? Readers have always imagined there would emerge a lurid "truth" behind the letters. . . . But everything in the letters is mentionable: indeed, everything is mentioned.[43]

Though I have considerable sympathy with this position it is, I feel, also rooted in contemporary debates over sexual politics. While Mowl may have turned Walpole into a camp gay man, Haggerty, at least in this

40. J. Campbell (1998), p. 250.
41. J. Campbell (1998), p. 240.
42. P. Rogers (1996), p. 33.
43. Haggerty (2006c), p. 560.

passage, is in danger of rendering him into a queer only insofar as he cannot be fitted easily into an accepted paradigm of sexual identity.

Another approach is to situate Walpole in the context of his circle and friends by employing Whitney Davis's concept of "queer family romance."[44] Walpole's writings show a tendency to blur the boundaries between real and possible ancestors, relatives, and friends, notably in relation to overlaps between the forbidden realms of incest and same-sex desire.[45] It is useful to compare Strawberry Hill, with its varied, intimate closet spaces, with those inhabited by the heroine of Samuel Richardson's *Clarissa* (1748). Karen Lipsedge has argued that none of the rooms called closets in this novel "are represented as exclusive sites for one member of the family alone. Instead, they are all depicted as places that can be shared with others."[46] Equally, Clarissa's abusive family could violate the privacy of her closet and drive her out of her home. Walpole constructed his own closet chambers not so much as spaces in which he could be alone, but where he could meet and talk frankly with those with whom he was intimate. Thus he hung portraits of his circle of bachelor friends so as to evoke not so much his erotic desires for them as his polite and cultivated relations with those who shared his own tastes.[47]

Walpole's discretion is one of the reasons that allegations of sodomy concerning him have been so heavily contested. The dangers of anachronism are, after all, such that I have been careful to talk of the presence or absence of same-sex erotic desire in this chapter, rather than trying to place individuals into particular categories of sexual identity. But even a man who was profoundly sexually attracted to women might still be aware in the eighteenth century, as today, that if he appeared overly effeminate his gender performance might lead to incorrect assumptions being made about his sexual tastes. One thing that Horace Walpole definitely was not, in physical terms, was a terrifyingly muscular giant. This became pertinent when the time came for him to publicly defend his cousin, the British general and statesman Henry Seymour Conway, from a series of political attacks. William Guthrie responded in 1764 by saying that Walpole was "by nature maleish, by disposition female," by drawing attention to "the delicate structure of his frame" and by suggesting that his literary style was that of a woman.[48] Now all of this might, of course, indicate nothing much to do with sexuality, but simply that Walpole was being sneered at as an effeminate (that is, as a weak

---

44. Davis (2011).
45. J. Campbell (1998), p. 239, Frank (2003), and Townsend (2009).
46. Lipsedge (2006), p. 119.
47. Reeve (2013b), p. 431, and see also (2013a). It is interesting to compare this with the way in which the Onslow family used portraiture of youth and then of marriage to edit out the scandalous side of Edward Onslow's life; see Stanworth (1993).
48. Mowl (1996), pp. 177–189.

and enervated runt). However, when Guthrie said that "it would very much puzzle a common observer to assign him to his true sex," he was not evoking so much the weak male as another exotic sort of creature, the hermaphrodite, which was kin to certain of the above-mentioned macaronis who were just in the process of making their London debut. Moreover, Walpole seems to have thought that this attack was about more than his supposed lack of potency since he wrote to Conway that "they have nothing better to say, than that I am in love with you, have been so these twenty years, and am no giant."[49]

Walpole had indeed written various passionate letters to Conway and had stated that "I love and honour Mr Conway above any man in the world: I would lay down my life for him." He made him the chief beneficiary in his will.[50] Mowl presents Walpole as having written his novel in an anguished state of distraction after what he refers to as the "outing" at the hands of William Guthrie. We have already seen that a range of men were liable to experience sodomitical panic at this time. It seems comprehensible that Walpole was terrified of being *seen* as a sodomite, whether he was one or not. The false accusation of sodomy was treated by the courts in the late eighteenth century as being as serious as highway robbery by virtue of the "overwhelming terror" this accusation could cause.[51] Moreover, Walpole had stood as a witness for his brother, Edward, who was probably not a sodomite, when he had been accused of buggering one John Cather in 1751.[52] Furthermore, there is another reason that Walpole, who had just brought out his *Anecdotes of Painting in England* (1762), may have feared public denunciation: there was a rising perception since the 1750s that sodomites were associating themselves with connoisseurship and the arts.[53]

I am not convinced by Mowl's contention that by publishing "a rip-roaring, red-blooded romance" Walpole attempted to distract others (and perhaps himself) from his own sexual inclinations.[54] The novel, to me, evokes similarities to the formations we have seen in the case of Burke; and I see it as an attempt to explore his fears and desires in a way that provided an alibi for his predilections. In the case of the Irish writer, personal interests in power and pleasure were rationalized into a supposedly universal aesthetic schema. As has been seen, Burke presented the ecstatic horror of the encounter with masculine power as a subspecies of the subservience that all men must both endure and glory in before the throne of God. By contrast, preoccupation with armor in general and the helmet in particular suggests that fantasies of Conway's

49. Walpole (1937–1983), 38, p. 437.
50. Samson (1986), p. 149.
51. G. Dyer (2012).
52. Walpole (1937–1983), 43, p. 365; see also Fincher (2007), p. 31, and Trumbach (2007a), p. 38.
53. Senelick (1990), p. 56.
54. Mowl (1996), p. 186.

potency may have played an important role in forming and firming Walpole's giant. On September 28, 1749, Walpole had written to George Montagu, concerning an occasion on which Conway had tried on an old helmet found in a gothic church, that "you can't imagine how it suited him, how antique and handsome he looked."[55] A few years earlier (on October 24, 1746, to be precise), Walpole had enthused to Conway himself about his appearance, saying that he would write him up in a romance thus: "Elmedorus was tall and perfectly well made, his face oval, . . . his complexion sentimentally brown, with not much colour; his teeth fine, and forehead agreeably low, round which his black hair curled naturally and beautifully."[56] What did get written was a nightmare in which a father figure destroys a castle and leaves a son in power. What may underlie this is a script of insecurity toward Walpole's own extraordinary father. Thus Walpole himself has been identified as "the kind, handsome, somewhat ineffectual hero Theodore, who, like himself, is 'no giant' " and who is the grandson and heir of Alfonso, and also looks like him.[57] Yet the ending of the novel can also be read as a fantasy of phallic violation that shatters the gothic facade of the castle of Otranto and, by coded implication, implies that Strawberry Hill is a flimsy and theatrical masquerade.[58] In fiction Walpole could flirt with fantasies of erotic self-actualization through masculine violation that could easily, if acted out in real life, have led to the ruin of his reputation.

Walpole expended a great deal of energy on constructing an apparently unthreatening form of domestic environment and to deliberately avoiding such imputations of violence as were implied by sodomy. He emphasized lightness and diminutiveness (the world of Burkean beauty) to make his life seem unthreatening. This saved him from the charge of libidinous sodomy, but opened him to Guthrie's calumny as an effeminate at a time when the classical discourse of the hermaphrodite was informing the construction of a subspecies of man-woman whose street counterpart was the molly. But if in real life Walpole surrounded himself with paper-light architecture, "by contrast the bodies that Walpole characteristically images [in his novel] as actually or potentially engaged in incestuous sexual relations are emphatically, even exaggeratedly material."[59] Walpole was haunted by the very real social and criminal danger of illicit contact such that, in his life and writings, "honorable love among men, enacted in discourse and in the fanciful reconstruction of a house, cannot finally be kept separate

55. Quoted in Walpole (1998), p. xxvii.
56. Walpole (1937–1983), 37, p. 261.
57. Bentman (1997), p. 285, and Walpole (1998), pp. 54 and 88.
58. Note that the novel was inspired by the theater in general and Shakespeare in particular and that the first half of the eighteenth century saw concerted attempts to purge the theater of its bawdy aspects, on which see Senelick (1990), p. 42.
59. J. Campbell (1998), p. 246.

from the appalling and destructive energies of an embodied incestuous desire" (such as for his cousin).[60]

Just as the feathers on the helmet on the armorial bearings painted on the ceiling of Walpole's library could be imagined as coming to quivering life, so could the rakes depicted in his collection of paintings. Walpole recorded that on the night of May 1, 1760, he dreamed of visiting the Palace of Westminster in the seventeenth century and of seeing there "a very odd picture; it seemed a young king in his robes to his knees, sleeping and leaning on his hand thus [Walpole inserted a small sketch of the picture in his ms]. I immediately knew him to be Richard 2[n]d. He waked and came out of the frame, & was exceedingly kind to me, & pressed me to stay with him—no, thought I, I know the assassins are coming to murder you."[61] This not merely prefigures the moving painted figure of Ricardo in the novel but implies that Walpole had dreamed of looking at a young man who lay open to his gaze in sleep, and who, on awakening, wanted the two of them to be together. Moreover, it is significant that this is Richard II since he, as implied by Shakespeare, had stood accused of presiding over a dissolute and sodomitical court.[62] Moreover, in *A Description of the Villa of Mr. Horace Walpole* (1784), Walpole stated that the idea of a portrait walking from its frame had been inspired by the portrait he owned of Henry Cary, Lord Falkland. Cary was widely associated with interests in courtly sodomy because of the following publication: *The History of the Most Unfortunate Prince, King Edward II. With Choice Political Observations on Him and His Unhappy Favourites, Gaveston and Spencer . . . Found among the Papers of, and (Supposed to Be) Writ by the Right Honourable Henry Viscount Faulkland, sometime Lord Deputy of Ireland* (London: John Playford, 1680). Though the authorship of this work was (and is still) uncertain, the implication is that Walpole was fantasizing about the possibility that aristocrats with interests in sodomy might come back to life in Strawberry Hill.[63]

The Castle of Otranto was, therefore, a nightmare about the outbreak of masculine energy, but it also contained and concealed elements of homoerotic fantasy. The framing device of art as a species of *travesti* transformed Walpole as the potential subject of masculine violence into the empowered spectator of the Burkean sublime. *The Castle of Otranto*, therefore, was a safe space from which to exercise one's perverse

60. J. Campbell (1998), p. 256.
61. Horace Walpole, *Book of Materials*, Lewis Walpole Library, Yale University, MS 49.2615, 63–64, in Snodin (2009), p. 342.
62. Frost (2012), pp. 183–198.
63. Walpole (1784), p. 51; and, on the authorship of the Falkland text, see Skura (1996), p. 79, and Kelsey (2008). Note that in his novel *Caleb Williams* (1794), William Godwin made the chivalrous aristocrat Falkland a sodomite; on which see Corber (1990), p. 88, Markley (2004–2005), paras. 12–18, and G. Dyer (2012).

fantasies—which is, after all, one of the reasons for the ensuing popularity of the genre of gothic literature based on this novel—establishing, as Anne Williams argues, "conventions familiar in Gothic narratives from Walpole to the present: a vulnerable and curious heroine; a wealthy, arbitrary, and enigmatic hero/villain; and a grand, mysterious dwelling concealing the violent, implicitly sexual secrets of this *homme fatal*."[64] Insofar as the function of the spectacle of the closet is to act as a distraction for desires that lie in secret elsewhere, we can see Walpole's two (physical and fictional) castles as being implicated in such a project. Their function was *not* to spell out the nature of Walpole's sexual desires. Part of the very purpose of engaging with femininity on the part of those with secret same-sex desires may be specifically to try to place themselves into a space of refined safety where they would be safe from phallic aggression. However, in that soft and jeweled closet they have also set themselves up as an illuminated target for male desire, which, if it enters, can be represented as a violating horror that they abhor (and yet, of course, also desire). Thus Strawberry Hill, itself, as a sort of costume for Horace, can be seen as a precursor of the spectacle of the closet.[65]

FALLEN ANGELS

Just before his death, Horace Walpole received a set of drawings illustrating scenes from the *Castle of Otranto* from a young admirer, Bertic Greatheed (1781–1804). On February 22, 1796, Walpole wrote to Bertie's father, the dramatist of the same name, to relate his admiration of the scenes (Figures 4.2 and 4.3).[66] There is in these pictures a "clear emphasis on terror," according to Cynthia Wall.[67] And there is also, more remarkably, an emphasis on the body, since Greetheed's ghost is shown only partly dressed in armor. [68] His bare toes and sandaled foot, in particular, seem to be derived from the world of classical sculpture. This image bears comparison with Henry Fuseli's (1741–1825) *Drawing of a Figure Slumped before the Scale of Antique Fragments* (*Der Künstler verzweifelnd vor der Grösse der antiken Trümmer*) (1776–1780).[69] The torso of the original colossal stature was probably wooden and has not survived, leaving the marble elements which had been used for the visible areas of flesh, such as the hands, feet, and face. This is a drawing of what is thought to be the artist himself fainting, seemingly in despair, next to the remains of a gigantic cult statue of the Emperor Maxentius (reigned 306–312), which was subsequently reworked as Constantine, the first

64. A. Williams (1995), p. 38.
65. A. Williams (2006), p. 30.
66. Mishra (1994), p. 259, n. 9.
67. Wall (2007), p. 186
68. Silver (2009), p. 553.
69. In the collection of the Kunsthaus, Zurich.

Figure 4.2 Bertie Greatheed,
*Manfred's Servants
Frightened* (ca. 1796),
bound into Horace Walpole,
The Castle of Otranto, 6th
ed. (1791). Courtesy of the
Lewis Walpole Library, Yale
University (Strawberry Hill
ID: sh-000542).

Christian emperor.[70] The muscular solidity of the foot emphasizes, by
contrast, the fluidity and lack of musculature displayed by the figure of
the artist.

Jonah Siegel has pointed out that shortly after this time, Fuseli sent
a scabrous drawing of himself to the artist James Northcote in a letter
from Lugano. This shows the artist as a sprawling nude male in the
languorous pose of the "sleeping faun" from Herculaneum. With one

70. Brandenburg (2011), p. 54.

Figure 4.3 Bertie Greatheed, *The Destruction of the Castle* (ca. 1796), bound into Horace Walpole, *The Castle of Otranto*, 6th ed. (1791). Courtesy of the Lewis Walpole Library, Yale University (Strawberry Hill ID: sh-000542).

foot he gestures toward some mice in England, which represent his rivals, while, seated on a giant commode, he defecates on Switzerland while watching a winged phallus flying back in the direction of Italy.[71] This implies that the antiquities of Roman Italy were powerfully associated by Fuseli with phallic potency. Füssli, the original name of Fuseli, means "little foot" in Swiss German, and this might similarly imply

71. Siegel (2000), pp. 49 and 64, and Myrone (2005), p. 189, fig. 189.

that his despair in Rome may have had more to do with physical inadequacy than metaphysical angst.[72] Rome and its emperors were frequently read in Britain through an orientalist lens in which the lurid tales related by Suetonius in his *Lives of the Caesars* blended with fantasies of the Islamic master of a harem. That overwhelming sexual pleasure was central to the orientalist construction of the tyrant has been argued powerfully by Alain Grosrichard in his *Structure du sérail: la fiction du despotisme asiatique dans l'Occident classique* (1979) [translated as *The Sultan's Court: European Fantasies of the East* (1998)].[73] In his introduction to that translation, the philosopher Mladen Dolar explains that the fantasy of oriental despotism relies upon the construction of a "place of unalloyed excitement."[74] Imagining oneself as a glamorous tyrant, therefore, could provide an alternative to queer self-creation via the polite closeting of excessive desires.

William Beckford's (1760–1844) life recalled the forms and aspirations of the libertine sublime of a century earlier. His (in)famous novel *Vathek* (composed in 1782 in French, and first published in 1786), offers stronger erotic fare than appears amid the coded excitements of Walpole's *Otranto*. Beckford's novel, according to Andrew Elfenbein, "tossed taste, judgment, and heterosexuality to the winds in favour of rampant consumerism, boy love and necrophilia."[75] The oriental tyrant, Vathek, was also modeled, according to Mark Booth, on the Sun King, such that "the fearsome eyes of Vathek . . . capable of knocking people backwards with just a glance, are the fabled eyes of Louis XIV."[76] Most editions of the novel went unillustrated, but the eye of the Caliph appears under a turban on the title page of an edition from 1815 (Figure 4.4). This is the eye as representing supreme male scopic authority and, perhaps, here it also evokes the homosocial secrecy of Freemasonry, the attribute of which it was at this time.[77] The image on the frontispiece of this edition, by Isaac Taylor, shows a scene at the end of the novel where the satanic—and well-built—lord of evil, Eblis, is shown presiding over his underground kingdom:

> An infinity of elders with streaming beards, and afrits in complete armour, had prostrated themselves before the ascent of a lofty eminence; on the top of which, upon a globe of fire, sat the formidable Eblis. His person was that of a young man, whose noble and regular

72. Lindsay (1986), p. 483.
73. Grosrichard (1998).
74. Dolar (1998), pp. xi and xvi.
75. Elfenbein (1999), p. 39.
76. M. Booth (1999), pp. 75–76.
77. Note that Beckford was a freemason: McCalman (2007), para 11, says that he had been "initiated in the more occult Continental strains of the movement." See also Mulvey-Roberts (2003), p. 262, on Hogarth's use of sexual innuendo in relation to the symbol of the all-seeing eye.

features seemed to have been tarnished by malignant vapours. In his large eyes appeared both pride and despair: his flowing hair retained some resemblance to that of an angel of light.[78]

Figure 4.4 Isaac Taylor, Jr., frontispiece and title page, William Beckford, *Vathek* (London: Clarke, 1815).

The inspiration for homoerotic visions concerning the Devil in the late eighteenth century can be traced back to John Milton's description of the fallen Satan in the epic poem *Paradise Lost* (first published 1667, and a key site of the sublime for Edmund Burke).[79] For instance. Blake's series of illustrations, as studied by Christopher Hobson in *Blake and Homosexuality* (2000), appear to have been inspired by the relative leniency of the poet who "treats sodomy as a sin against oneself or others, but not as uniquely depraved or a sign of social decay."[80] However, in *Vathek*, unlike *Paradise Lost*, "the equation of demonism with evil comes undone," or at least the connections between the two become somewhat unclear.[81] Eblis appears almost as a handsome, romantic

78. Beckford (1786), p. 209; see also Châtel (2011–2012), p. 50, n. 3.
79. Burke (1998), pp. 55–57, 111, and 159–166. On the romantic cult for Milton in the context of the sublime, see Crawford (2011).
80. Hobson (2000), p. 13; see also Connolly (2002), Howard (1982), p. 134, and Stevenson (1996), pp. 23–48, on Blake and the "androgynous sublime."
81. During (2007), p. 277.

Figure 4.5 John Robert
Cozens, *Satan Summoning
His Legions* (ca. 1776),
watercolor on paper, 28.8
x 33.4 cm. © Tate Gallery,
London (2014) (T08231).

hero thrown into despair by defeat. One of the earliest illustrations in this mode, inspired by Milton, was by John Robert Cozens (1752–1797): *Satan Summoning His Legions* (ca. 1776), which was painted while the American revolution was in full swing, and it was hotly debated whether the rebellious colonists had been inspired by God or the Devil (Figure 4.5).[82] Cozens painted this work at the time when he was setting out for Italy with Richard Payne Knight, who was gathering notes for his aforementioned work on phallic worship. When Knight returned to England in late 1779 or early 1780, Cozens took up with Beckford who, along with Knight, was to remain a patron for the rest of the artist's life.[83] Both Cozens's and Taylor's works appear to have provided inspiration for John Martin's (1789–1854) engraving *Satan Summoning His Legions* (1824). Martin had been entertained by Beckford around the time of the sale of his estate at Fonthill, and the painter used part of the garden as the setting for another Miltonic scene, *Adam and Eve Entertaining the Angel Raphael* (printed descriptions also claimed that Milton's imagery had provided the model for the garden in the first place).[84] All this can be seen as a romantic rebellion against the

82. For other examples of such imagery, see Myrone (2006), pp. 92–93.
83. Rousseau (1991), p. 73.
84. Pointon (1970), p. 241, n. 6, and During (2007), p. 280. See also M. Campbell (1992).

patriarchal authority to which Burke's sublime would have them so painfully, if transcendently, submit.[85] Thus Beckford refused to vanish into permanent exile and, not only that, inscribed his queer architectural visions onto the landscape of his native county.[86]

Contemporaries would not have found it hard to explain Beckford's preoccupation with heaven and (particularly) hell because he was perhaps Britain's most notorious sodomite. His sexual tastes seem to have included an interest in both sexes, but his public identity was fixed when news was published in 1784 of his having been previously caught *in flagrante* with a boy, William Courtenay (1768–1835), the future Earl of Devon. Beckford, after retreating abroad for a period, showed a studied lack of remorse.[87] He even adopted the motto of the Mervyn family—his estate at Fonthill place having been owned by them before 1631 when Mervyn, Lord Audley, Earl of Castlehaven, had been executed for unnatural crimes with his servants and son. Beckford owned a copy of the rare pamphlet describing the trial. In modern terms, he had been "outed" as a sodomite, but he was in the extraordinary position of being one of the richest men in England due to the inheritance of Jamaican sugar plantations worked by slave labor. He was able to embark with great resources, and without Walpole's fear of exposure, on constructing what Whitney Davis has referred to not as a jewel closet but as an overt "site of sexuality."[88]

This extraordinary house—if house is an adequate word—was built in stages by James Wyatt between 1793 and 1813, the literal centerpiece of which was a vastly disproportionate tower, which Timothy Mowl has hailed as a "perverse triumph."[89] There is a letter in the Beckford papers that purports to pre-date the construction of the tower (but may in fact have been faked up in retrospect) in which Beckford writes that "sometimes when our minds are exalted by the sublime reveries of philosophy we will ascend a lofty hill which till lately was a Mountain to my eyes. There I hope to erect a tower dedicated to meditation."[90] But it is clear that Beckford was dreaming of towers that outraged proportion and morality from an early age. The Caliph Vathek, for example, is described as

> having ascended, for the first time, the fifteen hundred stairs of his tower, he cast his eyes below, and beheld men not larger than pismires; mountains, than shells; and cities, than bee-hives. The idea, which such an elevation inspired of his own grandeur, completely

85. Meller (1996), on how the "patricidal" imagination in Schiller, Blake, and Fuseli can be compared with Beckford's action in pulling down his father's house at Fonthill and in aligning its replacement deliberately away from its predecessor; on which, see Davis (2000), p. 109.
86. Gill (2003), p. 247.
87. O'Rourke and Collings (2004–2005), para. 8.
88. Davis (2000) and (2011).
89. Mowl (1998), p. 160.
90. Beckford quoted in Mowl (1998), p. 52.

bewildered him: he was almost ready to adore himself; till, lifting his eyes upward, he saw the stars as high above him as they appeared when he stood on the surface of the earth. He consoled himself, however, for this intruding and unwelcome perception of his littleness, with the thought of being great in the eyes of others; and flattered himself that the light of his mind would extend beyond the reach of his sight, and extort from the stars the decrees of his destiny.[91]

Beckford's obsession with towers as a way to see and be seen continued after he moved out of Fonthill: the final home he had constructed was Lansdown Tower in Bath, which was complete by 1828.[92]

That these constructions were acts of phallic symbolism and scopic assertion, overt attempts to challenge and defy the developing structures of legal surveillance and closet concealment, is suggested by the fact that Beckford had been highly interested in studies of comparative religion that focused on this very topic. For instance, he bid, two years before his death, albeit unsuccessfully, for Walpole's copy of Payne Knights's book when it was included in the dispersal sale of the contents of Strawberry Hill in 1842. The argument that oriental fertility cults had spread to the West had been developed in detail by Charles Vallancey (ca. 1726–1812), a man of French Huguenot parentage and a military engineer. As a founding member of the Royal Irish Academy, he elaborated a then influential, although now long discredited, theory of the oriental origins of ancient Irish civilization, in which he focused on standing stones, and also round towers, as being related to minarets, and also to phallic worship.[93] His ideas were to be taken further by Henry O'Brien, who argued that the Irish round towers took their "architecture after the model of the *membrum virile*, which, obscenity apart, is the divinely-formed and indispensable medium selected by God himself for human propagation and sexual prolificacy [*sic*]" (Figure 4.6).[94] It is in this context that we can view Fonthill's architecture as not simply darkly sublime, but visibly rampant, as represented by John Rutter veritably penetrating the heavens (Figure 4.7). [95]

91. Beckford (1786), pp. 7–8. See also Fincher (2001), p. 236, and Fothergill (1990), p. 40, who argues that "architectural influences had as strong a bearing on the composition of *Vathek* as did impressions drawn from the 'gothic' grandeur of the Alps."
92. Mowl (1998), p. 290.
93. Vallancey (1786) and W. Love (1962), p. 184.
94. H. O'Brien (1834), p. 101.
95. I am at pains to stress that it was eighteenth-century ideas that influenced the development of Freud's ideas concerning phallic symbolism. Nevertheless, for an exploration of such ideas as an ongoing conceptual tradition in modernity in relation to high-rise buildings, see Janes (2011b), pp. 66–68; and compare William Golding's *The Spire* (1964), p. 8, in which it is Dean Jocelin's obsession to build a terrific spike on his cathedral, even in the absence of suitable foundations. The phallicism of the spire is made explicit in Golding's description of the model of the Cathedral: "The model was like a man lying on his back. The nave was his legs

Figure 4.6 *Clondalkin*, published in Henry O'Brien, *The Round Towers of Ireland; or, the History of the Tuath-de-Danaans*, 2nd ed. (London: Whittaker, 1834), facing p. 101.

Excessive architecture, as in the palace of Eblis in *Vathek*, appeared to evoke not only a range of possible transgressions and enormities, but also, in the process, the inevitability of its own moral and physical collapse—hence, perhaps, the equanimity with which Beckford viewed the collapse of the tower at Fonthill.[96]

placed together, the transepts on either side were his arms outstretched. The choir was his body; and the Lady Chapel where now the services would be held, was his head. And now also, springing, projecting, bursting, erupting from the heart of the building, there was its crown and majesty, the new spire."

96. Fincher (2007), p. 84.

FONTHILL ABBEY.

VIEW OF THE WEST, & NORTH FRONTS.
From the End of the Clerks Walk

Published June 2nd 1823 by J. Rutter Shaftesbury.

The consciousness of pain and melancholy never left Eblis, and it never left Beckford either. He did not share William Blake's optimistic visions of spiritual redemption in which Albion would throw off the shackles of repression, both political and erotic, and display resurrected flesh that towers over beholders as if in a glowing realization of Walpole's vision at the end of *Otranto* (Figure 4.8).[97] Beckford was resisting a distinction that would separate the sublime from the beautiful, just as the sodomitical closet was coming into existence as the shadow of its spectacle. When the huge sale of furniture, art, and ornamental objects from Fonthill was held in 1822, that sight produced a splenetic review from the journalist William Hazlitt in the *London Magazine*, one so extreme that, in the view of Anne Richter, he can be said to have given way to "nearly irrational loathing."[98] Such phobic disgust foreshadows the homophobic responses of the twentieth century and paved the way for the sneers of later "art historians who consider Beckford's collection a mere show for a depraved voyeur."[99] What then would Beckford have thought of the American fabric designer Marion Dorn's (1896–1964)

97. Bindman (1989), p. 170.
98. Richter (2008), p. 549.
99. Davies and Châtel (1999), p. 454.

Figure 4.8 William Blake, *Albion Rose* [also called *Glad Day* or *The Dance of Albion*] (first drawn ca. 1780, this version printed ca. 1794–1796), color printed etching with hand-drawn additions in ink and watercolor, 27.2 x 20 cm. © Trustees of the British Museum, Department of Prints and Drawings (1856,0209.417).

take on *Vathek*? In her illustrations of 1929, the all-seeing eye of the Caliph is replaced by the, as it were, all-seen green eyeshadow (Figure 4.9). That the Caliph was depicted so camply provides evidence of the triumph of the spectacle of the homosexual closet in the early twentieth century.[100] I imagine that Beckford would resist both Dorn's ornamentalism and Burke's attempt to conceal the radical potential of same-sex desire and position himself as seeing and being seen, beautiful and damned.

This section of the book has focused on a series of men who took distinct, but inter-related, approaches to male desire and

---

100. On Dorn see Boydell (1996). Compare the description of John Chute as having "fluttered about with his eyeglass and fan, astonishing the solid English 'Johns' who passed through Florence," in W. Smith (1952), quoted and discussed by Claro (2005), p. 159.

VATHEK
BY WILLIAM BECKFORD
A NEW TRANSLATION BY HERBERT B. GRIMSDITCH

WITH TEN ILLUSTRATIONS BY MARION V. DORN
THE NONESUCH PRESS
16 GREAT JAMES STREET, BLOOMSBURY · 1929

Figure 4.9 Marion Dorn, frontispiece and title page, William Beckford, *Vathek*, trans. H. B. Grimsditch (London: Nonesuch Press, 1929).

self-presentation. In the course of the eighteenth century the polite interiorization of aspects of masculine desire was accompanied by a rising tendency to scrutinize the social landscape for visible signs of gender deviance. The fear of being viewed as a bloated figure of monstrous appetites appears to have led a number of men who sexually desired other men to adopt codes of cultivated politeness and discretion. The desire, however, for such men to spot each other from among the adepts of the fashion for polite behavior led to the development of distinctive profiles of taste, such as for the transgressive aspects of the gothic. However, the very production of such forms of coded expression led to a degree of popular awareness that aberrant sexual tastes could be signaled in code. Randolph Trumbach has indicated that "slim, delicate, good-looking" men were more likely to end up as the victims of blackmail for sodomy in the eighteenth century whether they were guilty of the offense or not.[101] Many of those who did not fit the evolving normative patterns of masculine appearance, whether due to being unduly fat or unduly petite, must have felt peculiarly impelled to assert their virtue, manliness, and utility. One way in which they could achieve respectability in an age that no longer

101. Trumbach (2007a), p. 38.

regarded rank as excusing moral license was through taking on public duties. In the next section of this book, I will look at the way in which the homosocial environments of the same-sex institutions of Victorian Britain provided a vital context for the further evolution of the masculine closet and its attendant spectacle of allegedly effeminate sexual deviance.

PART TWO

THE FIRST PART of this book charted the rise of various forms of sodomitical panic to which Edmund Burke found a solution in the form
of fantasies of private submission to masculine force. Horace Walpole
appears to have embraced a polite version of the ornamentalism that
Burke regarded as feminine, while Beckford attempted queerly to col-
lide ornamental indulgence and sublime experience. These cultural
formations formed the backdrop against which the closet, albeit not a
structure yet termed as such, would continue its process of formation
in the nineteenth century. When Proust described the vice of Sodom
as "flaunting itself, insolent and immune, where its existence is never
guessed; numbering its adherents everywhere, among the people, in
the army, in the church, in prison . . . ," he drew attention to the closet
as a key aspect not only of the lives of men, but also of homosocial institutions beyond the sphere of the family.[1] Armies, churches, prisons,
and many other institutions were organized around various degrees
of the separation of the sexes. As notions of sexual diversity and identity began to be elaborated during the nineteenth century, so tensions
also began to be further exacerbated between the wish to expel sodomites from institutional contexts and to deny their existence. In this
part of the book, I look at some of the ways in which the closet and its
attendant spectacle formed during the course of the long nineteenth
century through processes of tension between individual desires and
institutional imperatives. To begin with, I emphasise the importance of
recognizing the origins of sodomy within ecclesiastical classifications
of sin. The precedent for institutional secrecy toward deviant sexuality
lies in the structures of the prayer closet in which confession to God
was not incompatible with privacy and social secrecy. Moreover, resistance to sinful desires could be seen as a species of Christian heroism.
Therefore, a place could be found within Christian institutions (and in
nineteenth-century Britain this category included not just churches,
but also schools, hospitals, military units, and many others, since all

1. Proust quoted and discussed in Sedgwick (2008), p. 218.

of these possessed chapels, chaplains, and a Christian ethos) for those who resisted, or at least seemed to resist, sinful desires.

This structure, of course, was predicated on establishing strict limits to self-expression. This meant that it was a struggle to establish queer representations of the self that were not based on phobic stereotypes. Whitney Davis has, thus, highlighted the challenges facing homoerotic visual expression in this period, noting of the painter Simeon Solomon (1840–1905) that while he "seized the thematic significance of homoerotic inflections in cultural traditions," his pictures "too easily collapsed back into a distaste . . . for the homoerotic beauty that superficially they seemed to celebrate."[2] The gothic mode of the depiction of titillating but horrific secrets pervaded many nineteenth-century evocations of same-sex desire. Perhaps the most famous example of this is Oscar Wilde's *The Picture of Dorian Gray* (1890), in which the beautiful surface is presented as the sign, for those in the know, of the concealment of monstrous appetites.[3] Dorian keeps the ugly truth hidden in a locked room (i.e., a closet), and when he kills that vileness, he kills himself.

Much of the scholarly literature on nineteenth-century queerness has focused on the *fin-de-siècle* in general and the figure of Wilde in particular, who, for Allen Sinfield, for instance, played a crucial role in the production of modern sexuality.[4] I do not, by any means, want to go so far as Elisa Glick, who argued that after the trials of 1895 "it became impossible not to think of the dandy as gay."[5] Nevertheless, important changes had taken place between that date and the occasion of the previous most famous sodomy trial of the Victorian period, that of the cross-dressers Ernest Boulton and Frederick Park in 1871. In that case the defense had successfully been able to argue that it was the very ostentation of their behavior that showed that nothing was really amiss since one would otherwise expect to have to uncover "a secret hiding from the sights of men and women . . . [since, if guilty, they] would shrink and hide away and draw over themselves and their horrible deeds a pall of darkness."[6] After the downfall of Oscar Wilde, by contrast, those who appeared to be posing as sodomites were thought to be homosexual. It was in that retrospect that the indeterminate queerness of Dorian Gray was established in court as being the sign not simply of general criminality but of same-sex desire. What have been called Wilde's "strategies of *opacity*," as expressed in the novel [original

---

2. Davis (1999), pp. 201 and 205. See also Getsy (2007) and the comments of Prettejohn (2007), pp. 98–99.
3. Budziak (2004).
4. Sinfield (1994).
5. Glick (2001), p. 157.
6. *The Queen v Boulton and Others before the Lord Chief Justice and a Special Jury: Proceedings on the Trial of the Indictment,* National Archives DPP 4/6, quoted in McKenna (2013), p. 331.

emphasis], attempted to resist categorization on sexual grounds.[7] The state of having or not having a secret was replaced in court by that of being or not being revealed as a homosexual.

The tradition of dandyism to which Dorian Gray, and Oscar Wilde, belonged was ultimately descended from the styles of macaroni display that were mentioned in the previous section of this book.[8] Lytton Strachey (1880–1932) represents a later stage in this tradition of the spectacularization into existence of the queer self beyond the structures of phobic institutions. In Chapter 6, I look at the ways in which Strachey developed a satirical critique of a series of Victorian institutions as locales of the closet in the mode suggested by Proust at around the same date. In the aftermath of World War I, it was not possible openly to declare one's sexual deviance and be successful as a writer, but it was possible to mount powerful, if coded, attacks on the social practices and values of the nineteenth century.[9] The twentieth century was not, however, to see the end of the closet, but rather its establishment as a named social institution. In Chapter 7, the final section of this part of the book, I focus on a case study of the British public school and same-sex desire to show how the mode of secrecy coexisted in an uneasy dynamic with developing legal, medical, and psychological imperatives to describe and regulate sexual deviance. I believe that one of the key qualities of the British experience of homosexuality was the persistence of the open secret of the presence of queerness in same-sex institutions and concomitant unwillingness publicly to scrutinize the self as a locale of perverse desire. This state of affairs provided artists and writers with extraordinary opportunities to explore the social world as a realm of secrets that were both shameful and erotic.

7. De Villiers (2012), p. 3.
8. See J. Adams (1995), Schaffer (2000), and Horrocks (2013).
9. Joyce (2004).

CHAPTER 5

ATHLETICS AND AESTHETICS

"ATHLETICS V[ERSUS]. AESTHETICS," a cartoon that was published in *The Illustrated London News* in 1883, shows a scene by the river in Oxford populated by four men, two women, and a dog (Figure 5.1).[1] It seems clear from the direction of the gazes of these figures that the viewer is meant to interpret the two men at the center of the picture as being healthy specimens of youth who are, quite rightly, gaining the attentions of the attractive young ladies. Two poor specimens of manhood skulk past in the background to the left, their debilitation evident from their posture and eyeglasses. The only thing whose attention they attract is a small dog, which might, one could imagine, bark at them in alarm. Of course, this is twelve years before the trials of Oscar Wilde (1854–1900) firmly associated aesthetes and sodomites in the public mind, but that does not mean that there can have been no suspicion of sexual deviance concerning them at this date. After all, the joke is that these supposed aesthetes are, in fact, ugly—a point that the reader can only appreciate by admiring the fine physiques of the athletes, the buttocks of one of whom are positioned virtually at the center of the composition. The functioning of this cartoon, at least in relation to the male readers of the newspaper, therefore required the viewer to be complicit in a secret aspect of homosocial life: that of the admiration by men of each other's bodies.[2]

---

1. Maidment (2009), p. 383.
2. Compare the turn of the millennium metrosexual, as explored in Coad (2008), with George (2004) on "the emergence of the dandy" during the first half of the nineteenth century.

A few decades later, *The Times Literary Supplement* was reporting that "at English universities undergraduates classify themselves into the mutually exclusive categories of 'aesthetes' and 'hearties.'" This distinction was also expressed by the more euphonious phrase, "arties and hearties." By this period, the former were distinctly associated with the presence of homosexuality and the latter with its absence. However, as the *Oxford English Dictionary* proceeds to demonstrate, the earlier use of "hearty" as a noun, dating from the nineteenth century, indicated "a hearty fellow; a brave, vigorous man; *esp*. in phr. my hearty!, my hearties! used in addressing sailors. Hence, a sailor, a jack-tar."[3] Since

3. *Times Literary Supplement*, July 24, 1930; reported by Oxford English Dictionary online, definition of "hearty": http://www.oed.com/view/Entry/85142?redirecte dFrom=hearties#eid, accessed November 7, 2012.

sailors had long had an association with libertine sexuality, including sodomy, this might suggest that "arties" and "hearties" were, on occasion, a little more than simply good homophones. Sexual deviance as the basis for an identity was beginning to be formulated at the end of the nineteenth century, but there were still few people who could precisely explain what constituted an "invert" or a "Uranian," let alone a "homosexual." In that cultural climate of linguistic insufficiency, not to say of continuing legal and social danger, expression of same-sex desire was often necessarily coded through combinations of suggestive gesture, word-play, dress, and demeanor, an art of display that could be so well wrought into unambiguity that it drove Lord Queensbury to prosecute Wilde for assuming a pose such as could only be intended to indicate an incitement to sodomy. It was such forms of display that were spotlighted by Proust and, of course, by Sedgwick as spectacles of the closet.

From the point of view of traditional Christian morality, because all people were vulnerable to sin, including sexual sin, the sin of Sodom was on a different scale but not of a fundamentally different kind from other forms of evil. It might be thought that if even the sodomite could be redeemed, then there was hope of salvation for all. In this chapter, I will be exploring a period in which fear and hatred of the male sexual deviant coexisted with a desire for his moral forgiveness by God and for spiritual reclamation in the optimistic spirit of Victorian religious revivalism. A crucial element of both of these positions lay in the growing comprehension of same-sex desire. The deep structures of the developing closet were often located within the minds, bodies, and homosocial lives of the hearties as they stepped from their all-male schools, to single-sex battlefields and men-only parliamentary debates. The spectacle of the closet was also partly their creation. Whether it was true that Oscar Wilde was effete and effeminate—and in many ways, such as his physique, he certainly was not—it was important for the construction of the closet that he was seen to have been. By establishing the flamboyant aesthete *as* the site of Sodom, the rest of the populace could pretend to themselves that they were convinced of their own essential probity, even as they wrestled with their inner demons. This chapter begins quite literally at the site of Sodom in the Middle East, before moving on to explore the way in which "muscular Christianity" sought to purify the institutional structures of pious manhood of the overt evidences of same-sex desire.

In the course of 1854, the painter William Holman Hunt (1827–1910) could be found standing at the spot recently identified by Louis de Saulcy as the site of Sodom, where it was believed that the wrath of God had struck down the inhabitants of the cities of the plain for the enormity of their moral crimes. He was to spend some of the most productive years of his working life in Palestine, which he visited in

Figure 5.2 Anon., *William Holman Hunt Re-enacting the Painting of the Scapegoat* (ca. 1895), albumen print, 17.5 x 22.5 cm. © The Maas Gallery, London.

1854–1855, 1869–1872, 1875–1878, and in 1892.[4] On the first of these trips he spent February to May of 1854 in Cairo, before moving on from Damietta to Jaffa and then to Jerusalem, where he based himself from June of that year to October 1855. Sojourning long in the desert was not an easy option, to judge by the degree to which he emphasized the dangers of such journeys among wastes whose only inhabitants supposedly spent their time fighting and stealing from each other.[5] In old age he re-enacted the experience of working in such circumstances, posing with a gun clasped under one arm to ward off imminent attack (Figure 5.2). Hunt's bodily worries also appear to have had a specific sexual component, which Harry Cocks has referred to as bordering on homosexual panic. When John Everett Millais was contemplating a visit to the Holy Land, Hunt advised him to grow a beard because among those "peculiarly addicted people" he would then look less like a boy and escape attention.[6]

Holman Hunt produced some of the most important works of British religious art of the nineteenth century. He was, in essence, an Anglican who had bouts of agnostic doubt. But he was also, it is fair to say, somewhat anti-clerical and unwilling to fetter his vision as a result of institutional convention. He preferred that the individual believer follow his or her own search for spiritual meaning.[7] His account of the desert

4. Tromans (2008), p. 135.
5. Holman Hunt (1887), p. 21.
6. Millais, quoted in Cocks (2010), p. 26.
7. Cocks (2010).

Figure 5.3 William Holman Hunt, *The Scapegoat* (1854–1856), oil on canvas, 87 x 139.8 cm. Courtesy of National Museums Liverpool (Lady Lever Art Gallery).

landscape that he took such pains to depict in his two versions of his picture, *The Scapegoat*, contains more than a hint of the Burkean sublime in its blend of fear and ecstatic self-fulfillment (Figure 5.3). Writing in November 1854, he recorded that "if in all there are sensible figures of men's secret deeds and thoughts then this is the terrible figure of Sin—a varnished deceit—earthly joys at hand but Hell gaping behind."[8] It is important to situate Hunt in relation to an orientalist gaze that saw Eastern lands as being peculiarly unchanged from antiquity. [9] Sodom was, from that point of view, but freshly destroyed. He expressed the look and feel of the landscape by the Dead Sea in a manner that mixed attraction and repulsion: "the rose colour is the burnt ashes of the grate, the golden plain is the salt and naked sand, the sea is heaven's own blue like a diamond . . . but as it gushes up . . . it is black, full of asphalt scum—and in the hand slimy, and smarting as a sting. No one can stand and say it is not accursed by God."[10]

Reaching out to the naked sands, in the context of Hell's gaping behind, and coming back slimed seems unlikely for a devout Victorian traveler, but then he could have blamed it all on the climate. When Richard Francis Burton (1821–1890) penned his pioneering "terminal essay" on sodomy and same-sex desire as an addendum to his unexpurgated translation of the *Arabian Nights* (1885–1888), he theorized that such lusts were common in the "Sotadic zone" (the name being derived from Sotades, a Greek poet, who had written about male desire), which encompassed the oriental lands.[11] Though Muslims happened to be living in much of this rather extensive area, which was most notable for

8. Quoted in Boime (2002), p. 109.
9. Coleman (2002), p. 278.
10. Holman Hunt, November 1854; quoted and discussed in Jacobi (2006), p. 51.
11. Colligan (2003), p. 5.

pointedly excluding northern Europe, it was in fact the hot climate that predisposed anyone settling there to unnatural lusts.[12] There was a final reason that things sodomitical might have been on Holman Hunt's mind, at least in the later stages of the painting's development. In the course of 1854, a teenage boy was admitted to a school run by the inter-denominational Protestant diocese of Jerusalem.[13] Over the ensuing months, rumors of immorality erupted into a sustained public campaign of attacks, to which Hunt contributed, not only against that school, but against Bishop Gobat who was, ultimately, in charge of it.[14]

Holman Hunt put himself through all of this peril in order to make an image that was directly aimed at the conversion of the Jews. His aim was to depict the aftermath of the Festival of the Day of Atonement when, it was recorded in the Old Testament, a goat was driven out into the wilderness, bearing both a piece of scarlet cloth about its head and (supposedly) the sins of the community. For Hunt, this prefigured the sacrifice of Christ, who took the sins of the world upon himself, includ-ing the very worst, in a final act of atonement. There was no scriptural basis for setting such a scene on the site of Sodom and, thus, it was his choice to associate Christ's ultimate sacrifice as the taking on of the sin of what has often been understood to be, in effect, male rape. Not only did Hunt's pursuit of verisimilitude lead him to what he thought was the very spot of God's wrath, but he took a goat with him (although, in the event, he painted the animal back in Jerusalem). There are two ver-sions of the work, a smaller one with a black goat and a rainbow, which is now in the Manchester Art Gallery, and a larger one with a white goat and without a rainbow, which is now in the Lady Lever Gallery in Liverpool.[15] Inscribed on the frame of the latter version were the words "Surely he hath borne our Griefs, and carried our Sorrows / Yet we did esteem him stricken, smitten of GOD, and afflicted" (Isaiah 53:4), and "And the Goat shall bear upon him all their iniquities unto a Land not inhabited" (Leviticus 16:22) (Figure 5.3).

In her essay "Queers Are Like Jews, Aren't They?" Janet L. Jakobsen has argued that there are "longstanding associations, both implicit and explicit, of homosexuals and Jews, at least in terms of anti-Semitic and anti-homosexual discourses."[16] Seen from the perspective of the gothic imagination, the scapegoat also evoked the figure of the cursed wandering Jew popularized by Charles Maturin's novel *Melmoth the Wanderer* (1820).[17] Holman Hunt had driven himself out into the fearful

12. Kennedy (2000), pp. 336–339.
13. Jerusalem Diocesan (1854), p. 21.
14. Jack (1995), pp. 197–198.
15. Bronkhurst (2006), 1, pp. 177–178, *The Scapegoat* (1854–1855 and 1858), Manchester Art Gallery; and pp. 178–179, *The Scapegoat* (1854–1856), Lady Lever Art Gallery, Liverpool.
16. Jakobsen (2003), p. 65.
17. See also Boime (2002), p. 110.

wastes in order to encounter a vision of himself, menaced and faced by the evidences of death, just as Nichols Tromans notes, with reference to the Liverpool version, that "we can see that the backside of the animal seems threatened by the form of a member of the deathly skeleton of a camel in the middle-distance."[18] The goat's face, it can be suggested, has something of the quality of Hunt's own visage about it. Hunt chose to confront his fears by imagining himself in the position of an animal burdened by sexual sin, but, as the goat stares out from the picture, it also acts to involve the viewer in a process of engagement such that we too "thereby, became implicated in the landscape and stories contained in the picture."[19] It is hardly surprising that the critical response to this intensely personal work was distinctly lukewarm.[20] *The Art Journal* in 1860 was, for example, to characterize the composition as "having disappointed even his warmest admirers."[21] By depicting the sacrifice in all its ugliness, Hunt created a disjunction between admiration for Christ as redeemer and disgust at the death of a literal goat that could have had no such function. The scapegoat itself appears, therefore, as little more than a token sacrifice, which did nothing but provide a social alibi for the moral failings, including the sodomitical desires, of Jews past and present. This was a representation that, moreover, if its implications were fully understood, threatened to break open rather than to reinforce a sodomitical closet as the fundamental truth of the fallen male condition.

It is notable that the second major composition to emerge from these years in the Middle East had quite the opposite effect and was greeted with great enthusiasm. This was *The Finding of the Saviour in the Temple*, the larger version of which is now in the Birmingham Museum and Art Gallery, and a smaller version of which hangs in the Lady Lever Gallery, Liverpool (Figure 5.4).[22] F. E. Stephens wrote of the depiction of the young Christ in this work that

> He is no smooth-faced boy, a valetudinarian or feminine-featured child, half-babe half-woman in aspect, but a robust youth, of splendid physique, and exactly what the poet meant when he called him the ideal of a gentleman. . . . We heartily agree with Mr Hunt in not rendering this a simple type of passive holiness or asceticism, or merely intellectual power. A *man*, he is cast in the noblest mould: nobly beautiful, to express the glory of his origin and the greatness of his task—also strong and robust, to *be able to do it* [emphases in the

18. Tromans (2008), p. 152.
19. Coleman (2002), p. 281.
20. Landow (1979), p. 108.
21. Anon., "Picture Exhibitions" (1860), p. 182.
22. Bronkhurst (2006), pp. 173–177, *The Finding of the Saviour in the Temple* (1854–1855 and 1856–1860), Birmingham Museums and Art Gallery; and, pp. 195–196, *The Finding of the Saviour in the Temple* (1862) National Museums Liverpool.

The finding of the Saviour in the Temple.

Figure 5.4 William Holman Hunt, *The Finding of the Saviour in the Temple* (1854–1860), oil on canvas, 85.7 x 141 cm. © Birmingham Museums Trust (1896P80).

original]. Certainly painters have erred in representing Christ as the feeble ascetic hitherto chosen . . . it was no delicate frame that suffered the scourging and the cross.[23]

The viewer is encouraged to admire the beauty of the young Christ and can do so in safety because he does not *look* deviant. It is precisely because he is manly and attractive that he can be admired and even desired. The care with which this painting encodes exoticism and eroticism for the British audience can be compared with the less constrained French orientalism of Jean-Léon Gérôme (1824–1904), on display in his *Snake Charmer* from the late 1860s (Figure 5.5). This work was the subject of a celebrated article by Linda Nochlin on "The Imaginary Orient," in which she pointed out that the viewer of the picture is in this work more overtly directed to a perverse interest in the body of the young boy but at the same time absolved from being implicated in homoerotic desire because the child is shown performing for the benefit of a group of oriental men.[24] Compositionally, however, the two

23. Stephens (1860), pp. 72–73. The first section of this extract is copied from *The Athenaeum*, April 21, 1860, also by Stephens. See also Giebelhausen (2006), p. 167.
24. Nochlin (1991), p. 34; see also Aldrich (2003), pp. 152–153.

pictures are similar—in both a young boy is evaluated by a group of older men—but the Christian message of Hunt's painting acts as a further alibi, a sort of insulation against the appearance of overt homo-eroticism and, as such, enables the child, a suitably manly child, to make delicious eye contact with the viewer. *The Finding of the Saviour in the Temple* also shares with *The Snake Charmer* a fear, and yet also a thrill, at the thought of being alone in the company of other men.[25] None of this is to say that Holman Hunt was a sodomite himself (albeit that as an "arty" his manliness was potentially in question), but it does flag up that same-sex desire certainly cannot be expected to have obeyed the neat rules of late nineteenth-century sexology before they had been invented. This is particularly significant because the problematization of the desiring gazes of men toward other men (and boys) was something that was endemic to the homosocial environments that were so prominent in Victorian society precisely because they were constituted upon the script of the detestation of sodomy.

The Finding of the Saviour of the Temple secured the closet of unauthorized desire by creating a series of plausible alibis for the gaze. *The Scapegoat*, however, was a dangerously abject image because of its very ordinariness. It threatened to reveal perverse desire as an essential truth of fallen humanity and, thus, it confronted the viewer with his

Figure 5.5 Jean-Léon Gérôme, *The Snake Charmer* (ca. 1870), oil on canvas, 84 x 122 cm. Image © Sterling and Francine Clark Art Institute, Williamstown, MA, photograph by Michael Ages (1955.51).

25. Jacobi (2006), p. 76; see also Bendiner (1987), p. 128.

or her own complicity in sin. It did not allow for what Peter Gay has characterized as the nineteenth-century bourgeois trick of projection:

> [Freud] argued that so far as they are not justified by real exploitation or real persecution, people making an enemy will adopt the psychological maneuver of projection. They defend themselves against their unacceptable thoughts or wishes by expelling them from their own mind into the outside world, onto the convenient Other. This mechanism provides a highly supportive way of living with one's failings; it permits the denial that one is subject to those failings in the first place and then opportunely discovers them in strangers or adversaries, real or imagined.[26]

In *The Finding of the Saviour in the Temple* moral guilt can be projected onto the Jews, but in *The Scapegoat* it is bounced straight back onto us. Same-sex desire was born and nurtured as an art of the evolving nineteenth-century closet, in offhand gestures, sideways looks, and acts of denial. Oscar Wilde was to perfect all these arts before his own scapegoating reconfigured the closet in the context of a homosexual image that was no longer so delightfully and conveniently deniable.

Anthropological study has provided us with ways in which to compare theological and social meanings of scapegoating. In societies without a moral code framed in the Christian manner of "right" and "wrong," polluting transgressions could take the form of acts that were dangerous in terms of power rather than of personal morality. It is this that caused some confusion in the earlier literature on "taboo, that is, the avoidance of the socially dangerous."[27] Taboos were originally studied in South Pacific contexts, in which they often referred to emanations of supernatural power without reference to morality. Westerners saw this as being inherently magical and primitive. "Religion" was supposedly superior in that it did not simply highlight power, but classified it according to its position of good and evil. No longer was it sheer power that led to danger, but only the satanic elements of disorder. In the 1950s and 1960s the anthropologist Mary Douglas compared ancient Israel and contemporary tribal societies in Africa and moved the debate onward from the notion of taboo to that of pollution, by arguing that the latter was based on ambiguities of classification and was about preventing danger from anomalous situations. In her pioneering work, *Purity and Danger: An Analysis of the Concepts of Pollution and Taboo* (1966), Douglas presented an elaborated sociological theory of the concept of dirt and pollution. For her, dirt was "matter out of place" and, as such, dirtiness was produced by the regimes of classification that underwrote the social order.[28]

---

26. Gay (1995), p. 70.
27. Valeri (1999), p. 53.
28. M. Douglas (1966).

Fear of bodily transgression and impurity may lead societies into the production of rituals of containment or expulsion. René Girard built upon the notion of scapegoating as it appears in the Old Testament and constructed a theory in which this is seen as a sacred act that has the power to bring society back into a state of symbolic order.[29] Yet not all those who are driven forth from a community are treated with respect, as Giorgio Agamben identified in his reworking of the Roman category of *homo sacer*.[30] Those who transgressed certain rules in ancient Rome were to be killed but were not to be regarded as holy, sacrificial victims. It was in this mode, justified by spurious and inflexible racial "science," that the corpses of homosexuals were used to top up the kilns in Nazi Germany. The intense focus on victimhood in many works of art and literature that are sympathetic to or implicated in the desires of sodomites/homosexuals/gays is intended, by contrast, to establish the role that their sacrifice plays. As Butler notes in *Precarious Life*, the socially unintelligible is also the unmournable.[31] Douglas Marshall has argued that "sacralization theory provides a new perspective on such phenomena by suggesting that homophobia in males is a product of the homophobe's experienced collision between his own temptation to engage in sex with other men and the behavioural inhibitions on such behaviour."[32]

Christianity, therefore, can be seen to have played a key role in the evolution of socially phobic responses during the nineteenth century because of its insistence on the implication of all mankind in a state of sin. This means that the spectacle of the closet should not simply be seen as an abject diversion from the hidden truth of the closet, but also as the site where queer social martyrdom was displayed, as I discuss in my study *Visions of Queer Martyrdom from John Henry Newman to Derek Jarman*.[33] The spectacle of the scapegoated sinner did not, thereby, remove evil from the homosocial community so much as highlight a shared state of complicity. The closet as a space of shamefully concealed desire was, thus, reinforced rather than purged by the periodic and horrific spectacle of public expulsions from it. This, in essence, underlay Holman Hunt's critique of the ancient Jewish practice. What we will see in the remainder of this chapter is a peculiarly dogged preservation of the possibilities of desire in constraint by the religiously imbued eminences and institutions of Victorian Britain. In such hands, the closet was shaped not to preclude same-sex love but to preserve its essence as a shameful secret that was to be atoned for

29. Girard (1986).
30. Agamben (1998).
31. Butler (2004), p. 35.
32. Marshall (2010), p. 69.
33. Janes (2015).

by those *visibly* bearing the burden of such sin. Yet, as we have seen in the case of Holman Hunt, the too overt sight of such suffering was, in itself, still hard to bear, since it represented painful witness to the polluted state of the viewing self.

WORKING MEN

A few years before Holman Hunt took off in a cloud of moral angst for the Middle East, the Reverend Charles Kingsley (1819–1875), an emphatically robust and married man, had taken to hanging around at the British Museum. We know from several of his sermons that the heroic nudity of the ancient Greek marbles frequently inspired him to expatiate on the physically fallen nature of the modern world.[34] For instance, in *Nausicaa in London* (1873) he writes that

> fresh from the Marbles of the British Museum, I went my way through London streets [*sic*]. My brain was full of fair and grand forms; the forms of men and women whose every limb and attitude betokened perfect health, and grace, and power, and self-possession . . . those Greek sculptures, which remain as a perpetual sermon to rich and poor, amid our artificial, unwholesome, and it may be decaying pseudo-civilisation.[35]

For Kingsley the realms of art, or at least of what he thought of as *wholesome* art, and of manliness, were rightly to be brought together. In his sermon on "Picture Galleries" he argued that the function of great art was the validation of the self. Addressing the "working man," he wrote that such a person "begins, and rightly, to respect himself the more when he finds that he, too, has a fellow-feeling with noble men and noble deeds."[36] This piece was included in a posthumous collection entitled *True Words for Brave Men* (1878). In the same volume we find a text entitled "The British Museum," dating from 1848, that finds Kingsley absorbed in contemplation of the natural history displays that were still housed there prior to their removal later in the century to South Kensington. As he stared into the cabinet in front of him, he tells us that

> next to me stood a huge, brawny coal-heaver, in his shovel hat, and white stockings and high-lows, gazing at the humming-birds as earnestly as myself. As I turned he turned, and I saw a bright manly face with a broad, soot-grimed forehead, from under which a pair of keen flashing eyes gleamed wondering smiling sympathy into mine. In that moment we felt ourselves friends. . . . If we had been Frenchmen, we should, I suppose, have rushed into each other's

34. D. Pick (1989), p. 195.
35. Kingsley (1880), p. 107.
36. Kingsley (1878), p. 233.

arms and "fraternized" upon the spot. As we were a pair of dumb, awkward Englishmen, we only gazed half a minute, staring into each other's eyes, with a delightful feeling of understanding each other, and then burst out at once with, "Isn't that beautiful?" "Well, that is!" And then both turned back again to stare at our humming-birds.

I never felt more thoroughly at that minute (though, thank God, I had often felt it before) that all men were *brothers*; that this was not a mere political doctrine, but a blessed God-ordained fact [original emphasis].[37]

On the face of it, this is a simple and heartening piece of homosocial fraternizing in which Kingsley is sharing his enthusiasm for the progress of knowledge among the lower orders, and it has been construed, for instance, in relation to Kingsley's Christian socialism.[38] The two men are, after all, simply expressing their shared appreciation for one of the jeweled wonders of God's creation. Yet a cross-class same-sex meeting at the Museum centered upon aesthetic appreciation could have raised moral suspicions. Matt Cook has explained how the classical galleries, in particular, make repeated appearances in the late nineteenth- and early twentieth-century works of men such as A. E. Housman and E. M. Forster in the context of queer assignations in which "the scenario is redolent of fleeting urban encounters: the narrator 'loiters' in the museum and 'meets' the statue, which seems almost to be hanging around for just such contact and exchanged gazes."[39] Kingsley's encounters with statues were, if we take his word for it at face value, quite different. In an echo of Burke's experiences with the sublime deity, the classical statue was an exemplar of moral conduct and manliness, the encounter with which functioned to enhance one's own probity. Thus, when Kingsley meets the coal-heaver we are meant to understand that the two appreciate each other for their respective manly values before turning their attentions back to the delicate, ornamental (one might say, in terms of the codings of the time, feminine) forms of the little birds in front of them (albeit that there were likely to have been both male and female specimens in such displays because both sexes are equally brightly colored).

This setup, however, provides Kingsley with the opportunity not only to admire the birds, but also the coal-heaver. It enabled them to stand "for half a minute, staring into each other's eyes, with a delightful feeling of *understanding* each other" [my emphasis]. The verb to "understand" was sometimes used in the nineteenth century to express mutual recognition of same-sex desire, as when Peter Doyle said in 1895 of his first encounter with his lover Walt Whitman at the end of a tramcar ride: "we

37. Kingsley (1878), p. 245.
38. P. Jones (2003), pp. 212–213.
39. Cook (2003), p. 34.

were familiar at once—I put my hand on his knee—*we understood*" [original emphasis].[40] This happened in a different time and place, but it is possible to suggest that these two meetings had something significant in common. In 1855 Kingsley published *Westward Ho!*, a novel in which he based the character of Frank, an Elizabethan poet, on Charles Mansfield, a Cambridge classmate, whom Kingsley said later was my "first love." Frank and the (male) narrator of the novel stare at each other at one point in what is described as "eye-wedlock," which is elsewhere used in Kingsley's fiction as code for sexual desire and indeed for love-making.[41] The bedroom, for Kingsley, was a sacred erotic space. Shortly before his marriage, he wrote to his future wife, Frances (Fanny) Grenfell that "when I feel near to God I always feel such a need to undress, as if everything that was artificial jarred me. What bliss to see that you feel the same."[42] It should be recalled that the British Museum was also a temple of godliness and physical perfection (and nudity) for Kingsley, in contradistinction to the world outside. Therefore, it may be reasonable to compare his admiration for the coal-heaver with that of the Roman Catholic convert and poet Gerard Manley Hopkins's (1844–1889) homoerotic visual projection of Christ as a thrillingly strong, working man.[43] All of this does not imply homosexuality per se, but it does suggest processes of implication in aspects of same-sex desire similar to those suggested by Michael Hatt in his reading of Hamo Thornycroft's *The Mower* (1884), a sculpture of a young, working man, as being "situated on the boundary between the homosocial and the homosexual."[44] Further suggestive evidence for Kingsley's lively awareness and appreciation of the male physique, including his own, is implied by the series of sketches that he made of himself and Fanny.[45] For instance, in one drawing, dated October 31, 1843, Kingsley is positioned as the central element of the composition, carefully muscular, his hair cascading down over his face, while Fanny is set to one side, dutifully staring up at him in the customary pose of feminine adoration.[46]

From the point of view of Joseph Bristow, "Hopkins, like [John Addington] Symonds and Forster, takes Kingsley's and Hughes's novel

40. Quoted in Murray (1994), p. 13.
41. Compare the discussion of Beckford in Chapter 4. See Barker (2002), pp. 479–480, and Fincher (2007) on queerness and "the penetrating eye" in Gothic literature.
42. Kingsley, quoted in Chitty (1975), p. 84.
43. Bristow (1992), p. 694, comments that "the male body, especially the working-class male body, has such potency, vitality, and it has to be said, no uncertain danger in Hopkins' aesthetics."
44. Hatt (2003), p. 26. Compare R. Griffin (1995), p. 78, on Thomas Eakins, *The Swimming Hole* (1883–1885): "hidden behind a screen of classical allusions and a general tone of Mark Twain-like rural innocence, Eros reveals himself in what has been occluded" (i.e., overt homosexuality).
45. Klaver (2006), p. 78, on the strong sensuality of his correspondence at this time.
46. This drawing was inserted into the diary kept in 1842–1843 by Frances Grenfell before her marriage to Charles Kingsley; see Maynard (1993), fig. 4, after p. 92.

concerns with 'muscular Christianity' to unforeseen [erotic] lengths."[47] The ascription of homosexuality to Hopkins has been the subject of considerable controversy as a result of objections from those who thought this a slur, applied gratuitously to a man of intense religious devotion. The ascription of same-sex desire to Kingsley is similarly not something to be taken lightly, bearing in mind that he was (in)famous in his final years for fighting what he saw as the rise of effeminacy within the Victorian Church through his endorsement, along with others such as Thomas Hughes (1822–1896), of a renewed drive toward Christian manliness which was then, subsequently, to be popularly referred to as "muscular Christianity." These battles centered, above all, on the person and example of John Henry Newman (1801–1890), who had received Hopkins into the Church of Rome. The Catholic revivalism that Newman embraced, first at Oxford within the Church of England before his conversion in 1845, was held up to suspicion by Kingsley for its advocacy of clerical celibacy. On the face of it, the accusation concerned a want of manliness, which primarily referred to a lack of moral and physical vigor. His jibes can be contextualized by reference to contemporary lampoons in *Punch* of Anglo-Catholic priests as being camp transvestites, such as the drawing "Sweet Thing in Christmas Vestments," which appeared in 1866.[48] However, Oliver Buckton has suggested that whether or not Newman's celibacy, friendships and behavior in the 1830s were "full of dubious sexual import and suggestive of a variety of 'perversions'—it is clear that they were so, or were becoming so, by the 1860s."[49] Kingsley's stand was intended not to get rid of same-sex desire but to prevent the Church from becoming seen as the epitome of effeminate spectacle. Indeed, his "profoundly erotic appreciation of the virile body" has been seen by James Eli Adams as providing an "essential precedent" for later Victorian homoerotic aestheticism.[50]

A piece in the *Saturday Review* (1858), "Parsons and Novels," was, moreover, far from clear in its support of Kingsley's style as representing natural behavior and honesty and that of his clerical opponents as artificial. The piece is not even clearly negative when it says that "clergymen are especially attractive to ladies . . . women regard clergymen as standing half-way between themselves and men."[51] It is argued, with only moderate irony, that well-bred ladies admire a man who takes the lead in domestic arrangements and who is "willing to superintend the distribution of petticoats."[52] Referring to Kingsley's fiction, the article says that his "parsonic gladiators may, from one point of view, be

47. Bristow (1992), p. 696.
48. Anon., "Sweet Thing" (1866), p. 11.
49. Buckton (1992), p. 380.
50. J. Adams (1994), pp. 216 and 235.
51. Anon., "Parsons and Novels" (1859), p. 708.
52. Anon., "Parsons and Novels" (1859), p. 709.

described as a trick by which the clergymen novelists wish to make themselves men amongst men. They rather resent the way that ladies regard them. They do not wish to be thought a kind of neutral body to which a woman is as near as a man. Accordingly they carry their parson heroes to the extreme of manliness."[53] Seen from this perspective, Kingsley was trying just a bit too hard to appear *like* a real man, placing himself eye to eye with a coal-heaver, to quite *be* a real man.

Kingsley saw the role of a clergyman as standing in a line of patriarchal authority from God, and he advocated the modeling of the self, in Burkean fashion, as the lesser reflection of the ultimate power of his sublime maker. As Fasick has argued, the concept was that "a properly masculine father, taking his authority from his resemblance to a patriarchal God, will transmit a tradition of male strength to his energetic sons."[54] Harrington has argued that "reading Kingsley, one realises that, estranged though he and his enemies doubtless were, the real estrangement was within himself. Opposing sides of his personality are represented by the split between masculine and feminine virtue, sport and domesticity, instinct and responsibility."[55] Thus the supposedly effeminate and reserved Newman, all robes and tears, functioned for Kingsley as the spectacle of his own closet that did not contain a homosexual but a man who on occasion enjoyed the experience of same-sex desire. The obvious "secrets" of others drew attention away from the secrets of his own, which included, among other things, a lively interest in sadomasochistic ritual.[56]

Yet, even as he plunged himself into ever more masculine worlds of work, sport, and the military, Kingsley's continued preoccupations as an art-appreciating clergyman threatened to reveal that he was *performing* manliness, that is to say, that he was involved in what has been studied in late twentieth-century contexts as "male impersonation."[57] This meant that his need for a weakly effeminate sacred/abject scapegoat grew apace. Kingsley's dilemma was far from unique. Generations of British men grew up having crushes in their single-sex schools and universities and were in search of an alibi. The appearance of the closet by the end of the nineteenth century as an artifact of same-sex desire, in association with a gradually growing awareness of sexuality as a core element of identity, was a result of this need. This meant that a split was able to emerge between those who saw their deviant sexual desires as a central element of their identity and those who did not, or did not want to do so. Performing the spectacle of the closet became a vital way of openly signaling sexual preference, but one that operated in collusion

53. Anon., "Parsons and Novels" (1859), p. 709.
54. Fasick (1993), p. 107.
55. Harrington (1977), p. 86.
56. Janes (2015) and (forthcoming).
57. Simpson (1994).

with those eager to hide in the closet. Kingsley was, thus, attempting to position Newman as being the spectacular performer when the Cardinal thought he was simply following his own sincere beliefs.

The public revelation of Oscar Wilde through his conviction in 1895 marks a crucial moment when the spectacle of the closet becomes dislocated from inchoate fears of sodomy, effeminacy, and male inadequacy and becomes more firmly anchored to the ascription of homosexual desire. The case of Wilde became paradigmatic for Proust and contributed to his characterization of de Charlus. Wilde's performance has been the subject of intense academic scrutiny and so does not necessitate lengthy recapitulation here.[58] But it is important to stress that his performance before 1895 only became canonical as the ideal form of the spectacle of the closet as a result of his conviction for gross indecency.

> If we read Wilde's containing inscription into discourse and his physical containment behind bars as the successful culmination of his efforts to construct a personal homosexual identity, then a solution to one of history's most perplexing psycho-mysteries can be offered. . . . [Instead of fleeing] he simply waited for the State to begin its inscriptory process. He allowed himself to be martyred. For almost fifteen years he had tried to achieve the construction of a homosexual social identity, and he needed the State to finish the job he had started.
>
> Wilde needed the state's dominance, with its control over signification, in order to complete the project by linking his transgressive reinscription of bourgeois masculinity to sexology's homosexual type.[59]

What he did, said, wore, smoked, drank, and who he flirted with were retrospectively inscribed within the boundary of the overt evidences of a homosexual secret that had been brought to light. The abject sight of Wilde in prison, and in exile on the streets of Paris, completed the work of transforming the public perception of what had been a sparkling dandyesque performance into a poisonous charade. In the long term, this shameful Wilde was to be contested by some of his defenders through the development of an alternative narrative—that of an "out" proto-gay who was scapegoated for his transgressions of society's rules. The reality was that before 1895 Wilde had operated in collusion with the closet. The abject outsider to society had then still been the ugly and vile low-life sodomite rather than

58. Some useful places to begin exploring this topic include Elfenbein (1993), especially in relation to the precursors of Wildean dandysim such as Byron; Neff (2002), Denisoff (1999), and Stephenson (2007) on the problematization of performance; Schultz (1996) on the media; McDiarmid (2001) on Wilde's speeches from the dock; and M. Meyer (1994) and (1995) and Bristow (1995), pp. 16–54, on camp and effeminacy.
59. M. Meyer (1994), p. 102.

the camp aesthete. The codes of affected behavior that we think of as camp only now were to become firmly bolted onto the freshly constructed concept of homosexuality as a state of mental and physical abnormality.

I do not wish to elaborate here on the cultural phenomenon of the *fin de siècle* literary closet because that is precisely what Sedgwick achieved in her study of 1990. What I have been eager to establish, however, is that the closet as a place of secrecy and insecurity did not spring into existence in the late nineteenth century because sexology had only now identified that there was such a thing as a "homosexual." Likewise, the shame of the closet in the twentieth century continued to encompass the fear of same-sex desire as but one component of an ugly brew of male insecurities that had long been in preparation. One key difference that the Wilde trial made was to entrench a particular set of surface appearances as being, supposedly, the signs of the spectacle of the closet. Thus when Maurice, in E. M. Forster's Edwardian novel of the same name, confesses to homosexuality, he does so by saying that "I'm an unspeakable of the Oscar Wilde sort," and he is not believed when he says this because he is manly rather than effeminate.[60] That book was not published in its author's lifetime, but just such a determinedly "Oscar Wilde sort," the poet Wilmot, did appear in the (at the time well-known) novel *Sinister Street* (1913–1914) by Compton Mackenzie. This character's idea of a good chat-up line to a youth is "what is the book, Hyacinthus?"[61]

> "I don't suppose you've seen any of my stuff. I don't publish much. Sometimes I read my poems to Interior people."
>
> Michael looked puzzled.
>
> "Interior is my name for the people who understand. So few do. I should say you'd be sympathetic. You look sympathetic. You remind me of those exquisite boys who in scarlet hose run delicately with beakers of wine or stand in groups about the corners of old Florentine pictures . . . "
>
> "Won't you smoke? These Chian cigarettes in their diaphanous paper of mildest mauve would suit your oddly remote, your curiously shy glance . . . shall I buy you *A Rebours*, and teach you to live?"[62]

The effect of this conflation of surface camp and hidden ("interior") same-sex desire was, of course, to strengthen the closet. If the homosexual was perceived to be wild(e)ly affected, then a moderate degree of effeminacy might, in comparison, pass under the moral radar. On the

60. Forster (2005), p. 138.
61. Mackenzie (1960), p. 215, and H. Booth (2007), p. 322.
62. Mackenzie (1960), pp. 215–216.

other hand, in due course, the prosecution of Wilde could be presented by his defenders as a persecution precisely insofar as weak effeminates were not, by definition, a threat to ordinary men. It was to be a cultural politics of victimhood, inspired ultimately by the idealized suffering of Christ, that was finally to underpin changes in public opinion concerning homosexuality in the context of AIDS. But it is important to remember that it was also only in the latter part of the twentieth century, as will be discussed in Chapter 9, that gay liberation movements successfully began to contest the closet by their very assertion that such a structure existed.

In the meantime, the golden age of the spectacle of the closet saw even the body and relationships of the "manly" proto-gay rights campaigner Edward Carpenter (1844–1929) re-inscribed within the very structures of gender difference and effeminacy that he was attempting to challenge. In the case history that he contributed to John Addington Symond's *Sexual Inversion* (1897), he stated that "my ideal of love is a powerful, strongly built man of my own age or rather younger."[63] Carpenter had met such a working-class man from Sheffield, George Merrill, in 1891, and seven years later they began living together. The couple remained together for the rest of their lives. The cross-class nature of their relationship was part of their radicalism. Forster tells us that his novel *Maurice* was directly inspired by visiting Carpenter, whom he approached as a "saviour" at his "shrine" at Millthorpe in Derbyshire. The character of Scudder was based on Merrell and was in turn to inspire D. H. Lawrence to create Mellors as the lover of Lady Chatterley.[64] Their home, paid for out of Carpenter's considerable inheritance, became a "sacred" locale, the place to which many socialists and Uranians (as increasing numbers of those with same-sex desires were beginning to refer to themselves) "made our pilgrimage."[65]

When *Personal Impressions of Edward Carpenter* by Edith Ellis (wife of the pioneering sexual-health researcher Havelock Ellis) was published, posthumously, in 1922, it included extensive commentary on the domestic arrangements at the house.

> What has always struck me most is the way the apparently incongruous in this atmosphere appears orderly and reasonable. In the little kitchen, where we eat and talk, there is a piano. It seems quite in place, though in our kitchens it would probably appear absurd. I remember smiling to myself one night when I sat between Carpenter and his factotum and friend in one. One was mending his shirt, and other a pair of socks. No incongruity struck me, because Carpenter's

63. Carpenter quoted and discussed in Roberton (2008), p. 176.
64. Forster (2005), p. 219, and see Piggford (1997).
65. Brooks (1915), p. 330. On the "Uranian identity," see Wilper (2010).

idea of life is simplification and a real division of work. His belief is, that what a woman can do a man can always share.[66]

The kitchen is described here as a place where the absurd has become natural. Merrell is described not as a lover, but partly as a friend and partly a servant. Moreover, the implication of the reference to the division of labor was not simply that men were mending their own clothes, but that this was more remarkable in the case of Carpenter, who was the master of the household. The lower-class Merrell has, therefore, been positioned as the woman in the relationship.[67]

Other sympathetic visitors also failed to identify a partnership of two manly men. Thus, in September 1914, Frederic Brooks and six other socialists visited Millthorpe. The visitors wondered about the domestic arrangements, but Brooks concluded that "I think I may say there was no evil history lurking in the dishes we had that day; the tea or the sugar possibly had a doubtful 'past' but that fact did not obtrude itself upon us just then."[68] On leaving, their doubts were seemingly eased by a quasi-religious vision:

As we passed through Chesterfield on our way home we looked again at the crooked spire [of the parish church], no longer an object of

66. E. Ellis (1922), p. 11.
67. On nineteenth-century queer manservants, see McCuskey (1999) for an interesting discussion of Thackerey and the flunkey and, for later twentieth-century counterparts, Medhurst (1984) on the film *Victim* (1961), starring Dirk Bogarde.
68. Brooks (1915), p. 329.

jesting amusement, but hallowed now by the fading glory of a rainbow. "Ah!" I said to myself, thinking of George and looking at the spire, "how often does man see truly into the heart of his fellow-man? Yes! Here indeed is a mystery like that of the Sphinx!"[69]

But what is the Sphinx doing here in the countryside? That epitome of the Wildean, metropolitan secret was not meant to be making itself at home in the very citadel of twentieth-century sexual progress. While Merrell was "rough" in terms of his working-class manners, photographs of him show a man positioned as the dependent.[70] Sheila Rowbotham captions one such image as featuring a "racy-looking Merrill," but to my eye his crooked pose has something of the Boldini Montesquiou about it (Figure 5.6).[71] At this date, even individuals whom we might regard as having "outed" themselves appear to have been in danger of re-inscription, perhaps even self re-inscription, under the sign of the spectacle of a closet that the fall of Wilde had consolidated as a stance of great utility to so many "normal" men.

69. Brooks (1915), pp. 330–331.
70. Rowbotham (2008), p. 181, and Robertson (2008), p. 177.
71. Rowbotham (2008), p. 181.

CHAPTER 6

STRACHEY IN EARNEST

IF THE HOMOSEXUAL sins of the Victorian closet were still un-nameable, they could, however, begin to be hinted at in earnest, at least from the standpoint of the changed cultural landscape of 1918. Lytton Strachey (1880–1932) sought to be excused from service in World War I on the grounds of physical debilitation. From the moment of his appearance at the tribunal in Hampstead in north London in March 1916, Strachey had been assiduous in presenting an image of advanced enfeeblement. After myriad relatives had arrived, along with "attendant spirits, Bloomsbury painters and pacifists,"

> the applicant himself, suffering, among many other disorders from piles, and carrying a tartan travelling rug, made his entrance. [Strachey's ally, the Liberal MP] Philip Morrell gravely handed him the air cushion which, to the astonishment of the chairman, he applied to the aperture in his beard and solemnly inflated. Then he deposited this cushion upon the wooden bench, lowered himself gingerly down upon it facing the mayor, and arranged the rug carefully about his knees.[1]

We are perhaps used to the spectacle of the closet as having something of the ornamental about it, but here Strachey, in an act of the camp grotesque, highlighted what was not about to be openly addressed— namely his sexual deviance—by drawing the attention of the members of the draft board to the sorry state of his anus.

1. Holroyd (1967), 2, pp. 178–179. Morrell was attending as a character witness for Strachey.

As this scene in Hampstead illustrates, Strachey was a master of queer dandyism and spectacle—of being able to "outrage," without being dangerously outrageous. You would think from this account that he was in his seventies, but in fact he was thirty-four years old when World War I began. In 1900, the year of Wilde's death, Strachey was at Cambridge, where he became one of the leading lights of the Apostles society.[2] He had various same-sex affairs without drawing great attention to himself beyond that association of friends and neighbors in the district of central London that was to give its name to them in the form of the "Bloomsbury Group." In 1918 Strachey, then still a little-known writer, published *Eminent Victorians* [hereafter *EV*].[3] This book consisted of a set of startlingly original essays on leading figures from the previous century. By the following year Strachey was famous.

The word "queer" in the age of the Bloomsbury Group meant "strange," but it was a sort of strangeness that was beginning to be applied to unusual and subversive gender roles and sexual preferences.[4] It is the purpose of this chapter to explore Strachey's literary practice as an act of queer exploration of others who, it could be alleged, lived deep in the closet, the aim of which was to draw attention to aspects of perversity at the heart of the normative structures of Victorian society. His goal was not to "out" any of his subjects, or indeed himself, as homosexual, but rather to shift the balance of social power by gently, but audibly, deflating the artificial cushions that supported the reputations of some of the major figures of the previous century. Julie Taddeo has argued that "since the 1960s, [Lytton] Strachey and the Bloomsbury Group in general have incited interest among feminist and queer studies scholars, not so much for their publications and art, but for their lifestyles."[5] I will suggest that sharing aspects of the space of the closet did not mean an inability to contest the precise nature of its covert operations, particularly for a man who could negotiate the terms of his own social inclusion and exclusion. This, Strachey did by subtly influencing how the Victorians and their Christian institutions were viewed, and he did this in reaction to the authoritarianism of wartime in the hope of creating a more morally flexible and interesting future.

Larry Lepper has argued that "at a time when some aspects of sexual orientation were criminalised, a sense of rebellion and elaboration permeates literary styles often not found in writers whose sexuality is not suppressed or hidden in some way."[6] The Bloomsbury Group is notable

2. Taddeo (1997), p. 211. See also Lubenow (1998).
3. Strachey (1918). A useful introduction to Strachey is Rosenbaum (2008), and other key studies include Holroyd (1994), Spurr (1995), and Taddeo (2002). Some of the following material appeared in an earlier form in Janes (2014).
4. Herrmann (2000), p. 6.
5. Taddeo (2002), p. 2.
6. Lepper (2010), p. 288.

for a variety of sexual expression that is hard to classify according to the simplistic binary opposition on which the distinction between heterosexuality and homosexuality is framed. However, at the time when Strachey published *EV* he had long been involved in the exploration of aspects of same-sex desire. Yet this man espoused a literary style that was anything but anarchic or revolutionary and which, in fact, looked back to the eighteenth century. As Barry Spurr has argued of Strachey's literary approach: it owed more to the adaption of "Augustan and Victorian styles *albeit for unconventional purposes* [my emphasis], than to any stylistic innovation."[7] John Sutherland, in his introduction to a recent edition of *EV,* has argued that this is "among the small corpus of books which have wholly changed the genre to which they belong."[8] But not only did Strachey's work dramatically influence the genre of biographical writing in English, it played a crucial role in the questioning of the nature of the achievement of Victorian Britain as a whole.

I have already noted that Lytton Strachey was an adept of queer performance. Particularly during World War I, he combined his ethical stance as a conscientious objector with a personal style of dress, behavior, and expression that was ostentatiously out of kilter with contemporary standards of normative manliness.[9] His striking combination of the visual and verbal expression of deviance placed him, in some ways, as the inheritor of the mantle of Oscar Wilde. Yet it is important to emphasize that if society was becoming more aware of same-sex desire in the aftermath of the trials of 1895, its main effect was to intensify public expressions of hostility. In relation to the coded nature of *EV,* it is perhaps pertinent to note the publication in *The Imperialist* newspaper in January 1918 of claims that the German secret service had the names of 47,000 British deviants and was blackmailing them to betray their country.[10] Strachey may have been especially scared of being publicly identified at such a seemingly unpropitious time. Indeed, it is likely that his work found its wide audience precisely because it was *not* obviously homosexual. In particular, Strachey eschewed the study of artists and aesthetes in the manner of the previous work with a similar title, *Some Eminent Victorians: Personal Recollections in the World of Art and Letters* (1908), by the critic Joseph Comyns Carr. Nevertheless, by applying a highly aestheticized literary technique, Strachey made a series of leading British figures of the nineteenth century appear not merely to be queer in the sense of strange, but to be so in ways that linked their private and public lives. Taddeo has noted the similarity between Strachey and his subjects by subtitling her book about him *The Last*

7. Lepper (2010), p. 297; see also Spurr (1990), p. 32.
8. Sutherland (2003), p. vii.
9. Fassler (1979), p. 249.
10. Hoare (1997).

Eminent Victorian, but I would argue that this similarity included allusion to putative sexual tastes.[11] Strachey's queer work was executed in ways that reflected on the contemporary conditions of World War I and implied that the recent disasters were at least partly the result of the persistence of Victorian peculiarities and repressions in British institutions (the Church, the medical professions, the public schools, and the army) that were led, as they overwhelmingly still were, by people who had grown up in the nineteenth century. As Todd Avery has recently argued, it is quite wrong to dismiss Strachey as a "mere stylist," because his work is concerned with the ethics of leadership, which he regarded as requiring a new moral code that accepted the "inherent, ineradicable complexity of erotic desire."[12]

EV consists of four chapters, the last three of which tell the stories of Florence Nightingale (1820–1910), Dr. Thomas Arnold (1795–1842), and Major-General Charles George Gordon (1833–1885), respectively; however, the first is, in effect, a dual biography of two Roman Catholic cardinals, Henry Edward Manning (1808–1892) and John Henry Newman (1801–1890). It is important to point out that this is something of an idiosyncratic lineup, but these figures were not chosen at random. For instance, one might expect that in the chapter on religion a leading Anglican would have been chosen, perhaps one of the archbishops of Canterbury, but Strachey decided to focus on two men who left the Church of England. The cultural politics of those who became Anglo-Catholic, or left for Rome itself, was to be openly associated with homosexuality by Geoffrey Faber (cofounder of the publishers Faber and Faber) in his book *Oxford Apostles* (1933), which was itself influenced by the picture of Newman given in *EV*.[13] Doctrinal suspicion of such behavior in a country with a long tradition of engrained anti-Catholicism is hardly surprising, but what is striking is the way in which gender performance had become a key issue in the Victorian church. Thus, as was discussed in the previous chapter, Charles Kingsley had attacked the Oxford Movement in general and, of its leaders, Newman in particular, for a combination of weakness and effeminacy. By the end of the nineteenth century, the bar against marriage for the Catholic clergy was one of a series of factors that had begun to establish Catholicism in general and its priesthood in particular as a queer cultural formation.[14] As Ellis Hanson says, in his book on *Decadence and Catholicism* (1997), the *fin de siècle* Anglo- and Roman Catholic clergy found, in priesthood, "a spiritualisation of desire, a rebellion against nature and the instincts, and a polymorphous redistribution of pleasure in the body. In the elaborate stagecraft

---

11. Taddeo (2002). This similarity also emphasized by Lubenow (2004).
12. T. Avery (2004), pp. 184 and 204. See also T. Avery (2010).
13. Faber (1933).
14. Janes (2015).

of ritualism they celebrated the effeminate effusions and subversions of the dandy."[15]

Current views on Newman's sexuality, in relation to such matters as the precise nature of the relationship between him and his "constant companion" Ambrose St. John, with whom he shared a grave if not a bed, suggest that "any interpretation must remain controversial. It is unrealistic to expect documented proof of overt homosexual behaviour."[16] There had, after all, been a tradition in England since the sixteenth century of two clerics being buried together. Such relationships have been seen as "wholly spiritual" and, in the view of Alan Bray, "not the less" for being so.[17] Sexual revelations, of course, are not what Strachey provides, but what he does give us is a reading of Victorian religion that is highly suggestive of various forms of unspecified queerness. The picture of Newman that appears in that chapter is of an aesthete who was seduced into religious obsession by the tenor of his times:

> under other skies, his days would have been more fortunate. He might have helped to weave the garland of Meleager, or to mix the lapis lazuli of Fra Angelico, or to chase the delicate truth in the shade of an Athenian palaestra, or his hands might have fashioned those ethereal faces that smile in the niches of Chartres. Even in his own age he might, at Cambridge, whose cloisters have ever been consecrated to poetry and common sense, have followed quietly in [Thomas] Gray's footsteps and brought into flower those seeds of inspiration which now lie embedded amid the faded devotion of the *Lyra Apostolica*. At Oxford, he was doomed. He could not withstand the last enchantment of the Middle Age.[18]

The "delicate" truth that he might have chased, and perhaps grasped, in an ancient Greek wrestling school (palaestra), or which he might have expressed through developing the coded homoeroticism of Thomas Gray, was closeted, therefore, in Newman's devotional writings.[19]

Newman is rendered intellectually effete as a result of "his delicate mind, with its refinements, its hesitations, its complexities—[and] his soft, spectacled, Oxford manner, with its half-effeminate diffidence."[20]

---

15. Hanson (1997), pp. 7–8; see also Janes (2011a).
16. Hilliard (1982); Dawson (1933), p. vii, and Cocks (2001), p. 165.
17. Bray (2003a), p. 97; see also Bray (2003b). But note also the reservations of Traub (2004).
18. Strachey (1918), p. 16. Classical Athens and Renaissance Italy were favorite loci for fantasies of homosexual desire during the *fin de siècle*; on which see, respectively, Dowling (1994) and Fisher (2008), p. 41, who argues that when the concept of the Renaissance was "introduced in England, the period was imagined as queer terrain."
19. On Thomas Gray and same-sex desire, see Chapter 4 of this book.
20. Strachey (1918), p. 68.

Masculine sexual agency is given to his friends, such that it was only "when [Richard Hurrell] Froude succeeded in impregnating Newman with the ideas of [John] Keble, [that] the Oxford Movement began."[21] Froude, a pupil of Keble, was further queered by Strachey's statement that "what was singular about him, however, was not so much his temper as his tastes. The sort of ardour which impels more normal youths to haunt Music Halls and fall in love with actresses took the form, in Froude's case, of a romantic devotion to the Deity."[22] Another member of the circle, W. G. Ward (who converted to Rome in 1845), appears simply as being a rather camp "young man who combined an extraordinary aptitude for a priori reasoning with a passionate devotion to Opera Bouffe."[23]

By contrast with all this, the picture of Manning does not suggest gender deviance. He is depicted as being an energetic specimen of the marrying kind. And yet there is something peculiar about the way in which Strachey presents the narrative of Manning's entire personal life in the following short paragraph:

> Just then he fell in love with Miss Deffell, whose father would have nothing to say to a young man without prospects, and forbade him the house. . . . Accordingly, in the first place, he decided that he had received a call from God "ad veritatem et ad seipsum"; and, in the second, forgetting Miss Deffell, he married his rector's daughter. . . . When Mrs. Manning prematurely died, he was at first inconsolable, but he found relief in the distraction of redoubled work. How could he have guessed that one day he would come to number that loss among God's special mercies? Yet so it was to be. In after years, the memory of his wife seemed to be blotted from his mind.

This hardly makes for glowing evidence of a life of manly devotion to women.

It was in a similar fashion to this that the only hint of marital vitality in the life of Florence Nightingale is presented as having been of little importance to her:

> It was only natural to suppose that Florence would show a proper appreciation of them [her parents] by doing her duty in that state of life unto which it had pleased God to call her—in other words, by marrying, after a fitting number of dances and dinner-parties, an eligible gentleman, and living happily ever afterwards. Mr. Nightingale suggested that a husband might be advisable; but the curious thing was that she seemed to take no interest in husbands.[24]

21. Strachey (1918), p. 16.
22. Strachey (1918), p. 12.
23. Strachey (1918), p. 32.
24. Strachey (1918), p. 123.

Strachey's portraits of Manning and Nightingale are similar in that they are presented as people who embraced a celibate life as a necessity for their ascent to power (Manning, after the death of his wife and his conversion, in order to rise in the hierarchy of the Roman Catholic Church, and Nightingale in order not to be forced out of public life into marital domesticity). But whereas Manning's rise is as unflatteringly depicted as one might have expected on the part of a writer with a distinct antipathy to religion, Nightingale's progress is much more sympathetically depicted, albeit that she is presented as, in essence, an invert, that is, as a person with a man's spirit in a woman's body. As Strachey put it, in her case, the conventional gender roles were reversed and, in her personal dealings "the qualities of pliancy and sympathy fell to the man, those of command and initiative to the woman."[25] Her aura of power was such that Strachey seems to imply that she was fantasized, on occasion, even as something of a dominatrix, as in the instance when

> an aristocratic young gentleman arrived [during the Crimean War] at Scutari with a recommendation from the Minister. He had come out from England filled with a romantic desire to render homage to the angelic heroine of his dreams. He had, he said, cast aside his life of ease and luxury; he would devote his days and nights to the service of that gentle lady; he would perform the most menial offices, he would "fag" for her, he would be her footman—and feel requited by a single smile.[26]

It is not that Strachey is calling Nightingale a lesbian, but he is most certainly queering her in this passage, and not merely by associating her with gender inversion, but also by talking of the public school institution of "fagging," and thus implying that she might be viewed as behaving like a senior schoolboy on whom a smaller boy had conceived a passion. Moreover, it is true to say that the model of inversion was one of the most widespread ones at large for understanding lesbian desire at this time. It underlay, for instance, the presentation of the tragic hero/ine Stephen in Radclyffe Hall's pioneering lesbian novel *The Well of Loneliness* (1928).[27] Deborah Cohler has noted in her study, *Citizen, Invert, Queer: Lesbianism and War in Early Twentieth-Century Britain* (2010), that the "first widespread public linkages" between female masculinity and lesbianism were established during World War I.[28] Thus, Strachey's response to Nightingale must be understood in relation to the cultural politics of his own times,

25. Quoted and discussed in Taddeo (2002), p. 132.
26. Strachey (1918), p. 139.
27. Hall (1982) [first published 1928], Bauer (2003), and Vicinus (2001).
28. Cohler (2010), p. xx; see also pp. 116–149 on key events, which included the publication and banning of Rose Allatini's novel *Despised and Rejected* (1918) and the case of *Rex v. Pemberton Billing* (1918), on which see also Hoare (1997).

when large numbers of women were working as nurses on the front lines in Belgium and France.

Strachey's picture of Nightingale bears comparison with his later gender-bending presentation of Queen Elizabeth I, "Gloriana" (reigned 1558–1603).[29] And a perverse dynamic even crept into Strachey's portrait of the implacably heterosexual Queen Victoria, insofar as Benjamin Disraeli (1804–1881), when prime minister, is described as attempting to reinvent her as a "Second Gloriana."[30] This fantasy, described by Strachey as "an enchanted palace out of the Arabian Nights, full of melancholy and spangles," would appear to indicate a spectacular degree of erotic displacement if we accept William Kuhn's picture of Disraeli as not just a dandy but a man whose literature shows his strongest erotic and romantic attachments as having been with men; this he then sublimated into politics through his discovery that "power was the greatest pleasure of all, that it eclipsed the joys of dressing up, going out, or thinking about the Queen."[31] Thus, in what Barry Spurr has referred to as a moving paean to Queen Victoria on the part of Strachey, "homosexuality is obscured in the inconsequential peculiarity of personal eccentricity. . . . But circumlocution, as Strachey knew, can be the vehicle of a revelation more profound and haunting than more obvious observations." Thus, he simply leaves it to the reader to wonder at the implications when he tells us that Victoria never had cause for jealousy against another woman even though Prince Albert, her consort, "was not in love with her."[32]

This brings us to General Gordon, whose "unassuming figure, short and slight, with its half-gliding, half-tripping motion" perhaps reminds us of no one so much as Newman as depicted by Kingsley.[33] Far more than in the other portraits, Strachey resorts to almost blatant innuendo when he tells us that the soldier was "particularly fond of boys. Ragged street arabs and rough sailor-lads crowded about him. They were made free of his house and garden; they visited him in the evenings for lessons and advice; he helped them, found them employment, [and] corresponded with them when they went out into the world." Moreover, "except for his boys and his paupers he lived alone."[34] It is further implied that he had a distaste for women, as in the anecdote that Strachey tells concerning an occasion when Gordon left, apparently in disgust, from

29. Dobson and Watson (2002), p. 222. See also Strachey (1928), p. 29, and Fassler (1979), p. 238. Note Strachey's growing enthusiasm for psychoanalysis, Holroyd (1994), p. 610. See also the introduction to Part Three of this current book.
30. Strachey (1921), p. 261. Compare Watson (1997).
31. Strachey (1921), p. 261, and Kuhn (2006), p. 245.
32. Spurr (1990), p. 31, and (1995), pp. 226–227.
33. Strachey (1918), p. 217.
34. Strachey (1918), p. 228. Note that all of this is strangely reminiscent of Wilde's excuses for consorting with working-class youths and that Gordon was flagged up by Hyam (1990), p. 33, as being one of a series of military men of the time who "liked small boys."

a reception in Khartoum in 1874 that featured completely naked young women—he did so after having witnessed the Austrian consul fling himself with abandon into the melée and listened to the governor general "shouting with delight."[35]

This picture of one of the British Empire's greatest military heroes, famed above all for the supposed heroism of his final hours at Khartoum, should be seen in the context of the admixture of homosociality and homoeroticism that was associated with soldierly brotherhood in the trenches. Paul Fussell's *The Great War and Modern Memory* (1975) is a classic study of this process.[36] Fussell drew attention to the role of war in disrupting normal patterns of behavior, in promoting opportunities for illicit sex and for basic animality.[37] As he comments: "given this association between war and sex, and given the deprivation and loneliness and alienation characteristic of the soldier's experience—given, that is, his need for affection in a largely womanless world—we will not be surprised to find both the actuality and the recall of front-line experience replete with what we may call the homoerotic."[38] Fussell suggests that the same-sex regimes of the muscularly Christian public school trained young men to react in this way.

The remaining biography, that of the headmaster Thomas Arnold, is the only one of an apparently happily married person, yet the narration of that marriage fails to bring the figure of his wife into any great prominence and, in her stead, the visual imagination is left replete with ever renewing visages of generations of schoolboys. Strachey implied the prevalence of homosexuality in educational contexts when he quoted the Rev. Mr. Bowdler as saying that the public schools "are the very seats and nurseries of vice," and by saying, in relation to Manning's schooldays, that "at Harrow the worlds of danger were already around him."[39] Moreover, Strachey tells us that "there was an exceptional kind of boy, upon whom the high-pitched exhortations of Dr. Arnold produced a very different effect [from that they had on hearties]. A minority of susceptible and serious youths fell completely under his sway, responded like wax to the pressure of his influence, and moulded their whole lives with passionate reverence upon the teaching of their adored master."[40] These passively impressionable youths, apparently seduced by Arnold's falsetto voice (this detail is yet another of Strachey's queer notes), were precisely those who were to go on at university to take part in the emerging Oxford Movement. Beyond this, Arnold's system, according to Strachey, resulted largely in a substantial increase in corporal punishment, while "in the actual sphere of teaching, Dr. Arnold's

35. Strachey (1918), p. 245.
36. Fussell (1975), L. Smith (2001), D. Johnson (1982), and A. Harvey (2001).
37. Fussell (1975), p. 270.
38. Fussell (1975), p. 272.
39. Strachey (1918), p. 6.
40. Strachey (1918), p. 207.

reforms were tentative and few."[41] Arnold does father a string of children, and yet even here Strachey queers the headmaster's pitch by suggesting that they were produced in a spirit of diligence by a man whose major interest appears to have been in exhorting and punishing small children. The results of such exertions are also rendered somewhat questionable by Strachey's passing mention that "'the taste of the boys at this period,' writes an old Rugbaean who had been under Arnold, 'leaned strongly towards flowers': the words have an odd look to-day."[42]

At the time that Strachey was writing, the issue of moral standards in the public schools had been highlighted by the furor surrounding the publication of Alec Waugh's (1898–1991) novel *The Loom of Youth* (1917).[43] Waugh had been forced to leave Sherbourne School two years earlier in the wake of a homosexual scandal, and he had had the temerity to retell his school experiences, albeit in coded form, in the novel.[44] Jeffrey Richards sums up the general atmosphere of criticism at the time in which "most "serious" writers from the Great War onward excoriated the public schools as hotbeds of homosexuality, brutality, snobbery, and conformism. The system was seen as symbolic and symptomatic of the mindset that had caused the war."[45] Therefore, even though Strachey was ostensibly talking about the events of the early nineteenth century in his biography of Arnold, these can again be interpreted as having been presented in a mode of suggestive juxtaposition to contemporary concerns. In the next chapter I will look at the way in which expulsions operated to both contain but also retain same-sex desire within public schools during Strachey's lifetime.

In conclusion, I do wish to emphasise that if Strachey's *EV* was an act of queering, it was by no means an act simply of sneering at these figures, strangely deluded in some ways though they might appear to have been. In fact, the queerer the figure the more ambivalently sympathetic Strachey becomes, as in his rewriting of Nightingale into a masculinized woman of action rather than the feminized angel of legend.[46] And when it comes to Newman, and his mistreatment at the hands of Manning, Strachey turns almost sentimental:

> the Curate of Littlemore had a singular experience. As he was passing by the Church [that Newman had founded] he noticed an old man, very poorly dressed in an old grey coat with the collar turned up, leaning over the lych gate, in floods of tears. He was apparently in great trouble, and his hat was pulled down over his eyes as if

41. Strachey (1918), p. 192.
42. Strachey (1918), p. 212.
43. Alexander Raban Waugh, to give him his full name, was the older brother of the better-known novelist Evelyn Waugh.
44. Richards (1988), p. 230.
45. Richards (1988), p. 16.
46. Bostridge (2002), p. 174.

he wished to hide his features. For a moment, however, he turned towards the Curate, who was suddenly struck by something familiar in the face. Could it be? . . . He sprang forward, with proffers of assistance. Could he be of any use? "Oh no, no!" was the reply. "Oh no, no!" But the Curate felt that he could not run away and leave so eminent a character in such distress.

It is almost as though it was Strachey who was passing by the church and realizing to his sorrow that there was not more he could do to assuage the cardinal's anguish. After all, Newman and Strachey inhabited worlds that were sufficiently similar in their moral inflexibility that it was only in code and by implication that the latter was able to suggest that not only had many of the most eminent Victorians been inverted, but that they might have been considerably greater still had the issue of sexual tastes not been seen as a matter for shame and concealment. Further, by implication, Britain might never have found itself at war, or, driven forward as it had been by the Church, the schools, the army, and the medical professions, might have avoided many of the disasters of the last four years, had its subjects not been weighed down by their burdens of sexual self-constraint. The issue at stake here was not one of being "out" in the sense used by the gay liberation movement of the 1970s, but rather of degrees of self-awareness and of creative agency within the closet. Strachey sought, in essence, a world with more delightful spectacle and less pained obscurity.

CHAPTER 7

EXPULSION

WHETHER WE THINK of it as a kind of fame or of infamy, there were a number of well-known public-school teachers during the nineteenth century whose careers were interrupted by sexual scandal. Oscar Browning and William Johnson Cory at Eton and Charles Vaughan at Harrow were simply three of the highest profile men who were forced to step aside from teaching as a result of such circumstances.[1] I have been stressing that the tendency of the Victorian homosocial environment was, where it could, to contain and conceal but not eradicate (for how could it?) the homoerotic gaze (if not the erotic act). Schools present a particularly intense example of the operations of the closet because they were under scrutiny from fee-paying parents who were quite at liberty to take their children away should they feel qualms about the moral environment to which their offspring had been consigned. In this chapter I will be exploring the ways in which schools attempted to shore up their status by the selective use of expulsion in the case of homosexual offenses. However, as I will go on to argue, this mechanism was not entirely effective, partly due to a widespread belief that sexual experimentation was of less significance in the young than it was in the case of adults, and second, because those who were scapegoated by the system notably failed to match the effeminate stereotype expected from knowledge of the spectacle of the closet.

Childhood sexuality, in the wake of the rise of psychoanalysis, has been one of the most controversial issues in modern Western culture. The idea that boys ought, at least as teenagers, to be fascinated by girls only dates from the period after World War II. Before then, male

---

1. Kaplan (2005), pp. 102–165, and Gibson (1991). A good overall introduction is provided by Gathorne-Hardy (1977).

childhood was idealized as a space of purity in which manliness was to be fostered. However, the fact was that boys did, from time to time, express themselves sexually, most frequently through masturbation, on their own or with each other. This led to counter-perspectives that looked on public schools as being the source of sexual pollution in the young, rather than as the means of keeping it to a minimum. It was with this view in mind that, for instance, David O. Selznick, producer of *The Third Man* (1949), confronted Graham Greene with his concerns over the script by asking him, "what on earth motivates Martins in his curious and passionate interest in clearing up the reputation of a dead man who he hasn't seen for ten years. . . . The only conclusion I can draw from it is that they slept together, and I don't mean slept, all the way through Eton."[2] To Selznick, "passionate interest" on the part of one man in the reputation of another was a clear indication of homosexuality that he linked directly to the English public school system. Conversely, those who wished to celebrate the role of same-sex desire during this period have pointed to the public schools as being the source of what Florence Tamagne has referred to as a peculiarly British queer counter-discourse of the "cult of homosexuality" as a noble ideal.[3]

Since the 1960s immense advances have been made in the understanding of the cultural history of homosexuality and the role played in it by perceptions of adolescents and adolescence. Above all, considerable progress has been made in exploring discourses surrounding homosexuality in novels set in public schools and in the testimony of former pupils.[4] However, attempts to explore schools using official contemporary records have been less successful. For instance, one detailed survey that used correspondence with parents at Ellesmere College, Shropshire, concluded that the picture of homosexuality at the school remained "suggestive and mystifying."[5] The position remains similar to that outlined in the serious, if dated, work of T. W. Bamford on the general history of public schools. He argued that "expulsion with a capital E was the automatic penalty for stealing, riots, flagrant defiance and sexual offences." However, he does not back up this assertion with any detailed evidence. He does, however, highlight the challenges of achieving a more accurate level of insight by acknowledging that "the overall picture is scanty in the extreme, for schools have been secretive and no

2. R. White (undated). Greene's attitudes to public schools were shaped by his traumatic experiences at Berkhamsted where his father was Second Master and, subsequently, Headmaster.
3. Tamagne (2004), p. 105. She was inspired by Annan (1990).
4. Key materials exploring affective aspects of the history and literature of youthful friendship and homosexuality in more detail include D'Arch Smith (1970) and Kaplan (2005), p. 104, et passim. In relation to public school novels, Thomas Hughes, *Tom Brown's Schooldays* (1994) [1st edition 1857], has received particular attention, for instance from Puccio (1995) and Martin (2002). Hickson (1995) is perhaps the most detailed attempt to use anecdotes of "old boys."
5. Heward (1988), p. 157.

reliable figures, as far as can be traced, have ever been published. . . . An expulsion register or two would be a goldmine."[6] Bamford's study appeared in 1967, but no subsequent research has substantially altered this picture through the examination of school archives.[7] It is the purpose of this chapter to begin the process of remedying this situation by summarizing the current state of knowledge of same-sex eroticism in the public schools at this time, and then, by exploring the available archival records, assessing the degree to which these confirm or modify our picture of the presence of same-sex desire and the way it was viewed and dealt with by the institutional authorities.

Bearing in mind the scandal surrounding accusations of homosexuality in the late nineteenth and early twentieth centuries, it is hardly surprising that schools did not wish to draw attention to the issue. However, any such secretiveness would not have helped to diffuse emergent public suspicion, particularly in the wake of the trials of Oscar Wilde in 1895, which drew intense media scrutiny to the issue of the alleged seduction of boys.[8] According to the mid-twentieth-century American educationalist Edward C. Mack, "assuming the proportions of a real menace, was homosexuality. . . . Because of the prudishness of the Victorians, they offer little direct evidence of this fact, but their writings are full of veiled accusations, the meaning of which cannot be doubted."[9] However, he also fails to present any clear evidence in his study for the occurrence of this, other than by referencing novelists or by recourse to the opinions of Havelock Ellis.[10] However, turning to the pages of that pioneering study of "inversion" by Ellis and John Addington Symonds, first published in 1897, shows that even advanced sexology was ill-informed on this topic.[11] And, furthermore, it should be emphasized that, since most of the first edition of that book was pulped and the second edition was banned, even this work was in very limited circulation. The section on the effects of education comments that "in England we are very familiar with vague allusions to the vices of the public schools. . . . But, so far as I have been able to gather, these allegations have not been submitted to accurate investigation."[12] The discussion continues:

> The physicians and masters of public schools who are in a position
> to study the matter usually possess no psychological training, and
> appear to view homosexuality with too much disgust to care to pay

---

6. Bamford (1967), p. 71.
7. Further important works on same-sex desire and the public schools include Richards (1987) and (1988), Honey (1997), and Holt (2008).
8. Sinfield (1994) and Foldy (1997), pp. 48–66.
9. Mack (1941), p. 126.
10. Mack (1941), p. 127.
11. E. Cohen (1987).
12. H. Ellis (1897), p. 37.

any careful attention to it. What knowledge they possess they keep to themselves, for it is considered to be in the interests of public schools that these things should be hushed up. When anything very scandalous occurs one or two lads are expelled, to their own grave and, perhaps, lifelong injury, and without benefit to those who remain, whose awakening sexual life rarely receives intelligent sympathy.[13]

The social taboo concerning the subject appears to have inhibited both public discussion and detailed research on the topic. This meant that even a reforming tract such as the anonymous *Our Public Schools* (1881) has only this to say on the subject: "the scholastic mode of dealing with questions of morals creates an artificial atmosphere of mystery and suspicion which is not favourable to a sound and healthy morality. The subject is an extremely difficult and delicate one, and ill adapted for public discussion. We therefore leave it without further remark."[14] The only hint of an opinion on the issue of causation comes from the fact that this statement appears sandwiched between an exposé of poor discipline at Eton and a diatribe against the alleged deficiencies of a Classics-based curriculum. It would seem, therefore, that the author believed that the knowledge of ancient Greek 'boy love' might lead to contemporary impropriety.[15]

On the other hand, during the interwar years, certain former schoolboys began publishing highly frank accounts of their childhood experiences. For instance, Oscar Wilde's former lover, Lord Alfred Douglas, confessed in his *Autobiography* of 1929 that "when I was a boy at Winchester [1884–1888] and at Oxford [1889–1893] I had many fine friendships, perfectly normal, wholesome, and not in the least sentimental. . . . I had other friendships which were sentimental and passionate, but perfectly pure and innocent. . . . I had others again which were neither pure nor innocent. But if it is to be assumed that I was 'abnormal' or 'degenerate' or exceptionally wicked, then it must be assumed that at least ninety per cent. of my contemporaries at Winchester and Oxford were the same."[16] This claim may be compared with that in John Addington Symonds's (unpublished) autobiography in which he recalled that at the Harrow he attended in the 1850s

every boy of good looks had a female name, and was recognized either as a common prostitute or as some bigger fellow's "bitch." Bitch was the word in common usage to indicate a boy who yielded his person to a lover. The talk in the dormitories and the studies was incredibly obscene. Here and there one could not avoid seeing acts of onanism,

13. H. Ellis (1897), p. 37.
14. Anon., *Our Public Schools* (1881), p. 44.
15. Stray (1998), p. 44. For context see also Dowling (1994), Rousseau (2007), and Funke (2013).
16. A. Douglas (1929), p. 26.

mutual masturbation, the sports of naked boys in bed together. There was no refinement, no sentiment, no passion; nothing but animal lust in these occurrences.[17]

Without archival research in the records of the schools themselves, it is very hard to tell whether such lurid descriptions as these are exceptional, or even accurate. Nevertheless, they do fit into a pattern in which the topic of homosexuality in schools slowly came to be more openly addressed by the time of World War I. However, it is important to emphasize that much of such discussion as there was at that date still took veiled forms that, typically, did not clearly distinguish between sexual acts (often referred to by such euphemisms as "uncleanness" or "immorality"), romantic friendships between boys, and what we would refer to as homosexual relationships that combined sexual and emotional expression.

Arnold Lunn's novel *The Harrovians* (1913) was pioneering in its frank account of schoolboy discussion of (in this case, heterosexual) sex.[18] This work may have been the inspiration for Alec Waugh's aforementioned novel *The Loom of Youth* (1917), which featured a passion for a boy called Morcombe: "there began a friendship entirely different from any that Gordon had known before. He did not know what his real sentiments were; he did not attempt to analyse them. He only knew that when he was with Morcombe he was indescribably happy. There was something in him so natural, so unaffected, so sensitive to beauty."[19] But even more startling than the description of this (chaste) romance was the acknowledgment that it was only this platonic love affair that had saved Gordon from submitting to carnality with others:

> he saw the faces of those, some big, some small, who had drifted with the stream, and had soon forgotten early resolutions and principles in the conveniently broadminded atmosphere of a certain side of Public School life, he realised how easily he could slip into that life and be engulfed. No one would mind; his position would be the same; no one would think the worse of him. Unless, of course, he was caught. Then probably everyone would round upon him, that was the one unforgivable sin—to be found out. But it was rarely that anyone was caught; and the descent was so easy.[20]

Many of the responses to *The Loom of Youth* were hobbled by their very unwillingness to discuss this issue openly. Examples of this kind

17. Symonds (1984), p. 94.
18. Lunn (1913), p. 151.
19. Alec Waugh (1917), p. 284; see also Auberon Waugh (2011).
20. Alec Waugh (1917), pp. 284–285.

include Martin Browne, *A Dream of Youth: An Etonian's Reply to "A Loom of Youth"* (1918) and Jack Hood, *The Heart of a Schoolboy* (1919).[21] Waugh, unabashed, returned to the topic in *Public School Life: Boys, Parents, Masters* (1922), in chapters entitled "Morality and the Romantic Friendship" and "The Leaving Age with Regard to Morals." Waugh argues that what he calls "romantic friendships" are initiated by older boys who see younger boys as proxies for girls. These are very rarely sexually consummated and would not occur at all were it not that boarding school was an "unnatural system" that kept boys and girls apart.[22] However, analogously to those who had given into the sordid desires that Gordon resisted in *The Loom of Youth*, Waugh argues that, just as men would not sully the purity of a good woman that they were courting but might be tempted by a prostitute who had no good character to lose, so "there is at school a type that corresponds to the prostitute from whom boys refrain, when they do refrain, for many mixed reasons, of which fear of expulsion is generally not one. Boys are not afraid of punishments, nor do they think that a punishable offence is necessarily a moral offence."[23] To summarize, Waugh's position was that most schoolboy relationships were homosocial rather than homosexual, but that there were a few incorrigibly debased boys at school who, analogously to prostitutes in the outside world, acted as the focus for sexual expression on the part of "normal" males who lacked the outlet of relations with girls. This meant that he understood that there were two sorts of boys having sex at public school: the first sort were resorting to immorality because they had no other choice in a same-sex institution, but who did not have any moral concerns about doing this, and the second sort were inherent perverts. The logic of this, was, however, that these queer boys provided a useful service in the school because, were they not there, older boys might turn their sexual energies on their (unwilling) younger friends. This meant that expulsions would not solve the problem and that the only solution would be reducing the leaving age so that sexually mature boys were no longer kept in same-sex institutions. Waugh's discussion is the most detailed and frank to be found from the period. I will now go on to explore the evidence of school disciplinary archives to see if these support his view of the dynamics of same-sex desire in public boarding schools.

The *Public Schools Year Book* first appeared in 1889 as a guide for parents in the choice of school for their offspring. The establishments included were those that the editors, who were from Eton, Harrow, and Winchester, "regard as belonging to the same genus as their own."[24] In the autumn of 2011, I wrote to the persons in charge of the archives at

21. Browne (1918) and Hood (1919).
22. Alec Waugh (1922), pp. 128, 136, and 142.
23. Alec Waugh (1922), p. 156.
24. Anon, *The Public Schools Year Book* (1889), preface.

these schools to ask them if it were possible to determine the reasons for expulsions during the late nineteenth century, or shortly thereafter. Bradford, Brighton, Charterhouse, Dover, Haileybury, Lancing, Marlborough, Radley, Rossall, and Tonbridge said that there were no records available. At Bedford and Shrewsbury, records were available but these gave no reasons for expulsions. At Harrow, a record was kept in the form of a punishment book, but this had been closed for access by the headmaster. At Rugby, records were either not kept or, if they were, were kept private. At Eton, old headmaster's bill books were destroyed when they had been filled up, and housemasters' papers were regarded as private and were not, therefore, archived by the school.

This state of affairs was not simply the result of poor record-keeping. Anne Drewery, the archivist at Lancing, explained that no specific record was kept of boys expelled from the school because this was not a subject that colleges wished to publicize.[25] Terry Rogers, her counterpart at Marlborough, painted a similar picture, reporting that the only written materials would have been between parents and the school. Such matters would have been discussed at governors' meetings but were not minuted.[26] Clare Sargent at Radley provides a similar picture, saying that hearsay and gossip were the main sources of information about such matters. Moreover, in the case of her own school the nineteenth-century records were sent to be recycled during World War II.[27]

However, some of the schools' archives do preserve reasons for expulsion, as at Malvern, which opened in 1865, where the minutes of the governing council give occasional hints. Up to the turn of the century there are records of twenty-four boys having been excluded, for which no reason was given in sixteen cases. Of the others, there were three cases of theft and two of breaking bounds. Two boys were expelled in December 1885, one for making an unfounded charge of immorality and the other for intimacy with another boy.[28] This scanty record may be compared with the account given by C. S. Lewis in *Surprised by Joy* (1955) of Malvern from the time of his arrival there in 1913. In this book he openly discussed the system of "tarts": "a tart is a pretty and effeminate-looking small boy who acts as a catamite to one or more of his seniors."[29] Lewis says they were solicited, not forced, into relationships that were then sentimentalized. This was held to quite normal among the boys such that he found himself becoming bored by all the talk of "who had whose photo, who and when and how often and what night and where."[30] The archival record at Malvern was paralleled

25. E-mail to author September 22, 2011.
26. E-mail to author September 23, 2011.
27. E-mail to author September 22, 2011.
28. E-mail to author September 26, 2011.
29. C. Lewis (1955), p. 89.
30. C. Lewis (1955), p. 90.

by that at Cheltenham, where the prefects' book makes mention of punishments discussed at the weekly prefects' meetings that began in 1879. Jill Barlow, the archivist, reports that only two expulsions were recorded, one in 1882 and another in1898; these involved, respectively, a prefect and a head boy who was a relation of the president of college council.[31]

All this amounts to little more than the preservation of sporadic references; however, luckily, substantial disciplinary records survive and are available for consultation at Repton in Derbyshire, Winchester in Hampshire, and Clifton in Bristol. The key document at Repton is known as the "Black Book" and consists of a list of punishments with dates from 1900 to 1935.[32] A more substantial set of disciplinary records has been preserved at Winchester.[33] This was because it was, unusually, established as a statutory duty that the headmaster should report occurrences of expulsion to the governing body, and some of the related letters have been preserved.[34] Here the records from 1870 to 1914 reveal twenty-four cases that appear to be expulsion by the school authorities and four withdrawals by parents; the headmasters, however, sometimes used ambiguous language, such as a boy being "sent away," which makes it hard to be quite sure what category all the instances belonged to. This is particularly true of the early part of the period, which suggests a certain reluctance to play up the issue in any way. All of the cases were for some variety of immorality, other than, oddly enough, the earliest and the latest during the period, which were for violence and stealing, respectively.[35] Substantial records concerning expulsions also survive at Clifton where, as at Winchester, these were reported to the governing body and, in this case, recorded in the relevant committee minutes.[36] In addition, in two cases, legal action was feared, with the result that

31. E-mail to author, September 25, 2011.
32. Repton School, Derbyshire, founded in 1557, see http://www.repton.org.uk, and B. Thomas (1957). I am indebted to the transcription of the Black Book by Paul Stevens, archivist at Repton.
33. Winchester College, founded in 1382, see http://www.winchestercollege.org. There are many books on the history of the school, but a good place to start is Custance (1982).
34. The relevant headmasters were Rev. George Ridding in 1867–1884, Rev. William Andrewes Fearon in 1884–1901, and Rev. Hubert Murray Burge in 1901–1911.
35. Winchester College Archives [hereafter WCA], A3/12/1, May 27, 1874, expulsion of two boys for beating a smaller boy and A3/26, June 13, 1905, boy expelled for stealing.
36. Clifton College, Bristol, founded in 1862; see http://www.cliftoncollegeuk.com and Winterbottom (1990). It was originally a stock company before it received its charter in 1877. References to expulsions can be found in the run of Clifton College Company Minute Books [hereafter CMB] and Clifton College Minute Books [hereafter MB]. Further relevant archival materials are classified by reference to successive headmasters as follows: HM1, John Percival, 1862–1879; HM2, John Maurice Wilson, 1879–1890; HM3, Michael George Glazebrook, 1890–1905; HM4, Albert Augustus David, 1905–1909; and HM5, John Edward King, 1910–1923.

substantial documentation was produced and kept on file. Thirty-seven pupils were expelled between 1862 and 1914: eighteen for immorality, twelve for stealing, two for truancy, and five for unspecified offenses.[37]

To start with the Repton "Black Book": a comparison of offenses committed and punishments administered shows some interesting patterns.[38] There are only four expulsions, two for drinking and two for immorality; however, there were a substantial number of cases, fourteen, in which boys were required to leave without being formally expelled. This can be understood by reference to the notion that withdrawal effectively saved the embarrassment of both school and parents, and also made it easier for a boy to rebuild his reputation. Expulsion, therefore, was not, at least at Repton, the automatic penalty for sexual offenses.[39] It is also notable that, by modern standards, physical violence was not taken very seriously when compared with moral impropriety. Thus a boy was flogged on March 10, 1902, for writing an obscene word, as were three on March 13 of that year for dropping stones on a passing train. It is also notable that the precise species of immorality committed was often left unclear (a few entries include very brief additional details), but since the penalties ranged from caning to expulsion, it was clear that there was understood to be a considerable range of the seriousness of the acts that could be committed.

An interesting feature of the Black Book list is that most of the cases of "immorality" occurred in groups, rather than as single occurrences or as couples. This does not tend to support the notion that what we are

37. These figures include two cases described as "misconduct," on the basis that Anthony Swinburne's flagrant misconduct in the School House is likely to have referred to sexual behavior, MB1 414, June 10, 1881.
38. Summary of entries in the Repton Black Book, 1900–1914:

Absence	extra work 5, drills 3, flogged 6
Assault/bullying	flogged 2
Cheating/lying	caned 23, flogged 11, flogged+leave (at end of term) 1
Damage to property	extra work 2, caned 1, flogged 4
Drinking	loss of privileges 1, flogged+leave 1, withdrawn 1, expelled 2
False accusations	flogged 2
Gun offence	warning 1, Georgics 4, loss of privileges 1, flogged 5, withdrawn 1
Idleness	probation 1, on report 2, caned 1, flogged 6
Immorality	caned 6, flogged 13, flogged+leave at end of term 8, withdrawn 6, sent away 3, expelled 2
Minor/misc. offence	report 2, lines 6, Georgics 3, probation 1, loss of privileges 2, flogged 8
Pilfering	caned 4, flogged 1
Rowdiness	Georgics 5, bathing ban 2, rusticated 3, flogged 2
Smoking	caned 1, flogged 10
Swearing	loss of privileges 1, flogged 4
Writing indecencies	flogged 1, withdrawn by parent 1

39. Bamford (1967), p. 71.

seeing here is the victimization of homosexual couples, but rather periodic purges of small cadres of peers. However, only some of these boys found guilty of immorality were removed. For instance, on October 12, 1905, two boys were expelled for indecency and two were flogged. A similar pattern occurred on November 1, 1906, when three suffered withdrawal by parents as a result of immoral conduct and, in the case of two of them, solicitation. Three others were merely flogged. It appears that the difference in the punishment reflects a perception of a distinction between solicitor and solicitee. This is strongly suggested by the references to what happened between October 11 and 13, 1901, when five boys were disciplined for moral offenses. There appear to have been two instigators (one of whom was also accused of bullying), and these boys were, respectively, sent away and withdrawn, while two others who consented or showed moral weakness were merely caned.

The materials from Repton do not provide direct evidence of homosexual relationships, as opposed to casual sexual acts, nor do those from Clifton and Winchester. One exception might be inferred from the decision of Herbert J. Bubb and J. W. Meares, having been expelled from Winchester, to train together at University College London as electrical engineers.[40] It is also notable that there is only one case in which an expulsee can easily be connected with homosexual circles in later life; this is Arnold Charles Taylor, whose expulsion in 1885 for immoral conduct does not seem to have harmed his career, since he went on to Oxford and became a master at Uppingham School and an editor of Buddhist texts. He is mentioned as a friend in a letter written by the decadent poet Lionel Johnson when they were both undergraduates. It is likely that the two had also known each other at Winchester, where Johnson was later said by Oscar Wilde's executor Robert Ross to have slept with Lord Alfred Douglas.[41]

It would appear that it was much more typical for expulsion to be visited on hearty than on arty boys. A good example of such a scandal occurred at Clifton during World War I, during the investigation of which several parents appeared to have threatened both media exposure and legal action.[42] One of these parents was particularly well connected and brought his brother-in-law Sir George Toulmin (Liberal MP for Bury and a prominent newspaper magnate) with him to one of the interviews with the then headmaster John Edward King.[43] The

40. WCA, A3/19; Wainewright (1907), p. 442, and Leigh (1940), p. 67.
41. WCA, A3/16, June 30, 1885; Wainewright (1907), p. 399, Pittock (1987), p. 269, and McKenna (2003), p. 209.
42. Parental litigation had become more likely in the wake of the success of the legal case against the Admiralty over the expulsion of George Archer-Shee from Osborne Naval College in 1908, after he had been unjustly accused of stealing a postal order, see anon., "Law Report" (1910), p. 3.
43. The boys concerned were Cecil Bryant, Roger Edleston, and George Kay, all aged 16, John Bennetts, aged 15, and Alfred Aslett, aged 14.

matter came to light when a boy, Reginald Arnold, reported in March 1916, according to the headmaster's notes, that there was much filthy talk and misconduct taking place.[44] He said he had seen George Kay and Roger Edleston holding a third boy between them one evening. He alleged that it was known that Roger Edleston had been in Cecil Bryant's bed on December 20, 1915, and that other boys were corrupted. Although King refused to change his position that the boys must leave the school, he reached a compromise with the parents such that the boys were not formally expelled and were provided with references of good character: King wrote, for instance, to Mr. Bryant to say that if he would voluntarily withdraw his son then the lad would be given his school certificate since the aim was not to imperil his future.[45] In other words, the incident was hushed up. Bryant went straight into the Royal Engineers and Edleston into the Royal Flying Corps, after which he became a solicitor.

The College Registers at Clifton and Winchester do not record career details for all of the boys concerned, but many of them seem not to have been impeded from subsequent success. Thus, Thresher and Ward, two seventeen-year-olds who were thrown out of Winchester in 1887, went on to have careers in the army, the latter being noted as having been decorated in the Boer War.[46] G. Fanshawe, who had written immoral letters to another boy, was admitted to Lincoln College, Oxford (although he died there in 1906).[47] G. I. Moriarty proceeded to Edinburgh University and became a doctor. Many of these men went on, not surprisingly, to fight in World War I, but several of them held senior rank, notably N. Deakin (who was expelled along with Moriarty and two others for immorality in 1894) who became a major, as did A. G. Heales, who was expelled for indecency in 1904, and J. Cemlyn-Jones, who left three years later.[48] Although we cannot be sure of the sexual preferences of these men, it would appear from the way in which they were frequently able to move on to respectable careers, that they would appear to fit with Waugh's first group of those involved in homosexual activity at school, that is, boys who were seen as "normal" and as having behaved in deviant ways because of the limitations and temptations of the school environment.

The archives also preserve one case, Frank Anthony Jones, who was expelled in 1886 at the age of thirteen, which appears to fit into

44. The following quotations are all from Clifton, HM5, notes of J. E. King, March 1916. I am indebted to the archivist of Clifton, Charles Knighton, for his researches into these materials and for drawing these documents to my attention.
45. Clifton HM5, letter of J. E. King to J. B. Bryant, March 20, 1916.
46. WCA A3/17 and Wainewright (1907), pp. 425 and 438.
47. MB5 130, November 5, 1902, and Borwick (1925), p. 323.
48. MB4 108, October 24, 1894, and Borwick (1925), p. 292; MB5 188, March 3, 1904, and Borwick (1925), p. 357, and MB5 355, March 27, 1907, and Borwick (1925), p. 407.

Waugh's second category, that of the boy who was seen as inherently degraded. Nevertheless, it is notable that Jones served in World War I (and was killed in action in 1916) as a lieutenant-colonel, the same rank as his father. It was due to the latter man's bellicosity, and threat of litigation, that we have extensive knowledge of the son's case. An extensive correspondence between the father and the then headmaster of Clifton, James Maurice Wilson, survives in the form both of copies of the original letters and of printed versions of the key documents, which were circulated to members of the governing body.[49] It is also clear from his school record that he was anything but a pale, aesthetic flower. His school reports note that he was a shirker and that he had had to be caned several times for bullying. On October 9, 1885, his housemaster wrote complaining of the boy's dirty language, and on May 17, another master wrote that the boy was of a kind whose presence always causes unease. Wilson had solicited comments on Jones as part of his investigation of an incident that is only recorded in any explicit detail (as opposed to being expressed via euphemisms) in a private memorandum dated May 22, 1886. This explains that during the summer holidays a small boy had had his trousers opened and his genitals handled in the nearby Bristol Zoological Gardens by three boys aged between thirteen and fourteen. There was some suggestion that something of the kind had also happened on another occasion. Frank Jones was one of the three aggressors.

Colonel Jones contested Wilson's handling of the situation by complaining that only his son, the youngest of the attackers, had been expelled (one other had also been expelled but had been allowed to return on appeal). He contended that his son had been led into it by the older boys, but Wilson asserted the view that it was the young Jones who was the source of the uncleanness. It was alleged, for instance, that he had, on another occasion, climbed onto a roof in order to watch older boys bathing. The father wrote to Wilson on September 30, 1886, to contest what he claimed was the headmaster's belief that the boy had a natural depravity and that he possessed a vicious nature, by alleging that the boy was simply high spirited and that he had been made a scapegoat. Wilson, however, initially stood by his view that it was his duty, as he explained in a letter to the father on August 7, 1886, to get rid of boys who contaminate others. The father alleged that Wilson was acting outside his legal authority, and the headmaster countered that in that case they might turn the case over to the police. In October, however, the headmaster backed down and announced to the Senior School that, on close examination, the seriousness of Jones's role had been exaggerated and that he was no longer publicly expelled. A compromise had been reached whereby Colonel Jones had agreed voluntarily

49. MB3 21, 159, May 28, 1886; Borwick (1925), p. 173, and Muirhead (1948), p. 103. The letters are filed under HM3.

to withdraw his son, a move which, as Wilson put it to the assembled boys, allowed the boy to be admitted to another school and also to renew his acquaintance with his college friends. It appears that this must have been something of a public humiliation for the headmaster and, as such, makes clear that expelling a boy for indecency could, on occasion, rebound on the school authorities.

The appearance of supposedly vicious boys at public schools was clearly seen as an exceptional state of affairs, since it was understood that good parentage (that is, being upper or middle class) normally rendered such children capable of moral self-government. It is striking that poor children, especially those who lacked a conventional family background, were often spoken of as being "vicious" and as being both in danger and as socially dangerous.[50] Jones, from this perspective, did not so much appear to be a homosexual but as someone who had no moral self-control of any kind. He, and anyone like him, therefore, presented a potential threat to the entire moral economy of the school, thus justifying, from the point of view of the headmaster, an expulsion, which would not appear to have been warranted from the mere facts of the case. If Jones had been left in the school, Wilson clearly feared that he would spread moral contagion among the other boys by tempting them to act out of character.

The fear of the contagiousness of vice appears clearly from Winchester in the last years of the nineteenth century. For instance, in 1890, the then headmaster, William Fearon, reported to the governing body on the discovery of immorality in Mr. Turner's House, which would have led to expulsions if one boy had not been withdrawn by his father and another had not returned after the vacation. Fearon commented that misconduct was widespread.[51] He also appears to have been particularly distressed by the exposure of immoral behavior on the part of boys given authority in the school, possibly because this reflected badly on the judgment of the teacher who had so promoted them. Thus, in 1892, he commented on the expulsion of four boys that the matter was particularly awkward because it concerned a trusted prefect and took place despite the best supervisory efforts of his master, Mr Kensington.[52]

Fearon was even more upset by the expulsion of a boy from Mr. Toye's House for gross immorality in 1895. The case was regarded as especially distressing because the boy in question was head of house and captain of racquets and cricket; and, as such, a recognized leader. Again the headmaster was eager to stress that Toye, the housemaster, was not to blame.[53] It is notable that the name of the head of house was kept out of the report to the governing body, but it is most likely this

50. Mahood and Littlewood (1994), p. 549.
51. WCA, A3/20, January 27, 1890
52. WCA, A3/22, July 4, 1892.
53. WCA, A3/24; Leigh (1940), pp. 104 and 122, and Noel (1926), p. 128.

was G. H. Gibson, who was aged eighteen at the time and who (like his brother) became a tea planter in Sri Lanka (then Ceylon). Part of the reason for Fearon's distress may have been the high public profile of the brothers, bearing in mind, for instance, that they had both been members of the Winchester cricket team against Eton in 1894, but it may also have been related to the fact that sport was expected to inoculate boys against immoral urges. Sporty boys were thought to be those least likely to have unhealthy urges in the first place since they were athletes rather than aesthetes—a division that echoed, as I discussed in Chapter 5, the paired formations of the closet and its spectacle.[54]

In the early 1890s the number of expulsions had risen, and immorality had been exposed in several of the houses. For the first time, concerns about the issue appeared in substantial detail in one of the headmaster's annual reports to the governing body (that submitted in January 1896). He recorded that it had been a trying year with much worry and annoyance. His report began with physical ailments before moving onto their moral counterparts. Among various problems he recorded that the school had endured an outbreak of impetigo which, although contagious, was not the result of insanitary conditions. However, there were more serious matters to report which had required that steps be taken against the further spread of immoral behavior.[55] It is revealing that in his annual report submitted in January 1885, the first year of his accession to the post of headmaster, Fearon had described a minor outbreak of scarlet fever as not being attributable to local mischief and which, as such, did not warrant corrective measures; whereas, he continued, action still remained to be taken against serious mischief from before his accession to office. In the latter case, he was referring to "immorality." It is clear that Fearon thought of physical disease and sexual behaviour in similar ways. Both could be contagious, and both required swift investigation and the instigation of sanitary measures if the reputation of the school were not to suffer. There may have been more homosexual activity at Winchester in the later nineteenth century, or the prevention of sexual play may have been taken more seriously than it had been before. Another possibility is that the documentation of such issues was starting to be considered to be important. A particular reason, of course, for Fearon's jitters in 1895 appears in his annual report, where he notes that he was aware that certain public events were causing a particular sensitivity to such matters on the part of the parents. He was reporting, of course, when Oscar Wilde was newly transported to prison, and his lover, Lord Alfred

54. See Chapter 5. The enthusiasm of the ancient Greeks for sport might, perhaps, have provided pause for thought. Compare Harrington (1977) on Kingsley and sport.

55. The Annual Reports are bound together in one volume, WCA, A3/2.

Douglas, one of the most prominent Wykehamists of his day, was loudly petitioning for Wilde's release.

The supposed division between the amoral pervert who could infect a house with vice and the "normal" boy who might pick up such an infection was also emphasized by an anonymous correspondent whose letter was quoted by Ellis and Symonds in their study of "inversion." This writer, "whose experiences of English public school life are still recent," argued that a distinction should be made between two groups of individuals. First, there were "a very small number [of boys] who are probably radically inverted, and who do not scruple to sacrifice young and innocent boys to their passions. These, and these only, are a real moral danger to others, and I believe them to be rare." And second, there were others who "having been initiated into the passive part in their young days, continue practices of an active or passive kind; but only with boys already known to be homosexualists; they draw the line at corrupting fresh victims. This class realize more or less what they are about, but cannot be called a danger to the morals of pure boys."[56] Thus, apart from the rare "true invert" who, perhaps, possessed the soul of a girl in a boy's body, there were other boys who were either freed from danger once out of the same-sex environment, or who would retain strong moral scruples on such matters. Nevertheless, it would appear that those who were exposed to the wiles of a "vicious" boy might suffer lasting damage; such at least was the argument of Robert Graves in his memoir *Goodbye to All That* (1929), in which he claimed that "for every one born homosexual, at least ten permanent pseudo-homosexuals are made by the public school system: nine of these ten as honourably chaste and sentimental as I was."[57] In other words, he alleges that the effect of these schools was to manufacture and multiply a state of deeply closeted homosexuality.

It would appear that public school authorities were aware that homosexual activity in schools was a complex phenomenon that required a degree of nuanced response in relation to the age of the boy concerned, his degree of volition or coercion, his overall track record at the school, and his moral standing. Jeffrey Richards has, furthermore, drawn attention to the degree to which emotional homosocial bonds were actively encouraged by the public school system. In his view, the reaction of school authorities was to encourage "close noble friendships" until the 1880s as an antidote to "beastliness." Thereafter, with "perceptions sharpened and heightened by the scientific discussion of and increased legal and social hostility to homosexuality, schools tended to become wary of such close friendships" and tried to emphasize solidarity with the peer group as a whole through a focus on teamwork.[58] A "bad apple" theory appears to have developed in order to provide a

56. H. Ellis (1897), pp. 37–38.
57. Graves (1981), p. 27 [first published 1929].
58. Richards (1987), p. 117. See also Toda (2001), p. 143.

convenient explanation for how outbreaks of immorality could take place, even among groups of young men of good family. The logical function of expulsion would appear to have been the mechanism that would remove the dangerous invert from the school environment; however, it seems clear that the authorities believed that they were frequently sending away boys who had morally blundered, rather than those who were inherently degraded. The fact that many expulsees went on to have successful careers suggests that youthful experimentation was not automatically seen as blighting a boy for life and as indicating inherent degradation. Nevertheless, the presence of such cases did indicate an embarrassing failure of school mechanisms of moral hygiene.

In 1882 "Olim Etoniensis" ("a former Etonian") wrote in the *English Journal of Education* that, on making a list of the dubious boys he had known at Eton, he found that "these very boys had become cabinet ministers, statesmen, officers, clergymen, country-gentlemen, etc., and that they are nearly all of them fathers of thriving families, respected and prosperous."[59] This presents the view that temporary moral failure was a common danger of youth that the public school system could often address but, even if it did not, might well not lead to lasting ill-effects. That there were not many expulsions was not due to the rarity of homosexual behavior but because every expulsion, as in Wilson's sending away of the thirteen-year-old Jones in 1886, contradicted this optimistic script by suggesting that there was a limit to the moral effectiveness of the public school system. Moreover, as this case indicated, even when a headmaster was convinced that he had discovered the source of moral pollution, a wide range of factors might then intervene—ranging from the challenge of proving culpability to the social standing of the parents concerned—to limit the ability of the headmaster to act as he saw fit. Public schools, therefore, were spaces in which same-sex desire was not so much extirpated as managed and, at times, even accommodated. This may help to explain the rise of contemporary associations between the British boarding-school system and homosexuality.

Through the public assertion of the supposedly incommensurable scale of the gulf between the community of the school and the body of the expelled boy, schools attempted, in effect, to defend the institution of the closet as the place in which to conceal illicit desires through the display of a limited cadre of scapegoats.[60] However, the guilty boys tended to be virile troublemakers rather than effeminate dandies. This may not have been a problem in the early modern period before the likes of Thomas Arnold had worked so hard to implant a standard set of expectations for the behavior of the "normal" adolescent male.[61] But

59. Anon., "Olim Etoniensis" (1882), p. 85; see also Chandos (1985), p. 297.
60. Buckton (1998), p. 24.
61. Neff (2002), p. 400, argues for the preservation in the public schools of an older model of one sex and two genders (rather than two sexes and two genders),

those who were thrown out in the early twentieth century frequently failed to exhibit the signs of personal affection and bodily degeneration that were then expected of the spectacle of the closet.[62] Rather, as in Alec Waugh's *The Loom of Youth* (1917), the double standards of the closet were made apparent by comments such as "I heard men say about bloods [i.e. hearties] whose lives were an open scandal, 'Oh, it's all right, they can play football.'"[63] We can understand such men as having been shaped by the pressures of eroticized relations not only between older and younger boys at school, but also between boys and certain of their masters. Ari Ardut has suggested that the authorities in the late nineteenth century did not initially want to prosecute Wilde for his affairs with youths and that the general response to most such scandals was to hush them up.[64] The elaboration of a cadre of scapegoats threatened to produce an image of the deviant not as a self-serving poseur and threat but as the arbitrary victim of institutional discrimination. Even as the disciplinary institutions of the British establishment struggled to contain the sexually deviant, so that same sexual deviance shaped the key institutions of Britain and its empire. The closet and its spectacle, therefore, came to maturity hand in hand.

which promoted the notion that the differential development of men and women was gradual and contingent, rather than hard-wired from birth.

62. For the great masturbation scare from its eighteenth-century origins, see Laqueur (2003). For the nineteenth century, see Hunt (1998). Typical of this thinking was Acton (1857)—quoted and discussed in Chandos (1985), p. 291— who opined that "the signs [of abuse] began to appear by degrees, the thin lips, the pale cheeks, the haggard features, the irritable temper, the dank and cold hand"; on which see also Crozier (2000). On the debate over whether weak degenerates were prone to sexual deviation or whether moral weakness led to physical degeneration, see Crozier (2008), p. 79. The medical desire to find bodily proof of perversion was not to be seriously challenged until the postwar Kinsey Reports, on which see Seitler (2004).
63. Alec Waugh (1917), p. 60, discussed by Sinfield (1994), p. 67.
64. Adut (2005); compare Cocks (2006b) on similar responses in the early nineteenth century.

PART THREE

ONE OF THE less enthusiastically received elements of the celebrations to mark the Coronation of Elizabeth II in 1953 was the premier of Benjamin Britten's opera, *Gloriana*. The piece had been developed at the instigation of the Earl of Harewood, a first cousin of the Queen, who was on the board of the Royal Opera House, Covent Garden. The librettist was the homosexual South African writer William Plomer and the source text was Lytton Strachey's 1928 revisionist biography *Elizabeth and Essex: A Tragic History*. The musicologist Philip Brett has remarked on the adoption by Britten of Lytton Strachey's "outrageous Freudian view" of Queen Elizabeth I (reigned 1558–1603).[1] For Strachey's Elizabeth was, it has been argued recently, "not quite heterosexual."[2]

> She was a woman—ah, yes! a fascinating woman!—but then, was she not also a virgin, and old? But immediately another flood of feeling swept upwards and engulfed her; she towered; she was something more—she knew it; what was it? Was she a man? She gazed at the little beings around her, and smiled to think that, though she might be their Mistress in one sense, in another it could never be so—that the very reverse might almost be said to be the case.[3]

The moment in the opera when Essex bursts in on Elizabeth and finds her without her wig and makeup caused particular consternation. Plomer and Britten had elevated what is presented as something of a passing anecdote by Strachey into a pivotal scene that baldly, dare I say it, reveals the ugly and shameful truth beneath the façade of royal, feminine splendor.[4]

This closet drama enacted the fears of homosexuals who dreaded that their sexual secrets might be revealed to public humiliation. British

---

1. Brett (2006), p. 211; see also Alexander (1986), Banks (1993), and Wiebe (2005).
2. Dobson and Watson (2002), p. 222.
3. Strachey (1928), p. 29; see also Fassler (1979), p. 238.
4. Strachey (1928), pp. 212–213. Bearing in mind Bette Davis's subsequent status as a gay icon—compare R. Dyer (2009)—it may also be significant to consider her interpretation of the Queen in *The Private Lives of Elizabeth and Essex,* dir. Michael Curtiz (1939).

same-sex institutions had shaped the contours of the closet into a space connected with specific forms of power, as I argued in the previous chapter. However, in this third and final part of this book, I look at a series of strategies for creative engagement with the challenges of the twentieth-century closet. In Chapter 8, the dangers and limitations of public policing of the closet are seen to have produced opportunities for masochistic eroticization of sexual shame on the part of the painter Francis Bacon. The rise in the intensity of the policing of sexual behavior from the nineteenth to the twentieth centuries posed a problem for the authorities in that it threatened to publicize behavior that was supposed to be dangerously alluring. Those who were subjected to the visibility of a trial, even after the abolition of the public pillory, were inhibited from re-admission to the society of the "normal" and, hence, became, increasingly identified not as the performers of forbidden acts, but as a specific subset of persons whose numbers seemed only to increase in response to attempts at enforcement.[5] The fear that men in general might be subject to such lusts led to a desire on the part of the police only to arrest obvious "queens" during raids on queer clubs, and hence the institutions of the state participated in the construction of a fragile closet that was predicated on the potential vulnerability to legal prosecution of the secrets that it contained.

Chapter 9 finds its inspiration from Richard Dyer's comment, first published in the mid-1970s, that "it's being so camp as keeps us going."[6] In this chapter the apparently oppressive structures of the British state are seen to have provided rich opportunities for camp performance and production on the part of the photographer Cecil Beaton and others involved in the Coronation of 1953. This case study aims to draw attention to positive aspects of engagement with the cultural politics of the closet on the part of those who either lived prior to or did not wish to join the gay liberation movement.[7] The private life of the discreet homosexual home could be considered as involving an attempt to create a form of privacy that was not a species of shameful secret but rather one that sought tacit acknowledgment as a form of respectable cohabitation.[8] Conversely, the hard-won successes of the gay and lesbian liberation movement can be argued to have led, at the time of writing, to a diminution of queer cultural expression. The final chapter of this book looks at the way in which memories of the powerfully liberatory actions and imperatives of the openly queer filmmaker Derek Jarman have been partially erased by changing cultural and economic conditions in the twenty-first century. In such times it remains important to evaluate both the horrors and the consolations of past and present forms of queer secrecy.

5. Greene (2003), p. 225.
6. R. Dyer (1999), p. 6.
7. H. Love (2007), p. 71.
8. Cook (2012), p. 627.

CHAPTER 8

CRIMINAL PRACTICES

THE PUBLICATION OF *Sexual Behaviour in the Human Male* (popularly known as the "Kinsey Report") in 1948 played an important part in fueling a climate of popular concern about the prevalence of homosexuality. The Report's finding that, for instance, over 10% of American men between the ages of twenty and thirty-five were leading bisexual lives led to a sharp rise in the perception that society was not simply adorned with the occasional obvious deviant, but was riddled with perversion. In the United States the resulting paranoia was to become connected to fears of covert communism with the advent of the Cold War. In the United Kingdom the police were also spurred on to increased vigilance in the identification of vice, notably during the tenure of Sir David Maxwell Fyfe as Home Secretary from 1951 to 1954. Hushing up homosexual scandals was no longer the convenient option it once had been. All of this meant that the authorities participated in a complex compromise, which involved both attempting to maintain the closet and to police its boundaries to ensure that the attendant spectacle did not become overtly sexual.

That the boundaries of the postwar closet had become a subject not simply for spectacle but also for detection is clear from reading the pioneering novel *The Heart in Exile* (1953); written by a Hungarian émigré Adam de Hegedus under the pseudonym of Rodney Garland, this was one of the more prominent gay novels of its time.[1] The main character in the novel, Dr. Page, a psychiatrist, has some sexual inclinations toward women, but is otherwise homosexual. The action of the novel is largely generated as a result of his quest to discover the truth behind the suicide of a former lover. The novel presents a picture of

1. See the discussions of Ofield (2005), pp. 358–360, and Houlbrook and Waters (2006).

same-sex desire that is as complex as that depicted in Kinsey's research. The terms "homosexual," "invert," and "queer" are used, but in ways which suggest that the available terminology failed to do justice to the sexual gradations of real life. In particular, World War II features as a time when many men were having sex with men without being generally identified, or necessarily identifying themselves, as homosexual.[2] Scenes set in "queer" pubs (mixed bars where it was often possible to pick up other men) show that varying degrees of masculinity or femininity in dress and mannerism were carefully scrutinized as sources of information on sexual preferences.[3] As we are told, "most inverts are practised at spotting others."[4] Some deviants made themselves obvious and were viewed by the narrator with considerable disdain: "instead of physical exercise, which could help, they resort to plucked eyebrows and an excessive application of the wrong shade of rouge."[5] These men, in the narrator's opinion, did not represent the normative position for the homosexual, which was that of a closet constructed through masculine appearances. For such a man, "life is spent hiding his real passion," at least from those to whom he did not wish to display it.[6] The legacy of military service led many such men to take up exercise, the better both to pass as "real men" when they needed to, and to enhance their perceived attractiveness.[7] The normative viewpoint of the novel is also positioned firmly from within a middle class that eroticized the physicality and the (comparative) sexual open-mindedness of manual workers, thus turning its back on the supposed preference of effeminate homosexuals to seek solace in each other's company.[8]

Matt Houlbrook has undertaken some of the most detailed research into the queer life of London during the time when this novel was written. He confirms that behaviors and looks that were coded as effeminate were embraced by some homosexuals as a way of signaling both their own social nonconformity and their availability as queer friends and potential sex partners.[9] Some men, such as Quentin Crisp, as discussed in Chapter 1, "encapsulated the generalized aesthetics of being a quean [sic]—the dramatically enhanced and flamboyant style of demeanour, dress and display."[10] It was then precisely these things that the "respectable" closeted homosexual rejected by taking pains to ensure that his appearance was "nothing other than respectably masculine, his difference invisible," at least for that part of the week

2. Garland (1953), p. 58.
3. Garland (1953), p. 59.
4. Garland (1953), p. 159.
5. Garland (1953), p. 63.
6. Garland (1953), p. 120.
7. Garland (1953), p. 136.
8. Garland (1953), pp. 97–98.
9. Houlbrook (2005), p. 144.
10. Houlbrook (2005), p. 149.

when he was not with friends.[11] This meant that the masculine closet functioned in symbiosis with the effeminate spectacle of the closet represented by the queans/queens. And, moreover, it formed a vital semiotic challenge to those who carefully scrutinized masculine styles for secreted evidences of homosexual availability.

Men's homes, such as furnished rooms in inner-city London, were another source of clues. One such was found to contain a photograph of the man (hidden behind a photograph of a woman) who could explain the mystery of *The Heart in Exile*.[12] Houlbrook has pointed out that bedsits were, traditionally speaking, for the poor, or for others to occupy only in the years prior to marriage. Yet increasing numbers of men chose to occupy furnished rooms in particular areas of city centers where they could live with, or bring back, other men.[13] It was precisely in these areas and for precisely this reason that police activities were stepped up during both the interwar and postwar decades. The furnished room was often geographically at the center of the city, but it was also strangely dislocated and alienated from "normal" urban life. It was precisely away from the conditions of bourgeois order that one might expect to look, in either fear or excitement (or both), for criminal and sexual transgressions.

When the contents of the studio of the painter Francis Bacon (1909–1992) was catalogued after his death, a section of an American true-crime magazine from 1963 was found torn open to a page showing a violently disordered and bloodied bed.[14] Bacon's studio was strewn with piles of such images, going back to the time of his youth in the interwar period. I will now look at police evidence from a series of pre–World War II raids on queer clubs as a route into exploring some of the ways in which Bacon subsequently began to create powerful, masochistic images inspired by the supposedly abject and criminal world of the masculine closet. It was impossible for the police to enter into full awareness of the extent of homoerotic desires among men, such as themselves, who strove to appear "normal." Therefore, the shame of those figures of masculine authority who denied their own sexual desires was made available as a rich subject for artistic and erotic expression.

On February 14, 1938, Detective Sergeant Kenneth Murray of the Metropolitan Police entered flat 1 on the second floor of 29 Dover Street, London W1. He was there to gather evidence of suspected sexual offenses. His testimony formed a crucial element of the prosecution's evidence when the case was tried at the Central Criminal Court in London at the end of March. The defendants in *Rex v. Rosenz and Others*

---

11. Houlbrook (2005), p. 204, and Shaun Cole (2000), p. 61.
12. See Ofield (2005), on the finding of incriminating photographs.
13. Houlbrook (2005), p. 115.
14. Francis Bacon Studio, Hugh Lane Gallery, Dublin, RM98 F22: 72.

were accused of "keeping a bawdy house" (running a brothel), "keeping a disorderly house" (creating an immoral and corrupting assembly of persons), and of "attempted buggery with dog" (bestiality). On the night in question, Murray testified that a number of men arrived at the flat and were asked to pay around £6 each, ostensibly to cover the cost of the drinks. They then removed their clothes and went to watch women having sex in the space identified as "bedroom (1)" on the plan presented to the court by the police.[15] When the flat was subsequently raided, various "obscene" articles were discovered, such as books, belts, and "dill dolls." The police were, however, also interested in the visual as well as the material aspects of the flat. The plan was carefully annotated so that every light was shown in blue and every mirror in red. In particular, the many mirrors in "bedroom (1)" were carefully listed. The aim of this was to create a sense that this was not a "normal" private bedroom, but one that had been adapted to the purposes of total and obscene scrutiny of bodies.

On the night of his undercover visit, Murray had stood naked by the bed and was able to describe a variety of sexual acts in detail before a dog was brought in. In his sworn testimony, he explained what happened next: "Rosey put the dog on Harding. Harding played with its penis and pulled it toward her private parts. Rosey said, 'the dog's going to have a go now.' Just at that moment I left the room."[16] His departure is not explained, but it could be conjectured that the policeman's level of disgust was such that he could not bear to witness what was going to happen next. The success of the prosecution in this case was, therefore, not based upon total surveillance. Such a state of uninterrupted viewing was understood to belong to the realm of the criminal construction of this room as a chamber of mirrors. The legal authorities construed that others were having such obscene experiences through the accumulation of fragmentary evidence: an erotic book, a glass with lipstick on it, and the testimony of a policeman who left the room at the vital moment. Taken together, this accumulation of items of junk succeeded in projecting a sinister erotic meaning.

Such care not to reproduce for the court the full experience of being in such a flat on such an evening was important because of the nature of the offense of keeping a disorderly house. While a bawdy house was a brothel, a disorderly house was something more complex and dangerous. The Disorderly Houses Act 1751 had been designed to regulate places of entertainment, and it was employed against unlicensed venues of various kinds at which persons might "cause and procure and permit to assemble on the premises divers immoral, lewd and

15. Evidence presented at the Central Criminal Court, 1938, *Rex v. Rosenz and Others* (CRIM 1/1007). All the archival references in the footnotes are to files held at the National Archives, London.
16. Statement, Kenneth Murray, Detective Sergeant, at trial, 38–39 (CRIM 1/1007).

disorderly persons, using obscene language and behaving in a lewd, obscene and disorderly manner to the manifest corruption of the morals of His Majesty's liege subjects."[17] It was important that the evidence presented at the trial be partially obscured, otherwise the court itself might fall foul of this definition. The essential character of a disorderly house was not that sex was taking place there, although it might well be, but that, as the judge said in a case against those in attendance at a party in a nearby flat in Fitzroy Square in 1927, it was a place that was "not regulated by the restraints of morality."[18] Such moral restraints limited what the police might do, see, and recognize in the pursuit of their duty. The side effect of such restraint was that, of necessity, their knowledge of immoral behavior was based upon a degree of supposition. Evidence of criminal immorality had to be sufficiently fragmentary so as not to reproduce the disorderly house. In this section I will be using an art historical method of comparison between similar form and content in a set of photographs and a set of paintings to talk about the way in which homosexual transgression was often hinted at but not shown explicitly in the context of criminalization. The aim of this comparison is to resist the notion that the modern state, in panoptical fashion, was desperate to see the full truth of perverse desire. Rather, I suggest that the legal authorities colluded both in the fiction of the rarity of same-sex desire and, albeit unintentionally, in the production of forms of homoeroticism that participated in the pleasures of shame and concealment.

A photograph of the dog was presented to the court.[19] At first glance, this image appears not to obey the requirement of incompletion, because the dog appears friendly, is positioned centrally, and is shown on a step staring into the camera. But a second look confirms that the image is far from complete. The darkness of the background hints at the possibility of such an absence, but a telling detail is the dog's leash, which spirals up out of the shot. In Francis Bacon's *Man with Dog* (1953), we have a painting in which incompletion is made into a glaring attribute.[20] The black background ostentatiously imposes itself to the extent that it looks as though the top of the image has been somehow torn off. We infer the presence of a man from a suggestively shaped patch of darkness. There is a creature with four legs, but it is only inferred to be a canine by virtue of its suggestive juxtaposition with what appears to be a pair of trousers. Above all, neither the man nor the dog is given a clear face so that, just as we do not clearly see them, they, unlike the photographed dog, do not

17. B. Harris (2002), p. 300, and see Rendell (2000), p. 257.
18. Transcript *Rex v. Britt and Others*, Central Criminal Court, February 18, 1927 (CRIM 1/387).
19. Evidence presented at the Central Criminal Court, 1938, *Rex v. Rosenz and Others* (CRIM 1/1007). For discussion of interwar police photography, J. O'Brien (1937). My thanks to Les Moran for pointing me in the direction of this source.
20. In the collection of the Albright-Knox Art Gallery, Buffalo, NY (K1955).

engage us with their gaze.[21] Bacon's image actively leads the viewer on to notice the leash—that is, to notice the fact of a constraining device, and to wonder where it leads.[22] Furthermore, while the dog is photographed in precise focus, Bacon repeatedly depicts his humans and animals as blurred, as though they were present as smears and, in the view of one critic, therefore both "interchangeably unclean."[23] These paintings, therefore, play with the conventions of closet representation in that they draw attention to the fact that the artist is eager to hint that there is something more disturbing than that which we are being shown.

The significance of incompleteness in police evidence might appear to be a surprise since the development of regimes of power in modernity has generally been associated with the development of increasing efficiency in surveillance. As John Tagg has commented of the history of photography in *The Burden of Representation* (1998):

> If, in the last decades of the nineteenth century, the squalid slum replaces the country seat and the "abnormal" physiognomies of patient and prisoner displace the pedigreed features of the aristocracy, then their presence in representation is no longer a mark of celebration but a burden of subjection. A vast and repetitive archive of images is accumulated in which the smallest deviations may be noted, classified and filed. The format varies hardly at all. There are bodies and spaces. The bodies . . . are taken one by one: isolated in a shallow contained space; turned full face and subjected to an unreturnable gaze; illuminated, focussed, measured, numbered and named; forced to yield to the minutest scrutiny of gestures and features.[24]

However, the English law of disorder, as of sodomy, was based on pre-modern Christian principles that did not so much criminalize particular categories of individuals as outlaw gross breaches of the moral order. Such horrors were, by definition, essentially incomprehensible and unrepresentable by the "reasonable man" to whom the laws of tort and criminality repeatedly deferred as a gold standard of judgment.[25]

The representation of closeted desires involved, therefore, practices of visual scrutiny-as-detection, similar to those that were of central importance to the images in the "Scene of the Crime" exhibition held at the UCLA/Armand Hammer Museum of Art and Cultural Center, Los

21. Bacon was directly inspired by Eadweard Muybridge's studies of animal locomotion (first published 1887) for his dogs, so the above discussion is less about the dog itself, than about the sense of significant absences.
22. Hatch (1998), p. 171.
23. Gessert (2010), p. 137.
24. Tagg (1998), p. 64. See also Sekula (1986).
25. This "legal fiction" in the form of the man of ordinary prudence first made its appearance in English law in *Vaughan v. Menlove* (1837), a case about the spontaneous combustion of hay bales; on which, including aspects of gendering, see Parker (1993).

Angeles, in 1997. This exhibition explored thirty-five years of "artistic practices that address the art object as a kind of evidence, a clue to absent meanings and prior actions."[26] Bacon made use of photographs of crime scenes and he left a series of references to the idea of a "bed of crime."[27] He also moved in the homosexual underworld of London both before and after World War II, and he would have been familiar with the sort of venues that were raided. I will be asking whether the way in which certain police photographs hint at gross immorality can shed light on the forms and purposes of attempts to picture the closet in some of Bacon's earlier art works.

In the case of *Rex v. Britt and Others* (1927), Robert Britt and Mrs. Carre were accused of running a disorderly house at the Basement Flat, 25 Fitzroy Square, London W1.[28] The court was presented with evidence as follows:

Black Transparent Skirt
Red Sash
Pair Lady's Shoes
Material
Bathing Costume
A Pair of Slippers
Suit of Pyjamas
Set of Photographs
Plan
Letters to Britt
Letters to Summers.[29]

Chief Inspector Robert Sygrove testified that

the premises are the resort of what are known as "Nancy Boys." The premises consist of four floors. The basement which has been recently re-decorated, and well furnished, is in the occupation of Madame Carre, supposed to be of French nationality, and residing with her is a young man named Britt, who is employed in the chorus of "Lady be Good," at the Empire Theatre. They are supposed to be married, and sometimes take the name of "Britt," but there is a considerable difference in their ages. The basement has recently been made quite

26. Rugoff, Vidler, and Wollen (1997), back-cover text.
27. Cappock (2005), pp. 7–8 and 188, explains that there are many references to scenes of crime and that Bacon made four references in notes and annotations to pictures in his studio to a "bed of crime."
28. The woman's name is likely to have been Carré, but the police typewriter does not appear to have been equipped to deal with French accents.
29. List of exhibits in *Rex v. Britt and Others* (CRIM 1/387) and Houlbrook (2005), pp. 131–133. Houlbrook gives detailed readings of the sexual identity politics of the time but does not focus on visual and material culture issues.

Figure 8.1 Fitzroy Square, group, evidence presented at the Central Criminal Court, *Rex v. Britt and Others*, 1927 (CRIM 1/387). Reproduced courtesy of the National Archives, London.

distinct from the other part of the house, the staircase from the ground floor to basement having been removed.[30]

The flat had been kept under close observation by plainclothes police. In the course of one evening, various young men knocked at the door, which, on opening, let loose the sounds of laughter and of a gramophone. Then two "effeminates" were observed in bed together and laughing prior to the light being put out.

Having satisfied themselves of the commission of depravity though not having witnessed its commission, a warrant for a raid was obtained. At 12.40 A.M. on January 16, an officer, watching from a nearby roof, observed two men undressing in the back bedroom, one of whom "put a dark coloured bathing costume on and the other dressed in female attire." At 1 A.M. Superintendent George Collins knocked on door of the flat. Carre's response was to say that Britt was just going to give them "a Salome dance." The attendees then "sorted themselves out and got into the position shown in the photograph" (Figure 8.1).[31] Carre appears in the middle of the group, staring at the camera with an air of resigned amusement while, around her, the various young men appear to be, if not scared, at least unwilling to look into the camera lens. Britt himself sits bare-chested, wearing the black skirt that the police alleged to be transparent. On the other side of the wall behind the group was a small

30. Statement, Chief Inspector Robert Sygrove, Met. Police D Division, January 8, 1927 (CRIM 1/387).
31. Statement, Superintendent George Collings, January 17, 1927 (CRIM 1/387).

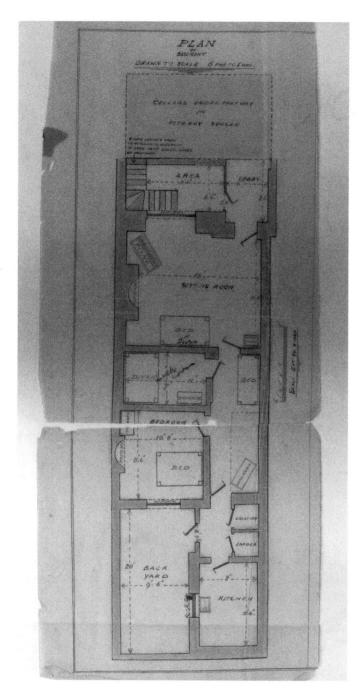

Figure 8.2 Detail, Fitzroy Square, plan, evidence presented at the Central Criminal Court, *Rex v. Britt and Others*, 1927 (CRIM 1/387). Reproduced courtesy of the National Archives, London.

room (Figures 8.2 and 8.3). As with "bedroom (1)" at Dover Street, the police were eager to show that this was not a normal bedroom, but was a closet space devoted specially to sex. Sygrove testified that "the small room behind the sitting room is decorated in an Eastern style. It is furnished with a bed furnished with 2 curtains and 3 fancy curtains. In front of the electric light was a Japanese umbrella. The walls were

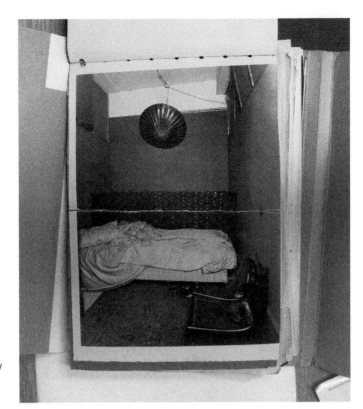

Figure 8.3 Fitzroy Square, small bedroom, evidence presented at the Central Criminal Court, *Rex v. Britt and Others*, 1927 (CRIM 1/387). Reproduced courtesy of the National Archives, London.

painted a bright red."[32] The suspect orientalism of this chamber was emphasized in the plan presented to the court, which indicated that the room contained not a bed but a "divan" (Figure 8.2). Red was a color widely used to signal prostitution, and there was also a red light outside the front door of the flat.[33] Moreover, the umbrella over the bulb would have further tinted the light. The air, it was noted, was scented.

In the photograph of the small room, there is a sort of low curved chair with a piece of clothing hung off it and the sign of a man in the form of a pair of shoes. In Francis Bacon's *Figure Study I* (1945–1946) a coat has been draped as if over a chair, thereby impeding comprehension that we are being shown a man wearing a hat (Figure 8.4). There is an umbrella in the photograph, but not in *Figure Study I*; however, such an item does appear in the place of a hat in *Figure Study II* (1945–1946) (Figure 8.5). In this painting, as in the photograph of Britt, a man appears naked to the waist, although in Bacon's composition the man is flabby and is bending over while staring blindly at the viewer. As with the comparison between the photograph of the Dover Street dog and Bacon's *Man with Dog*, *Figure Study II* differs from the respective

32. Statement, Chief Inspector Sygrove, Feburary 2, 1927 (CRIM 1/387).
33. Compare with the discussion of the supposed perversity of the Orient in Chapter 5. Statement, Sergeant Arthur Spencer, January 3, 1927 (CRIM 1/387).

Figure 8.6 Cropped page from J. A. Hammerton, ed., *Peoples of All Nations: Their Life Today and Story of Their Past* (1922), 1, p. 22. 35 x 22.7 cm. Reproduced courtesy of Dublin City Gallery, The Hugh Lane (RM98F1: 23), © The Estate of Francis Bacon, all rights reserved, DACS.

photograph in the same way: it implies unseen horror more overtly. The photograph implies that clothes have been removed, and that a make-shift bed has been employed, but the presence of immorality relies upon reading the "oriental" décor as inherently perverse. It also relies upon imagining Britt lying, or perhaps bending over, being buggered. Bacon, by contrast, gives us the figure (similarly set against a lurid red-orange backdrop) and endows it with a scream—which draws attention to incompletion through its tacit implication of piercing sound.[34]

Further light on the meanings of this assemblage are shed by two items that were found in Bacon's studio. The first is a photograph from a

34. Note Peppiat (2006), p. 35, comments that it is men who scream in Bacon's paintings, despite the fact that the acknowledged visual sources are women. He links the man screaming to the state of orgasm.

chapter on the "quaint folk, civilized and savage" of Annam (now central Vietnam), which has been torn from a copy of the first volume of J. A. Hammerton's *Peoples of All Nations: Their Life Today and Story of Their Past* (1922) (Figure 8.6). Bacon has drawn an architectural frame on this photograph, such as was common in his work from the 1940s to the 1960s, and this has the effect of confining the figures within an interior. The original caption read "young Chan dandies wear almost the same clothes as their sisters, with armlets and necklets for decoration. The umbrella is sheer vanity."[35] In the later nineteenth to early twentieth centuries, dark glasses and umbrellas were often associated with effeminate weakness of temperament.[36] This strongly implies that Bacon may have picked this image for its apparently queer "oriental" associations. A comparison for the dandified and arguably effeminate use of a black sun-umbrella can be seen, for instance, in a photograph of Lytton Strachey reading outdoors, in which his body effectively vanishes into obscurity (Figure 8.7). Further interesting evidence is provided by a black and white photograph of an unidentified old woman at a Francis Bacon exhibition in front of *Figure Study II* (1945–1946), which was also in Bacon's studio (Figure 8.8). Now clearly neither this woman, nor Strachey, fits the bill of the urban tough to whom the painter was sexually attracted, but they can both be understood to contribute to the imagery of bodily shame and abjection. As I will go on to argue, it was to the mental abjection of the supposedly tough, but actually fearfully closeted male, that Bacon repeatedly returns in his art.

Figure 8.7 Probably by Vanessa Bell (née Stephen), *Lytton Strachey* (1913), enlarged snapshot print on card folder, 21.1 x 15.9 cm, National Portrait Gallery, London (x21198). © The Estate of Vanessa Bell, courtesy of Henrietta Garnett.

While Dover Street seems clearly to have been used as a brothel, what the police broke up at Fitzroy Square was a private party insofar as there was no evidence that any money had changed hands. It is, however, likely that some, if not all, of these young men were selling sex, and may have used the flat to do so. The boys in Fitzroy Square were likewise not Bacon's type, bearing in mind that he preferred older, beefier men; however, both queens and rough trade were regulars at the (literally) underground venue, the Caravan Club, that operated from a basement in Endell Street, London WC1. If Francis Bacon

35. Vassal (1922), p. 147.
36. Janes (2012a), pp. 115–117.

was a member of this club, then he did not sign his real name in the membership book.[37] However, bearing in mind the appearance of such individuals there as Monsieur "Vrai-Homme," it seems likely that we will never know if he visited. However, Bacon's friend John Deakin, who was twenty-two at the time, certainly did, since he was one of the defendants in the ensuing court case heard in October 1934 in the aftermath of a police raid on the premises.

"Oriental" décor in clubs and brothels had an association not simply with sex, but with perverse sex, as Keir Hardy, the pioneering Independent Labour MP, signaled in his campaign against "white slavery in a Piccadilly Flat" in 1913. According to him—and it was unclear

37. Caravan Club, evidence presented at the Central Criminal Court, *Rex v. Neave and Others*, 1934 (CRIM 1/735).

how he knew this—Queenie Gerald's establishment there was "decked with 16 dozen arum lilies, with hot scented baths, whips and lashes, reminiscent of Oriental orgies."[38] The association of "orientals" with perverse sexuality appears to have been a particular inspiration behind not only the name of the Caravan Club—although this may also be a pun on the name of the highly respectable Caravan Club established in 1907 to encourage engagement with fresh air and country pursuits—but also its décor.[39] The Club was, in essence, a bare basement space that was hung with drapes and cheaply furnished with makeshift tables, chairs, and divans. Pictures were taken after the place had been emptied. The police made play of the supposedly Eastern character evoked by the furnishings, referring in a particularly arch manner to an "idol" (which was identified on the police plan). Cards for the venue termed it "London's greatest Bohemian rendezvous. Said to be the most unconventional spot in town." It opened between 9.30 P.M. and 4 A.M.[40]

The police observed the venue in plain clothes over several evenings before the raid. Constable Reginald Mortimer, for one, danced with both women and men and talked with them about male prostitution.[41] Overt sexual behavior was hard to identify because the venue was so dark and crowded. Therefore, the police proceeded to deduce the presence of rampant immorality through the process of accumulating a store of visual signs. Women were noted as embracing one another, and one was smoking a pipe.[42] Men were observed wriggling their posteriors in the manner of de Charlus and Jupien, as discussed in Chapter 1 of this book. The presence of colored persons was noted. After the room was emptied by the police, Detective Edmund Daws found two lipsticks, an eyebrow brush, a powder compact, and a powder puff. There was also a handkerchief bearing traces of rouge. Underneath the divan at the end of the room "which was occupied by men, I found a used rubber sheath, a roll of wadding and a lipstick-stained handkerchief." A tin of Vaseline was found under another divan. Police interest in these items was as evidence of homosexual transgression. Of the 103 persons arrested, 76 were discharged, including all the women. As one woman put it, when the (normative appearanced) male who was accompanying her started screaming, "for Christ's sake shut up. Make the best of it. It's the rotten 'cissies' they're after."[43]

These "cissies" (also referred to by the police as "nancies" and "sodomites" but never as homosexuals, but who are referenced as "queans" earlier in this chapter) were men who used makeup, allegedly to signal

38. Hardy (1913), p. 15, and Palmer (1920), p. 6.
39. Colligan (2003).
40. Letter, Divisional Inspector, Bow Street, to Superintendent, August 10, 1934 (MEPO 3/758).
41. Statement, Constable Reginald Mortimer, July 28, 1934 (MEPO 3/758).
42. Statement, Constable Reginald Mortimer, August 21, 1934 (DPP 2/234).
43. Statement, Inspector John Pollock, August 25, 1934 (DPP 2/244).

their availability as male prostitutes.[44] One such was Maurice Rowland Berkeley, age twenty-eight, an actor, on whose person were found "1 bottle of scent, tube of white lip salve, two pieces of paper with telephone numbers of men."[45] Another was Cyril "Coeur de Leon," who asked who was in charge and, on being told, said to the commanding officer, "Well I don't mind the beastly raid, but I would like to know if you can let me have one of your nice boys to come home with me, I am really good."[46] When his nearby one-room flat was raided, sketches of a naked man and a woman were removed, as was what was described as a photograph "of the penis of a man."[47] Daws stated that "at around 3 A.M., the same day, at Bow Street Police Station I took pieces of blotting paper and rubbed them on the cheeks [of six of the men] . . . all the pieces of blotting paper, which I produce, bear traces of rouge and all the men mentioned with the exception of Skinner had their eyebrows plucked."[48]

Matt Houlbrook has recently highlighting the importance of the case of "Thomas B." (1924) in which the presence on the accused of a powder puff, mirror, and powder was sufficient for the law to assert that he was soliciting for the purposes of prostitution.[49] This built on the case of *Horton v. Mead* (1913) in which, according to the Street Offences Committee,

> the accused was observed by two police officers to enter certain public lavatories and to remain a few minutes in each. While in the lavatories and also in the street he smiled in the faces of gentlemen and made certain gestures but did not speak to or touch anyone nor did anyone complain of his conduct. The accused when arrested was rouged and had a powder puff in his pocket. . . . [The case went from the magistrate to quarter sessions where] the Court held that in order to establish a case of solicitation under the [Vagrancy] Act it was not necessary to prove that the solicitation had actually reached the notice of any persons to whom it was directed. The evidence of solicited persons was thus held to be unnecessary in order to prove acts of solicitation.[50]

In other words, the word of a policeman, based purely on visual observation and judgment, was sufficient to secure a conviction. It was noted by the same official committee, reporting in 1928, that "although the

---

44. Houlbrook (2007). See also Weeks (1980–1981) and Bartley (2000), pp. 25, 30, and 157.
45. Statement, Inspector Stanley Chedzroy, August 27, 1934 (DPP 2/224).
46. Statement, Divisional Inspector to Superintendent, August 29, 1934 (DPP 2/224).
47. Statement, Detective Sergeant Leonard Stevenson, August 27, 1934 (DPP 2/224).
48. Statement, Edmund Daws, August 27, 1934 (MEPO 3.758).
49. Houlbrook (2007).
50. Street Offences Committee (1928), p. 48. See also Moran and McGhee (1998).

language of the Vagrancy Act, 1898, would cover the case of solicitation of women by men, the statute is generally regarded, if only by reason of the severity of the penalties, as applicable only to the case of solicitation of men by men." These provisions were further strengthened to a maximum of two years hard labor by the Criminal Law Amendment Act (1912), which also retained the earlier provision for private whipping in cases of a second offense.

These Acts did not apply in the case of the raids I have been describing because these statutes governed street prostitution; however, the discovery of men in makeup was a major preoccupation for the police because this was a key element in their argument for the venue being a disorderly house. Thus, in the case of *Rex v. Billie Joyce and Others* in January 1937 that ensued from the raid on Billie's Club on the ground floor of 6 Little Denmark Street, London WC1, just around the corner from Endell Street, the exhibits included seven powder puffs, powder, and rouge.[51] In the course of the trial, Constable Jack Smith was closely cross-examined over the suggestion that he had planted a powder puff on one of the prisoners, while Chief Inspector Donaldson testified that he had taken such care over his inspection of the arrested men that in the case of one of those whose makeup seemed to be unusually subtle, "I put him under the electric light as I wanted to be certain."[52]

During the 1920s, Francis Bacon had been a "man with a powder-puff" in Berlin, Paris, and London. And although the patronage of richer men, his own rising prosperity, and, in due course, advancing age kept him from the streets, he continued to use maquillage. Since he painted his face before he painted canvases, and he was a self-taught painter, it might seem that his training in the art of painting came from learning how to apply makeup. Moreover, he also made a practice of swirling makeup on his own face once his stubble had grown to the length at which it resembled the "wrong" (hairy) side of the canvas on which he painted.[53] Bearing in mind that Bacon's desires were centered on working class, masculine men in suits, some of his white, swirled figures seem like the aging abject remains of the painted pretty-boys of his youth.[54] Thus the scream of horror in *Figure Study II*, painted when Bacon was approaching middle age, has, perhaps, something to do with the horror of being revealed as old and ugly, and as having a body that is gradually slipping into a state of rot and abjection (Figures 8.5 and 8.8).

Despite having gained an interwar reputation for daring examinations of same-sex desire, it was a horror-filled portrait of rich old queens

51. Billie's Club, evidence presented at the Central Criminal Court, *Rex v. Billie Joyce and Others*, 1927 (CRIM 1/903).
52. Statement, Constable Jack Smith, December 2, 1936 (CRIM 1/903) and statement, Chief Inspector Robert Donaldson, November 16, 1936 (CRIM 1/903).
53. Farson (1994), p. 84, and O'Neill (2007), p. 113.
54. Farson (1994), p. 115.

that Rosamond Lehmann drew in her novel *The Echoing Grove* (1953).[55] Here is the artist Dinah talking to her sister Madeline about the handsome Rickie Masters:

> They got their rotten rotting teeth in him. They've got the belts and ties and rings and bracelet watches. And all the words. *Avant garde* passwords. And the freedom of the hunting grounds. All the happy hunting grounds mapped out, combed over. Barracks, pubs, ports, tube stations, public lavatories. How could he possibly be missed! The classiest piece of goods on the market. Bought and paid for. A whizzing beauty. Really but really a knock-out. And really but really amoral and uncorrupted and out of the bottom drawer! A natural gangster, a natural innocent. A natural. An enemy of society. *Done time!*—actually done time—for housebreaking! *Actually actively* anti-bourgeois [original emphases].[56]

From being an object of desire, Bacon could have imagined himself as having been rendered by time into a monster with a terrible appetite. His forensic imagination could also interpret the photographs of authority figures as the being tellingly incomplete evidences of other creatures with similarly bestial emotions and desires. The catalogue entry for Francis Bacon's *Painting* (1946), on the website of The Museum of Modern Art, New York, says that "*Painting* is an oblique but damning image of an anonymous public figure. Half-obscured by an umbrella, he is dressed in a dark formal suit—the unofficial uniform of British politicians of the day—punctuated by an incongruously bright yellow boutonnière. But his deathly complexion and toothy grimace suggest a deep brutality beneath his proper exterior."[57] Screaming under one umbrella, grimacing toothily under another, Bacon does not just present the abject body; he quite possibly presents his own body as representative of the secret of human bestiality. And he presents that body as a series of partial traces and smears, surrounded by objects fetishized as evidences of an unrepresentable ultimate amorality in which his erotic shame is brought to its climax by his domination by men who do not even have the courage openly to display their own perverse desires.

Though the police preferred to remain fixed on viewing effeminate spectacle rather than probing the full extent of the sexual secrets of the masculine closet, Bacon, in the course of the 1940s and early 1950s, was slowly developing from the depiction of monsters, to monstrous humans, and then to men as objects of desire. He said of *Painting* (1946) that, having started as a bird of prey alighting in a field, "suddenly the

---

55. Tindall (1985), p. 171, understands Lehmann to have here cast a "colder eye" on life, sex, and homosexuality than in her pre-war novels.
56. Lehmann (1953), p. 190.
57. Museum of Modern Art, New York (2011). The painting's reference no. is 229.1948.

lines that I'd drawn suggested some-thing totally different, and out of this suggestion arose this picture. I had no intention to do this picture; I never thought of it in that way. It was like one continuous accident mounting on top of another."[58] It is as though the figure of a predatory animal had fused with the erotic associations of "mounting" to produce the half-emergent human figure of secrecy and fleshy violation that is the subject of the completed painting.

In his "Man in Blue" series of 1954, Bacon presented us with images of an anonymous man whose "suit and tie are rendered in a black-blue, darker than the indigo blue of the surrounding space, painted as a flat ground. . . . As such, it is in keeping with the sartorial principle of a midnight blue suit's ability to register darker than black suiting, first innovated by Edward, Prince of Wales in the 1920s in response to having his photograph printed by the press. In the painting, the authority of the suit is made attractive by the suggested anonymity of the man wearing it, thus positing a homosexual" (Figure 8.9).[59] In November 1954, while working on the *Man in Blue* pictures, Bacon told David Sylvester in a letter that he was "excited about the new series I am doing—it is about dreams and life in hotel bedrooms."[60] And, indeed, these seven paintings were based on a figure "met (and possibly seduced)" at the Imperial Hotel, Henley on Thames.[61] Whereas Strachey was content to imply that the Victorian closet was ornamented with far more queer spectacle than it had been given credit for, Bacon was attempting to represent the closet states of secrecy and self-disgust as erotic in themselves. Thus, if Strachey viewed Cardinal Newman crying in distress, Bacon famously depicted his Popes screaming in sublime horror.[62] The implication is that he could represent the closet as a place that contained the terrible secret not of the obvious homosexual, for that was openly put on display by the queens, but of the fact that various "normal-looking" men had desires for other men—or even, more radically, that abject desires were universal. Such shameful knowledge was, for him, powerfully erotic.

The threatening moral chaos of disorderly places and persons was conjured by the police through their own fantasies of disgust as inherent to regimes of effeminate display. The effect of these was not to reveal the secrets of the closet so much as to reinforce the visually obvious queen as the supposed truth of the homosexual. Just as visual evidences of skirts and makeup were presented as crucial indicators of the existence of corruption, so the presence of scent in the air was understood to be a suspicious act of concealment. At the trial of *Rex v. Neave and Others* (the Caravan Club case), Constable Reginald Mortimer was cross-questioned in detail about this. He argued that "it is not unusual for people to spray

58. Sylvester (1993b), p. 11, and see also (1993a), p. 26.
59. O'Neill (2009), p. 285.
60. Quoted from Hammer (2012), p. 369.
61. Peppiatt (2006), p. 46.
62. Davies (2002) and Arya (2009a).

something into a thick atmosphere. That is what Neave did. I did not examine the machine which Neave used. I agree that there are many disinfectants supplied specially for such purposes. I agree it might have been any disinfectant but it might have been scent."[63] Such attempts at ladylike concealment of the abject homosexual body and its needs were projected as woefully inadequate. The lavatory, it was noted, "was in a disgusting condition. The floor was running with urine, there was no seat to the W.C., and on the door of the W.C. was painted a big mark of interrogation" (this question mark on the propped-open door can be seen reflected in the mirror in Figures 8.10a and b).[64]

63. Cross-examination, Constable Reginald Mortimer, *Rex v. Neave and Others* (DPP 2/224).
64. Statement, Constable George Church, September 5, 1934 (DPP 2/224).

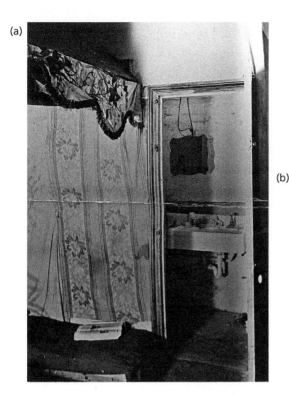

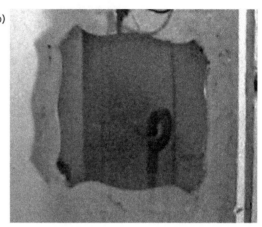

So horrifying was the toilet that the police photographer did not take a picture of it. Instead, he placed himself outside, with the result that the court was presented with a partial view of a sink, seen through a doorway. This was the entrance to the only toilet in the club and, it was noted with horror, both men and women were of necessity using it— hence, humorously, the sign on the door. The dirtiness of the space was, in other words, composed of two elements. On the one hand, there was physical dirt and disorder, and on the other hand, there was the moral disorder and gender confusion upon which the chances of conviction depended. Moral and conceptual pollution were held to be directly inter-related.[65] Judge Holman Gregory's summing up at the trial on October 23, 1934, returned repeatedly to images of dirt and pollution, as when he described the Caravan Club as "a vile den of iniquity that was likely to corrupt, in fact, did corrupt, the youth of London to a considerable extent." He commended the police, saying that he "would particularly mention the splendid work done by P.C. 453 'E' Mortimer [who], along with colleagues, entered this filthy place and associated himself in so discreet a manner with such disgusting companions."[66]

The legal concept of the "disorderly house" was posited not on specific transgressive acts, but on there being a state of transcendent moral

Figures 8.10a and b Caravan Club toilet and detail of mirror (reversed), evidence presented at the Central Criminal Court, *Rex v. Neave and Others*, 1934 (CRIM 1/735). Reproduced courtesy of the National Archives, London.

65. Compare the discussion of anthropological readings of boundary transgression in Chapter 5.
66. Letter, Divisional Inspector, Bow Street, to Superintendent, October 30, 1934 (MEPO 3/758).

confusion in which boundaries between right and wrong had broken down, a state that Bacon recognized as one of erotic truth in which the individual self was sublimely surrendered. This might explain why Bacon was such an enthusiast for Nietzschean nihilism.[67] William Miller, in his study *The Anatomy of Disgust* (1997), has argued that "disgust is very ambivalent about life itself, particularly human life. Life soup, *human* life soup, lies at the core of the disgusting [original emphasis]. And that makes disgust unavoidably misanthropic in its cast. Disgust recoils at what we are and what we do, both the voluntary and the involuntary."[68] Bacon responded to states of disgust and abjection by embracing them. The apparent chaos in which he worked has become iconic in itself; and he posited this quality as inherent to the human condition, rather than specific to those who appeared to transgress boundaries of sex and gender.

Bacon was certainly interested in problematizing the masculine subject by exploring the ways in which such a thing could be represented, as Richard Hornsey has argued in his interesting examination of Bacon's use of photo-booth strips, which show him turning from the camera lens and so disrupting the expected representation.[69] And there were times when it looked as though he might move to more open expression of same-sex desire, as Simon Ofield has argued in relation to *Two Figures* (1953), a painting in which wrestling figures can be contexualized in relation to the development of queer eroticization of body-building and contact sports.[70] But even these figures, which can be related to imagery that is more widely recognized as homoerotic, fail to develop a powerful sense of sexual subjectivity. Rina Arya has argued in her paper on "Constructions of Homosexuality in the Art of Francis Bacon" (2012) that this quality of his art can be explained by reference to alienation, nihilistic despair, and the supposed incapacity of same-sex eroticism to create a complete sense of connection.[71] But this fails to explain how it was that, even if Bacon's art was rooted in closet despair, it was, for him, an art of powerful eroticism.

One way to shed light on this issue is to situate Bacon in relation to the search for "limit experiences." Thus, in his famous interviews with David Sylvester, Bacon said he wanted to "paint the one picture that will annihilate all the other ones."[72] Such masochistic yearning after fantasies of self-destruction can be compared with the writings of Georges Bataille into the search for the destruction of self as a moment of "jouissance" (unbounded pleasure through the temporary loss of self).[73] Bacon

67. Arya (2009b), p. 155.
68. W. Miller (1997), p. 204.
69. Hornsey (2010), p. 122, fig. 17.
70. Ofield (2001), p. 116; see also Nealon (2001), pp. 99–139, on muscle magazines.
71. Arya (2012), p. 59.
72. Bacon quoted in and discussed by Brintnall (2011), p.168.
73. Ishii-Gonzalès (2000), p. 635.

stepped, in his imagination, into the space of the Burkean sublime and painted his own ecstatic terror in the face of reconstitutive dissolution by scopic authority. This imaginative stance is seemingly dangerous and disorderly when brought back into the light of day in the form of art.[74] However, Bacon's paintings flicker and blur between concealment and revelation of what is taking place. They were inspired by film and evoke movement, but fail to spell out a transparent narrative that unambiguously challenges homophobic assumptions. They are, thus, parasitic on a closet that could contain and heighten sadomasochistic as well as homosexual desires.[75]

Bacon's art was, of course, transgressive, but it was not, in fact, too transgressive for his age, or he would never have sold his works and become immensely wealthy. Just as Laurel Brake and Justin Bengry have argued that the "pink pound" had been discreetly courted by elements of the media and commerce since the 1890s, so Bacon can be situated in relation to an evolving market for culturally queer art in the postwar period.[76] His fractured bodies hung nicely in modernist interiors as fashionable statements of contemporary fracture and dislocation.[77] In some ways, Bacon, like Burke, can be seen as a conservative figure who was eager to view the extremes of experience as a form of re-constitutive tonic for his own insecure sense of self. His masochism can be understood as a way of accommodating appetites that he conceptualized as bestial and monstrous. His art, therefore, ultimately comes into erotic identification with the disciplinary gaze of the police since he was intent, as were they, on reinforcing the closet as a crucial structure in the maintenance of the masculine as sublime.[78] But while the police were looking at the queens, Bacon was, in effect, looking back at the police. He was transgressive, therefore, insofar as he detected the evidences of a universal closet of furious drives and desires in public exhibitions of masculinity. He recognized that the phobic construction of the camp spectacle of the closet had the effect of de-eroticizing the body of the allegedly effeminate homosexual and building up the erotic capital of the (supposedly) controlling and self-controlling "normal" male. By masochistically using the closet as a source of pleasure, he found a way in which to reposition the punishment of queers as being, in itself, an act and expression of same-sex desire.

74. Hammer and Stephens (2009).
75. As I argue in Chapter 3. Also see Savran (1998).
76. Bengry (2009) and Brake (2000), pp. 271–272.
77. Though Mellor (2011), p. 220, n. 98, suggests that Bacon's art can also be connected to realistic depictions of torn-up buildings and bodies as seen in the London blitz.
78. Barber (2008), p. 135.

CHAPTER 9

THE UNLIBERATED

"WE'VE GOT A criminal practice that takes up most of our time," observes one of a pair of lawyers in a comedy sketch broadcast shortly before the partial decriminalization of homosexual sex in England in 1967.[1] The flagrantly camp "friends" Julian and Sandy, who regularly appeared on the hugely popular BBC comedy series *Round the Horne* (1965–1968), have been celebrated as "the peak of radio's glorious gay liberation . . . [with] some jokes almost too defiant for straight audiences. (Singing and composing in a 'Bona Musicals' sketch: 'Julian's a miracle of dexterity on the cottage grand')."[2] I remember listening to this sketch (or to one of their many similar routines) when I was a child living with my homophobic grandparents. Apart from thinking that the wording was "a cottage upright," I also recall us all laughing heartily. I had no idea precisely what it meant, and I very much doubt my grandparents did either. The skit employed "polari" slang words, such as "bona" in place of good, which had once been in widespread use in urban queer subculture. The surface meaning of the phrase, that he's good at playing a small piano, is not necessarily obvious, and the other meaning, that he's good at having sex in a cramped public toilet, is even less so—which is, of course, why the joke could be broadcast at all. This is the spectacle of the closet as a place of apparently asexual camp enacted in sound for popular amusement—a fact that is reinforced by the knowledge that the self-hating diaries of the actor making the joke, Kenneth Williams (1926–1988), reveal him to have thought that to be a homosexual was a tragic fate.[3] However, it is worth noting that his camp did provide Williams with an opportunity to become a celebrity,

1. Medhurst (2007), p. 100.
2. A. Beck (2003), p. 132; see also Baker (2002) on polari and gay identity.
3. Butt and Langdridge (2003), p. 485; the diaries are K. Williams (1993).

and part of the power of his humor as a way of reinforcing an outsider identity may precisely have lain in the fact that the straights could not fully understand what he was talking about. I will now proceed to look at some of the ways in which the very structures of the British establishment could be colonized in the furtherance of queer pleasures and self-expressions in the closet.

The celebrity photographer Sir Cecil Beaton's (1904–1980) career rested on making women look beautiful. Therefore, it is perhaps not surprising that if one of the high points of that career was being chosen to take the official photographs of Queen Elizabeth II in her coronation regalia in 1953, his artistic encounters with Francis Bacon were not. For instance, in a series of images taken by Beaton in 1960 at Bacon's then studio at Overstrand Mansions in Battersea, where the artist would wipe his paint-spattered hands on the curtains, the painter is shown apparently propped up as just another abandoned canvas in a sea of junk.[4] Beaton was, in his turn, horrified by the portrait of him by Bacon, which he found hideous. The face that looked back at him, like that of the aging Dorian Gray, sorely failed to reflect the shiny image of a fashionable and successful socialite.[5] Bacon's images of abjection failed unambiguously to depict the homosexual partly because they aimed to make universal statements about the human condition, but the effect of this was, nevertheless, to equalize the status of queers and straights. Cecil Beaton's artistic project provides a parallel case study, but one of someone whose creative métier was the spectacle of the closet, rather than the secrecy of the closet itself, and whose transgressive fantasy was to imagine that all men could be queens.

In the official press release for "Theatre of War," an exhibition held in 2012 at the Imperial War Museum in London, it was stated that although "Cecil Beaton is widely remembered as the leading British portrait and fashion photographer of his day, the fact that Beaton was one of Britain's hardest working war photographers during the Second World War is less well known."[6] Although the exhibition included many images of male service personnel who had been chosen for the camera with an eye to their good looks, no mention was made of the photographer's homosexuality.[7] This would, at first sight, appear to be appropriate for a man who was what Martin Francis has called a "romantic Tory" and who, from suburban origins, rose by idolizing the aristocracy and profiting from their patronage. The art historian Sir Roy Strong suggested that Beaton's royal image-making helped save the monarchy after the abdication crisis of 1936, and that this was the reason that

4. Images held at the Cecil Beaton Studio Archive, Sotheby's, London. Discussed in Oldfield (2006).
5. Ofield (2006), p. 35.
6. Imperial War Museum (2012).
7. Beaton (2012).

the photographer's own knighthood, long delayed in case of sexual scandal, was finally conferred in 1972.[8]

Susanna Brown has extensively studied the impressive body of photographs that Beaton took of members of the royal family and has concluded that the 1953 images show him at "the height of his powers."[9] For his representations of Elizabeth, the photographer found inspiration in portraits of Queen Victoria, notably those by George Hayter and Franz Winterhalter.[10] Beaton recorded in his diary that "I suggested that she sit alone for some pictures by herself against my abbey background. The lighting wasn't very good but no time to readjust. Every minute of importance. Yes, I was banging away getting pictures in the can at a great rate, but I had only the foggiest notion of what I was doing, if taking black white or colour, if getting the right exposure. The queen looked very small under her robes and crown."[11] If one compares the images derived from this photo shoot, it becomes apparent that Beaton has subsequently cut out the periphery and blacked out the carpet so as to disguise the fact that these official images were taken in Buckingham Palace against a backcloth, rather than in the Abbey itself (Figures 9.1 and 9.2). Beaton was a sincere devotee of the monarchy, but that did not mean that he was unaware of the staginess and artificiality of royal display: in fact, he reveled in it, as evidenced by his *faux* memoir, *My Royal Past* (1939).

In this book Baroness von Bülop, a very plain and stupid Austro-Hungarian aristocrat, is constantly humiliated by her glamorous aunt, the Grand Duchess, before making an unwise marriage to a homosexual: "I discovered my only attraction for the Count was my friendship and near relationship to the Grand Duchess, and I soon became acquainted with the rumours that the man I had married

Figure 9.1 Cecil Beaton, *Queen Elizabeth II* (1953), semi-matte cibachrome print, 33.1 x 24.9 cm, acquired from Sir Cecil Beaton, 1986, in conjunction with the "Elizabeth II" exhibition, National Portrait Gallery, London (x35390). © Victoria and Albert Museum, London.

8. Francis (2006), p. 115.
9. S. Brown (2011a), p. 302.
10. S. Brown (2011a), p. 304, and Millar (1992), p. 105 and MS, St. John's College, Cambridge. See also Beaton (1973), p. 138, but note that this published version has been edited and variously tidied up by the author prior to publication and so the text is not always identical.
11. Beaton (1973), p. 147 and MS, St. John's College, Cambridge.

was addicted to vices only supported in the days of ancient civilisations. However, we continued the honeymoon."[12] One evening she relieves her boredom while the Count is being "massaged" by his valet next door by learning how to play the "cymballo."[13] Court life is then interrupted by the outbreak of revolution, and the Baroness retires to a convent. Beaton appeared in drag for a Cambridge footlights review in 1925, and he seems to have relished the chance to get some of his friends into ugly period frocks—notably the bisexual playboy Antonio de Gandarillas (who claimed to be descended from Catherine of Aragon)—for the extraordinary illustrations to this book.[14] These images make clear that Beaton viewed royalty, and its practices of self-presentation, as participating in the world of queer camp (Figure 9.3). The homosexual art collector Peter Watson said that "it is in fact a masterstroke even to see the book with its sinister undercurrents of sex, perversions, crass stupidities and general dirt, beaming severely from Maggs Bookshop in Berkeley Square."[15]

So how did Beaton get away with it? To start with, the book did not directly make fun of the *British* monarchy, and it also mocked styles of the period before World War I, rather than of its own time. This may explain why George VI's wife, Elizabeth Angela Marguerite Bowes-Lyon (1900–2002), was said to like it, but George V's wife, Queen Mary (Victoria Mary Augusta Louise Olga Pauline Claudine Agnes) of Teck (1867–1953), did not.[16] There is also a slight suspicion in my mind that the latter severe and formidable lady may have been an inspiration for the Baroness. Further light is shed on the matter by the behavior of Sir (Charles) Michael Duff (1907–1980), a Welsh aristocrat, who was not

12. Beaton (1939), p. 79.
13. Beaton (1939), p. 85.
14. S. Brown (2011b), p. 15, and Faulks (1996), p. 11. These aspects were brought further into prominence in the second edition of 1960 in which the drag element is rendered even more obviously transgressive by adding such images as one taken "on our honeymoon," Beaton (1960), opposite p. 58.
15. Letter of Peter Watson to Beaton, December 12, 1939, quoted in Vickers (1985), p. 231.
16. Vickers (1985), p. 230. See also Vickers (2004).

only a godson of Queen Mary but also liked to dress up as her at bachelor dinner parties. Beaton wrote of him that "there is surely no one who knows more than Michael about the private lives of any reigning family, in no matter what country; in fact, it can be said that he is 'royalty struck.' He collects stories and gossip about any royal personage, and treats his hierarchy with a mixture of complete reverence and a realization of how ridiculous their more exaggerated characteristics can become."[17]

There is yet another aspect of queer taste at work in these photographs: the coronation dress, which was designed by Sir Norman Hartnell (1901–1979), whose entry in the *Oxford Dictionary of National Biography* opines that he "was a much loved man" but does not say by whom, other than to note that he was unmarried.[18] His greatest rival as dressmaker to the Queen was Sir (Edwin) Hardy Amies (1909–2003), whose upbringing was also modest and suburban, and who said that Hartnell and he respected each other, but the difference was that he himself was a "bitchy old queen" while his counterpart was a "soppy old queen."[19] In his autobiography, *Silver and Gold* (1955), Hartnell describes his childhood love for actresses.[20] He "lost his heart to Gaby Deslys in the musical *Suzette* where she appeared 'like a humming bird, aquiver with feathers and aglitter with jewels.'"[21] He was fascinated by female excess, noting with awe that "her succession of gorgeous dresses was quite overshadowed, however, by the even more colossal headdresses that towered, twice her height above her. These were surmounted by fountains of aigrettes and foaming ostrich feathers, cascade upon cascade of paradise plumes and clouds of ospreys."[22] Deslys, with her "vacantly

Figure 9.3 Cecil Beaton, *Antonio de Gandarillas as Baroness von Bülop* [first published as *Myself "en Grande Tenue,"* in Beaton, *My Royal Past* (1939), p. 121]. Reproduced courtesy of the Cecil Beaton Studio Archive at Sotheby's.

17. Beaton (1973), p. 155. I must thank Charles Duff for fascinating discourse on this topic.
18. Rayne (2004).
19. M. Pick (2012), quotation at p. 9; and see also pp. 163–168, and Ehrman (2002), at pp. 138–140.
20. Parts of this book were ghostwritten, but these particular passages do appear to relate directly to his own personal experiences. My thanks go to Michael Pick for this information.
21. T. Beck (1985), p. 71. The quotation within this quotation is from Hartnell (1955), p. 17.
22. Hartnell (1955), p. 17.

Figure 9.4 Norman Hartnell, *A Suggestion for the [Danish] State Opening of Parliament* (1956). Reproduced courtesy of Michael Pick.

parted lips like a split plum," was a sugary mouthful of excess.[23] In 1953 Hartnell sat in Westminster Abbey at the coronation sucking sugar lumps and watching the peeresses "mounting towards the very roof. They look like a lovely hunk of fruit cake; the damson jam of the velvet, bordered with the clotted cream of ermine and sprinkled with the sugar of diamonds."[24] "My hand is trembling," he records, "for soon I shall be seeing the dress I had made, worn by Her Majesty the Queen for her Crowning."[25] He seemed to regard the clothes he designed as consumable items for his own delectation.

If, as Jane Hattrick argues, the interiors of Hartnell's country home can be read as an expression of his queer sensibility, then I would argue that the coronation dress can be viewed in the same light.[26] At this time he was joined by a new assistant, Ian Thomas (1929–1993), who "often spent weekends at Lovel Dene, the designer's country house, exchanging ideas, [and] polishing his sketches," including those of the various coronation robes.[27] Thomas appears to have shared similar tastes to Hartnell, or as his obituary in *The Independent* put it, "in private life he lived for his horses. . . . An unassuming man, he lived in a charming country house in Oxfordshire filled with beautiful objects he had collected over the years."[28] The wedding dress, which was far more complex than that of Elizabeth's mother or grandmother, may be situated in relation to some of Hartnell's more restrained designs (Figure 9.4); or even to the kitsch, complete with sparkles and bluebirds, displayed in sketches included in *Silver and Gold* (as his own, but probably by Ian Thomas) as part of the spectacle of Hartnell's closet, the ornamentations of which included not only his assistants and their design efforts, but even the Queen herself.[29]

Beaton's and Hartnell's devotion to the Queen looks rather like a species of "gay diva worship," as described by Daniel Harris in relation

23. Hartnell (1955), p. 17.
24. Hartnell (1955), p. 132.
25. Hartnell (1955), p. 134.
26. Hattrick (2012).
27. M. Pick (2007), pp. 158 and 187. See also McDowell (1985).
28. Etherington-Smith (1993).
29. I further thank Michael Pick for his insights into the attribution to Thomas of various sketches such as "A mimosa tulle dress worn in Australia by Her Majesty the Queen" and "A dress of moonlight-blue tulle and stars for Her Royal Highness Princess Margaret," published in Hartnell (1955), opposite pp. 80 and 96.

to his experience as "an insecure gay teenager stranded in the uncivilised hinterlands of North Carolina, [to whom] the gracious ladies of Park Avenue and Sutton Place embodied a way of life more glamorous and less provincial than his own."[30] Or as Brett Farmer has argued, "queers had had quite literally [sic] to invent their own modes of selfhood from the ground up, and the transcendent, value-adding economies of divadom have been a rich resource for this process of queer self-making and legitimation."[31] The life of the diva presents a fantasy space of limitless possibility and, thus, "the diva is nothing if not a consummate figure of self-authorization, a magisterial image of triumphant identificatory production."[32] The identification of middle-class homosexuals with the monarch might seem strange, but it is important to remember that the Queen's role was to maintain a gorgeous constitutional façade. As David Cannadine has pointed out, ceremonial invention in Britain centered on a position of royal weakness, and the monarch was put in the position of, in effect, performing as spectacle in the context of the reality of Parliamentary power.[33] Moreover, as Adele Patrick has argued in her article "Women's Taste for Jewelry Excesses in Post-War Britain," the monarch set a precedent for flamboyantly "queening it" among the lower classes—a tendency that could be copied, in the case of these men, by proxy.[34] Finally, royal service brought with it the pleasures of glamorous company and, in due course, a knighthood. Thus the spectacle of the closet could not only encompass the self-adornment of a camp man, but also profoundly influence the iconic images of the nation. This can be viewed as an attempt to bring the conservative separation of the sublime and the beautiful back into alignment, in this case via the figure of the monarch, for whom exalted social position legitimated what otherwise might be publicly condemned as queer displays of excess.

Beaton and Hartnell would not, in 1953, have said that they were in the closet, simply because that term was not in contemporary use in Britain. The metaphor of the closet, as was discussed in Chapter 1, appears to have originated in the postwar United States. As Henry Urbach has pointed out, this was the period when the closet as a physical space had become a prominent element in the design of American bedrooms.[35] The function of the walk-in wardrobe was partly to accommodate an ever-increasing desire for, and possession of, clothing and other household goods within a modernist design preference for clean lines and surfaces. Closets grew physically larger as a wealthier public gained ever more things that attitudes to décor and cleanliness demanded be

30. D. Harris (1996), p. 167.
31. Farmer (2007), p. 146.
32. Farmer (2005), p. 189.
33. Cannadine (1983), pp. 161–162.
34. Patrick (2004).
35. Urbach (1996).

cleared away from view. Moreover, unlike the cupboard, which was an ostentatious substantial item of furniture in its own right, the closet did not simply conceal its contents, but was so positioned within a recess that it effectively did its best to conceal its own existence.

The picture that I have been painting, however, is of the presence of a wide range of states beyond a simply binary divide of being, physically or metaphorically, in or out of the closet. These included varying degrees of self-recognition, self-identification, display, concealment, and even the queering of the "normal." However, as it was formulated by civil rights activists in the 1970s and 1980s, coming out as gay required specific forms of self-acknowledgment and public avowal. This was intended radically to challenge and, in due course, even to eradicate the separation of camp spectacle and the closet as phobic constructions, furthering the development of the community life of gays and lesbians, and bringing personal relief and self-fulfillment. Even as it did so, however, it deepened awareness of their closeted status as abject for those who had not come out.

It was during this period that Keith Haring (1958–1990) created an image filled with apparent vibrancy, rather than with anger and doubt, for National Coming Out Day in the United States, which was held on October 11, 1988 (Figure 9.5). His vibrant yellow figure does not just step out, for it is vibrating, but rather almost dances out of a

Figure 9.5 Keith Haring, *National Coming Out Day* (1988). © Keith Haring Foundation, used by permission.

PICTURING THE CLOSET

dark rectangle that we understand to represent the interior space of the closet. Yet this figure is, on second glance, strangely equivocal. It might appear to be shivering rather than dancing, and looks almost as if it has been pulled off balance and is being dragged back out of sight by one arm. The tragedy of AIDS confronted gay liberation with a situation of crisis in which the political climate in Britain, the United States, and around the world began to turn even more vehemently homophobic. At the time when Eve Kosofsky Sedgwick was writing *Epistemology of the Closet* (1990), both gay activists and conservative Republicans were making calls to "out" closet homosexuals.[36] On the one side of the political divide, the aim was to show the true numbers of lesbians and gay men, and to shame those who were, it was thought, hypocritically colluding with repression; on the other, the wish was to enable regimes of compulsory testing for HIV and even plans for segregation.[37]

Seen in retrospect, the late 1960s and early 1970s, a time when "out" gays and lesbians were in a tiny minority, could appear as a golden and heroic age of dreams that turned into actions. This was, after all, a period when desires for a life of peace within the closet, far from police harassment, had begun to be rejected as grossly insulting and inadequate. In her important analysis of the lesbian and gay liberation movement, which was published shortly after Sedgwick's study, Margaret Cruickshank wrote that "although revolutionary movements do not usually have a single spark, most gays believe that June 27, 1969 is the date marking their passage from homosexual to gay"; although she does partially qualify this by adding that "Stonewall would not have had such an electrifying effect, however, if pioneering advocates of equal rights for homosexuals had not worked from 1950 to 1969 to lay the groundwork for a broader movement."[38]

The Stonewall riots have, thus, emerged as a key element of gay "mythology"—and not just in the United States.[39] Armstrong and Crage have discussed the constructed nature of the Stonewall story, explaining why a range of other raids and fights did not become immortalized in the same way as transcendent acts of the rejection of official repression.[40] The implication was that Stonewall contained something far more radical than could be found amidst the pleasurable propositions formulated for those in the know by closeted artists. The liberation struggle could be viewed as "an attempt to envision an exit from the closet that would not also be a trap, [and] that would also be unnameable and unimaginable of all that needs the closet in order to continue to exist."[41] This was what was held by many to have shone forth from

36. L. Gross (1993) and Mohr (1992).
37. R. Meyer (2002), p. 225.
38. Cruickshank (1992), p. 3.
39. D'Emilio (1992), p. xv.
40. Armstrong and Crage (2006).
41. Casarino (1997), pp. 205–206.

the Stonewall Inn as a portent of the coming revolutionary dissolution of sexual boundaries. It was now time for the truth of sexual diversity not only to be told, as Kinsey among others had attempted to do, but also to be *seen*. Stonewall was thus, above all, about emergent visibility, as the paradigmatic collection *Out of the Closets: Voices of Gay Liberation* (1972) attested in its poetic introduction in the form of verses by Fran Winant on "Christopher Street Liberation Day, June 28, 1970," which were followed by an essay by Allen Young, "Out of the Closets, into the Streets," which begins "On a June evening in 1969. . . ."[42] The seeming darkness of the closet would be replaced, it was hoped, with a state of brightly visible sexual truth.

Yet mainstream society, if that is an appropriate term, continued to treat the emerging gays and lesbians via the techniques of the spectacle of the closet, which posited their visual exceptionality as the proof of the normality of the masses. Even the cover of the first edition of *Out of the Closets* highlighted the power of the image of the sexual secret because it was adorned with a prominent keyhole of the kind often employed to illustrate cheap murder mysteries. The situation with the later editions was much worse. The cover of the 1977 paperback edition shows a group of men and women standing just outside a very tidy closet who are not glamorized, but who, nevertheless, seem to evoke the Village People in their varied choice of uniforms (Figure 9.6a). One of the women has been shopping, and no one looks like they are about to start a revolution. They are not even flirting with each other. One woman is young and attractive and it is her right breast—perky under a tight pullover—that is placed at the center of the composition. Things do not get any better on the back cover, where a light bulb has gone on inside the dark rectangle that signifies the closet (Figure 9.6b). "Who are *they*? What do *they* want?" [my emphases] asks the headline text, strongly implying that the reader of the book is not expected to identify as one of "them." It would seem that this edition was either being marketed to "straights," or at least to those straights who had reasons, perhaps even reasons of the closet, for being interested in this subject. As John D'Emilio pointed out in his introduction to the 1992 reissue of the volume, it had not taken long for the revolutionary idealism to fade out in the course of the 1970s.[43]

Yet, as Martin Duberman attests in his pioneering 1994 study of Stonewall, the riot remained the "*the* [original emphasis] emblematic event in modern lesbian and gay history" which "occupies a central place in the iconography of lesbian and gay awareness."[44] The importance of evoking a sense of liberated and ecstatic self-expression in the aftermath of Stonewall appears from posters produced by gay

42. Young (1992), p. 6, originally printed in Jay and Young (1972).
43. D'Emilio (1992), p. xxiv.
44. Duberman (1994), p. xvii.

liberationists in the 1970s. These make for a striking comparison with the conservative styles of earlier campaigns for homosexual law reform, as in the manner with which the rights protest in front of the White House on May 29, 1965, was conducted.[45] Yet, as Duberman recounts, the seemingly spontaneous and joyous "Come Out" poster, based on a photograph by Peter Hujar, which was created for the aforementioned 1970 Christopher Street Liberation Day march, was staged with equal care. It had been hard to get people who were willing to be photographed in this way, and those who came were dressed deliberately in what Duberman refers to as the "pseudo-shabby workers drab then fashionable" so as not to distinguish themselves from other protest movements of the time.[46] As Richard Meyer has discussed, much of the visual culture of gay liberation, and indeed of queer art in the ensuing decades, gained much of its punch from ongoing play with images that made a point of contrasting display and concealment.[47]

None of this should be read as indicating any sense of derision toward the course that gay liberation took both in the United States and in Britain. I wish simply to point out that the movement for lesbian and gay rights after Stonewall depended on references to the closet and to its spectacle for the constitution of its own political agenda of coming out, and for many of the forms of visual self-expression with which it sought to make its points. One particular aspect of the spectacle of the closet, the association with effeminacy, was to cause particular problems. On the one hand, some people hoped that liberation would allow individuals to express themselves however they wanted. For others, Stonewall, despite having been led by drag queens, marked the point at which the non-effeminate men (and indeed non-masculine women) could make themselves known.[48] The flamboyantly effeminate male posed a problem. Was he not simply the grotesque product of the repressive and hateful regime of the spectacle of the closet? As Thomas Waugh pointed out, writing in 1977, the effeminate gay man was often not just scapegoated by straights, but also by other gays.[49]

Nor did everyone want to come out, at least not in the way championed by many gay rights activists. It is instructive, for instance, to think about the way in which Peter Pears (1910–1986) talked about his partner Benjamin (Baron) Britten (1913–1976), whom he had met in 1936, on coming out to the press in the course of newspaper interviews and a TV documentary in 1980. I found a copy of one such article, "The Good Companions" by Gillian Widdicombe, tucked into the back cover of my secondhand copy of the musicologist Donald Mitchell's *Benjamin*

45. R. Meyer (2002), pp. 165–166, and (2006), p. 450.
46. Duberman (1994), pp. 274–275. Note that the poster was used on the cover of this paperback edition.
47. R. Meyer (2006), p. 459.
48. Sinfield (2004), p. 268.
49. T. Waugh (1977), p. 16.

(a)

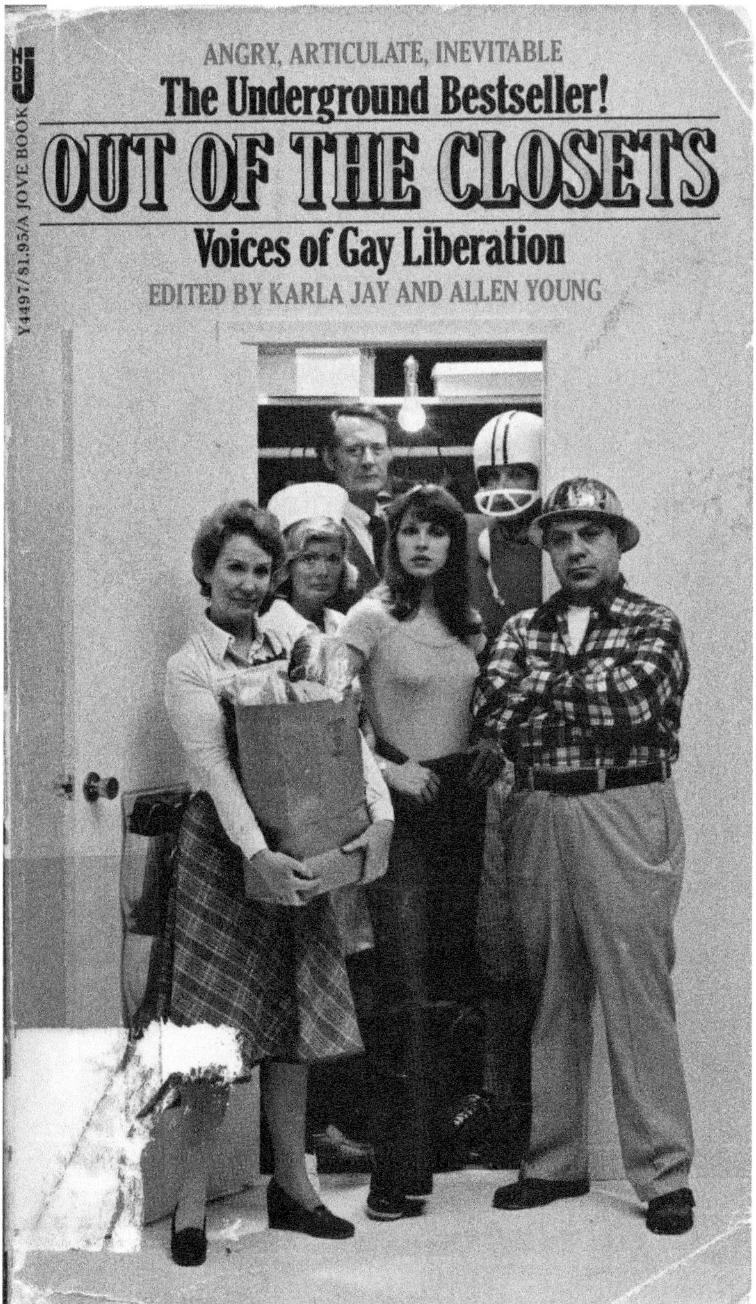
HBJ
Y4497/$1.95/A JOVE BOOK
ANGRY, ARTICULATE, INEVITABLE
The Underground Bestseller!
OUT OF THE CLOSETS
Voices of Gay Liberation
EDITED BY KARLA JAY AND ALLEN YOUNG

Figures 9.6a and 9.6b Front and back covers, Karla Jay and Allen Young, eds., *Out of the Closets: Voices of Gay Liberation* (New York, Jove/HBJ, 1977). Reproduced courtesy of Penguin.

(b)

WHO ARE THEY?
WHAT DO THEY WANT?

Gay. Lesbian. Homosexual.
These are the names they
have chosen; the names
they now wear proudly and
openly as they state their
case for equal treatment
and justice under the law
and in society.

Fag. Dyke. Queer. These
are the names they have
been called—the better
ones—by a world that
fearfully mocks what it
refuses to understand.

Here, in their own words,
are the voices of gay
America: white, black,
brown, yellow, conserva-
tive, radical, rich, poor,
male, female, believers,
atheists. People—who
have chosen to love others
of the same sex...and have
paid a bitterly high price
for that choice.

FEATURING AN UPDATED
GAY BIBLIOGRAPHY AND INTERNATIONAL
DIRECTORY OF GAY ORGANIZATIONS

Figures 9.6a and 9.6b

(*Continued*)

Britten, 1913–1976: Pictures from a Life (1978). Widdicombe records that she met Pears at the Reform Club in central London, but they had to adjourn for tea at the upmarket department store, Fortnum and Mason, as the Reform did not admit women in the afternoons. Pears stressed that Britten had not identified as gay; and not only that, but "the word 'gay' was not in his vocabulary . . . Ben thought that decent behaviour, decent manners, were part of a fine life. Gracious living, if you like. But 'the gay life,' he resented that."[50] Such a stance alerts us to the dangers of reading the cultural politics of the closet, as constituted by gay liberation, back into earlier decades, or even as devaluing those holding contrary viewpoints in more recent times. Should we see Britten's denial of the label "gay" as the result of self-hatred imposed by the constraints of the closet, or should we say that he simply could not have "come out" as gay if he did not think he was gay—that gayness for him indicated a lifestyle choice and a political stance, rather than being the only route, as it clearly was not, to authentic same-sex love?

As Pears also noted, Britten had not attempted to censor his personal papers and, besides which, the two men's relationship was well-known. Philip Brett has asked, "what if Britten had been forced out of his already transparent closet by some unthinkable event? It is hard to believe that any public disclosure of his homosexuality would have harmed his career greatly" (although it is certainly arguable that the result in the 1970s would have been rather different from what it might have been thirty years earlier).[51] Byron Adams has written, in connection with Britten, of a situation in which "the 'open secret' becomes by inference synonymous with the 'glass closet,' a situation in which the putative hiding place functions merely as an uneasy convenience for both the frightened inmate who seeks refuge within and the hostile society that decides to remain without."[52] But another way to look at this situation is to say that mid-twentieth-century British society was straining to find the means by which to accommodate the existence of "respectable" homosexuals. This is certainly one way in which the Sexual Offences Act (1967) can be understood to have operated through its attempt to distinguish the private lives of homosexual couples from the opportunities of free-for-all sexual expression.[53]

The aforementioned *Benjamin Britten, 1913–1976: Pictures from a Life* (1978) is a fascinating biography of Britten told through photographs. The word "homosexual" is nowhere mentioned, but associations with Auden and Forster are included. There are lots of pictures of Pears and Britten together. But, as in the painting of the two men by Kenneth Green (1943, image no. 231; Figure 9.7), while Pears is sometimes shown

50. Widdicombe (1980), p. 33.
51. Brett (2006), p. 220.
52. B. Adams (1993), p. 1406.
53. Moran (1996), pp. 33–65.

looking at Britten, we do not get to see Britten looking at Pears, nor are there any images of laughter and intimacy between them—although we do see Britten sharing jokes with other people. Yet the caption to image no. 231 says that from the point when Green designed the costume and sets for the 1945 production of *Peter Grimes*, "what this book documents is not one life, but two" (referring to Britten and Pears). In no. 296, a photograph taken in January 1956, the couple appear in drag in the company of Prince Ludwig of Hesse and the Rhine and his wife Margaret: "Ben . . . looked like a governess at a fancy dress party. Peter looked like a Rhine maiden." However, and rather more seriously, nos 394–395 are positioned so as to overlay a photograph, taken in Aldeburgh in June 1973, of Von Aschenbach (played by Pears) reaching out to Tadzio, onto the final lines of Britten's manuscript sketch of *Death in Venice* of 1972.[54] This then, and touchingly, contextualizes the final photograph of an elderly Britten holding Pears by the arm.

This *is* moving stuff, but my interest in this commemoration of a closeted, or should one say semi-closeted, life should not be taken to imply nostalgia on my part for a supposed golden age of the closet. I simply wish to sketch an indication of the complex history and variety that this cultural formation has displayed over the course of modernity. Life in the closet was not necessarily more distorting and damaging than life outside it—which is not to deny that a world without the closet would be better than one with it. However, just as experiences of the closet varied over the time, so did the nature of the secret that it was

54. Mitchell and Evans (1978), unpaginated, figs. 394–395.

asked to contain. As has been seen, the *homosexual* closet, although it had its precursors, was primarily an unstable and contested creation of the twentieth century. It was in the eighth decade of that century that Sedgwick was spurred on by the terrible experience of AIDS to interpret and denounce the closet and its attendant spectacle. With the passing (one hopes) of the worst of that crisis, at least in certain parts of the world, aspects of gay life have come to be increasingly incorporated into mainstream society. Yet in the final chapter of this book I will ask whether neo-conservative (economic) liberalism is giving the closet a new lease of life.

CHAPTER 10

AFTER THE OUTRAGE

AT THE TIME when I was a student and "coming out" as gay in 1990, Derek Jarman (1942–1994) represented "the face of AIDS," insofar as he was probably "the most publicly prominent person with AIDS in the United Kingdom."[1] Jarman was one of the leading queer artists, film-makers, and writers of late twentieth-century Britain.[2] He came to prominence in 1976 with the release of his film *Sebastiane*, and his work was associated first with gay liberation and later with the rise of queer cultural politics in the 1980s, which advocated the validity of same-sex desire in the context of a wider challenge to normative personal and commercial behaviors. He died at a time when to claim to be queer was a powerfully countercultural stance. The Conservative Party had governed the United Kingdom since 1979 and had focused on combining economic liberalism with social conservatism.[3] Ian Lucas, writing in *Impertinent Decorum* (1994), a study of theater and drama in gay culture, powerfully evokes the confrontational nature of sexual politics at the time of "a media backlash against AIDS during the campaigns which resulted in Section 28 of the Local Government Act [(1988) which required that a 'local authority shall not intentionally promote homosexuality or pub-lish material with the intention of promoting homosexuality . . . shall not promote the teaching in any maintained school of the acceptabil-ity of homosexuality as a pretended family relationship']. For many of us, Margaret Thatcher and her government were the impetus into not only gay politics but a particular form of rebellion against repression and coercion."[4] All of this was happening just as police activity redoubled

1. Hallas (2009), p. 220.
2. For a good introduction to Jarman's cinema, see Richardson (2009).
3. Durham (1991), P. Thomas (1993), and Reinhold (1994).
4. Lucas (1994), p. xi. For the Act see www.legislation.gov.uk/ukpga/1988/9/section/28.

such that 1989 saw the "highest ever number of arrests and prosecutions for consensual sexual activity between men since records began."[5] The result was that sexual activism was strongly associated with left-wing politics at this time, even though in the mid-twentieth century, as Lucy Robinson has pointed out in her book *Gay Men and the Left in Post-War Britain* (2007), "homosexuality was characterised [by many socialists] as a bourgeois decadence and feminised threat to working-class respectability if it was acknowledged at all."[6]

By contrast, the first decade of the twenty-first century has seen the rise of a powerful movement for the assimilation of those who regard themselves as gay, homosexual, or queer into the core power structures of society in Britain and in many other countries.[7] Associated with this has been a "widely acknowledged growth in consumerism over politics in the gay community."[8] Whether this has resulted in a queering of mainstream society or a post-queer erasure of activism and creativity is being hotly debated.[9] The final chapter of this book explores a case study of the post-queer legacy of Jarman's seaside retreat at Dungeness in Kent. This explores the afterlife of the closet and the fate of queer visibility. The work of architects, publishers, and journalists will be discussed in order to illustrate how sexual and economic nonconformity has been progressively erased from what had been the outcast landscape of Dungeness.

Derek Jarman divided the last years of his life between central London, where he had a small studio flat, and Dungeness in Kent. I know that no one bothers to look at Phoenix House, a nondescript block of flats on the Charing Cross Road, because I used to live there. However, the garden that Jarman created at Dungeness around a cottage by the sea has become so famous that *The Guardian* newspaper commemorated the tenth anniversary of Jarman's death with a piece saluting his "still flourishing" "avant garden":

> The public perception of Dungeness unexpectedly underwent a sea change one day in 1986 when the film maker Derek Jarman took the actress Tilda Swinton for lunch at the Pilot [Inn], which was said to serve the best fish and chips in England. He was struck by the area's otherworldly atmosphere and its unusual light, and driving past he saw a shack for sale, Prospect Cottage, which he bought on impulse for £750. A similar property would now set you back upwards of £100,000, and possibly cheap at the price. Before Jarman, no one realised that tarred weatherboard and corrugated iron could

5. Cook (2007), p. 206.
6. L. Robinson (2007), p. 4.
7. Shepard (2001) and Goldstein (2003). Note the attempted rehabilitation of Thatcher as a "gay icon"; on which see Janes (2012b) with R. Dyer (2009).
8. L. Robinson (2007), p. 188.
9. For instance by Simpson (1999), Waites (2000), Maskovsky (2002), Ruffolo (2009), and Ghaziani (2011).

be things of beauty. Most of the other shacks have been smartened up; some now look as though they have just been photographed for the latest style magazines, and possibly have.[10]

The figure of £750 is often quoted in news stories concerning the property. In fact, Jarman paid £32,000 for the house, and the much smaller sum widely quoted in the print media may have been derived mistakenly from the £700 he paid for some extra land. It is revealing, however, that media excitement has been focused on the supposedly extraordinary bargain that a £750 purchase price would have implied. Nevertheless, it is still clear that property prices in Dungeness have accelerated out of proportion to those in the local area. At the time of writing, a similar cottage was on offer for £199,999, even though property prices in most of Britain had been weak in the aftermath of the financial crash of 2007–2008.

In 2003 the architect Simon Conder redeveloped a cottage close to Jarman's, rotating it on its axis so that it faced the sea and cladding it in black rubber as a more durable replacement for the traditional wash of black tar. Discussing this building, Hugh Pearman explains that "Dungeness started, very slowly, to get fashionable when the artist, film-maker and gay activist Derek Jarman bought a little house, Prospect Cottage, here in the 1980s, shortly after having been diagnosed with AIDS."[11] However, the couple who commissioned Conder came to Dungeness because "it reminded them of one of their favourite places, the California desert."[12] A 1950s Airstream trailer, itself an icon of American design, is kept permanently parked by the house (Figure 10.1).[13] The effect of this juxtaposition is to efface the quirky Englishness of this landscape and re-present it as if it were in the United States. The stark composition of the photograph used on Conder's website at the time of writing recalls that seen in paintings such as Edward Hopper's *South Carolina Morning* (1955) (Figure 10.2). This painting was inspired by what Gail Levin refers to as the erotically intense moment of seeing a "mulatto girl" come out of a cabin at Folly Beach, South Carolina.[14] It is as if not only the script of Englishness, but also of same-sex desire, has been written out of Dungeness.

Moreover, the anti-commercial aesthetic and ethic that attracted Jarman to this formerly scorned location has also been under attack. An admiring online commentary said of Conder's house that it "shows that it is possible to design a building in the context of the bodged 'squatter architecture' that typifies Dungeness Beach."[15] This process can also be

10. Mallalieu (2004).
11. Pearman (2009). See also Simon Conder Associates (undated a).
12. McGuirk (2004).
13. See http://www.airstream.com.
14. Levin (1998), p. 105.
15. Anon., "Black rubber" (undated).

read into Conder's design for a second beach house.[16] In that project "the old cottage was stripped back to its original core of a section of railway carriage—which itself dates from the 1870s. But instead of extending that, Conder designed a house that absorbed it, like an amoeba. Now the old carriage—treated as a found object, complete with scabby paintwork and with some entirely unpainted sections—stands in the main living-dining area and acts as the house's kitchen."[17] In contrast to Jarman's externalization of found objects in a publicly viewable garden, in Conder's design a cottage itself has become a found object that is enclosed within private space—expensive private space: this property was, at the time of writing, on sale for £450,000 through the Modern House Company. This company was marketing the building as enjoying a "wonderful location, right on the shingle of Dungeness beach," as having won the Royal Institute of British Architects/Marco Goldschmied Foundation Stephen Lawrence Prize, and as being in an area that "has been a draw for numerous artists over the years, most famously the filmmaker Derek Jarman whose house and garden continues to attract numerous visitors."[18]

The critic Matthew Collings commented that "the sheer delight of the contrast of the picturesque carriage, with its distressed surfaces and peeling blue paint, and the clean planes and lines surrounding it, is unforgettable. The effect is like . . . Tracey Emin's beach

16. Simon Conder Associates (undated b).
17. Pearman (2009).
18. Modern House Company (undated).

hut in the Saatchi Collection."[19] Beach huts were utilitarian wooden structures in which families could change at the seaside. There was a major stir, therefore, when the artist Tracy Emin sold hers in 2000 for £75,000 to the collector, and former advertising guru of Margaret Thatcher's Conservative Party, Charles Saatchi. Peter Lamarque has argued that the idea that items such as Emin's beach hut "become in some sense 'transfigured' by being put on show and invite a different kind of attention when removed from their original contexts is now a commonplace even if it remains problematic to say exactly what their new status is."[20] But the commercial, if not the artistic, implications were quite clear to *The Daily Telegraph* when it reported under the headline "Tracey Emin enters her blue beach hut period" that "traditional beach huts are not only hot property—in fashionable Southwold, Suffolk, they change hands for £30,000—but, as from today, they are art. And worth even more."[21] As *The Times* reported in 2008, "the humble beach hut has grown into a luxury bolthole." In this process *"the owners' lives are irrelevant* [my emphasis]; what counts

Figure 10.2 Edward Hopper (1882–1967), *South Carolina Morning* (1955), oil on canvas, 77.2 x 102.2 cm, Whitney Museum of American Art, New York; given in memory of Otto L. Spaeth by his Family, 67.13. © Heirs of Josephine N. Hopper, licensed by the Whitney Museum of American Art. Digital image © Whitney Museum of American Art.

19. Collings (2008), p. 121.
20. Lamarque (2010), p. 228.
21. Reynolds (2000).

Figure 10.3 Credit card advertisement, *The Garden,* dir. Jarman (1990).

is the sense of nostalgia, of recapturing tranquillity in a quintessentially English beachside setting. For this, you can expect to part with well over £100,000."[22]

In 1991 Derek Jarman wrote that "we are all richer, have more opportunities, more information, but are dispossessed. The city no longer belongs to us . . . as I approach 50, London is foreign—all the nooks and corners of my student days sanitised, scrubbed."[23] This is the voice of Jarman, the savage critic of the values of commerce over those of love; the voice of the man who presented Judas, having sold Jesus for thirty pieces of silver, in a mock a credit card advertisement, dangling enthusiastically against a backdrop of yuppie offices in his film *The Garden* (1990) (Figure 10.3).[24] It took the forces of commerce only fifteen years to overwhelm Dungeness, but the irony of this is that, had it not been for Jarman, it is quite likely that this would never have happened. Thus *The Guardian* may have found Jarman's garden "still flourishing" in 2004, but his values seemingly were not.

The appearance of *Derek Jarman's Garden, with Photographs by Howard Sooley* (1995) was an early danger sign.[25] This book was sold as an aesthetic artifact (as opposed to a work of queer literature) to a mass (and, therefore, mostly straight) audience by the art publishers Thames and Hudson. Jarman's seaside garden has come to be enthusiastically consumed as an aesthetic exemplar by the middle classes. Even in the critical literature, it is rare to find a voice such as that of George Mckay which asserts that Jarman created a "queer garden" that was a "monument to

22. Wade (2008).
23. Jarman (1992), pp. 176–177.
24. Perriam (2000), p. 120.
25. Jarman (1995).

Figure 10.4 Sebastian's death, *Sebastiane*, dir. Jarman (1976).

fragility *and* defiance" [original emphasis].[26] Far more typical of contemporary responses is the extended discussion in Alexandra Harris's article, "Seaside Ceremonies: Coastal Rites in Twentieth-Century Art," which talks of Jarman's film *The Garden* (1990) as an "elegy for friends who had died," but makes no direct reference to Jarman's sexuality or to HIV.[27] Jarman himself appears in several of Howard Sooley's photographs, but it is as if his figure, too, is itself slipping from sight, as in the recent reprint of *Dancing Ledge* (1984) by the University of Minnesota Press, which replaces the cover image chosen by Jarman himself (featuring an object by Christopher Hobbs that "looked like a death mask of Jarman's face— albeit with the cheeky addition of an ear-ring") with a photograph taken in the garden in Dungeness.[28] This shows a piece of driftwood around which spirals a metal coil that ends in a spike. That image can also be read as evoking death insofar as it might appear to be an abstract counterpart of the highly aestheticized display of martyrdom in Jarman's pioneering film *Sebastiane* (1976), in which the saint's body twists in a ritual of erotic penetration against a bleak backdrop of shingle (Figure 10.4). But the cover of the new edition evokes merely the *frisson* of danger and elides the issue of eroticism, so illustrating the fact that aspects of Jarman's literary legacy are being marketed in ways that appear to play down queerness.

I do not endorse what has happened, but I do wish to suggest that the origins of the partial commercial erasure to which Jarman has been subjected can be found in the particular nature of his visual self-presentation beyond the closet. In literal terms, Jarman's death

26. Mckay (2011), p. 145.
27. A. Harris (2009), p. 233.
28. Jarman (1984), cover, and (2010), cover, and Peake (1999), p. 325.

came about as result of infection with HIV, but he ironically styled himself as "Saint Derek of Dungeness" as both a queerly ascetic and aesthetic choice that evoked the Catholic imagery of martyrdom.[29] The retreat to Dungeness itself was part of this post-diagnosis agenda of re-presentation which was repeatedly referenced by the print media. Simon Garfield found the artist to be a "picture of wrecked beauty" who lives in a "tiny, sparse flat" (in Phoenix House) like a monastic cell.[30] AIDS was, in such accounts, being aestheticized with reference to ascetism as style:

> in the eighteenth century consumption was the ultimate poet's disease: the stricken became thin and pale, specter-like. Much closer to the spiritual. Now there is AIDS: all those nice artistic young men wasting away. Illnesses which reduce body size as cleanly as possible (or, just as importantly, are *perceived* [original emphasis] to do so—those with TB cough into handkerchiefs; people with AIDS generally disguise their Kaposi's Sarcomas) are viewed as more aesthetically pleasing, almost romantic.[31]

Jarman's apparent embrace of ascetic chic needs to be placed in the context of deep-seated views in Britain, ultimately rooted in a long history of anti-Catholicism, that saw perverse self-abasement, rather than spiritual value, in such styles of behavior.[32] Such viewpoints helped to shape "sainthood" into a site of queer desire for Jarman, but also left him open to cultural re-inscription. So, while right-wing commentators condemned Jarman for supposedly having brought destruction on himself through gay promiscuity, the liberal media had a tendency to present him as a picturesque victim.

It is true that thinking of the self in this manner is one way to give meaning to suffering.[33] Victim culture can transform the endurance of oppression into an act of self-sacrifice and so create an oppositional economy with which to contest power relations. But this stance does entail the danger that attention will cease to be focused on ways to prevent future horrors, and the politics of victimhood may also trap individuals and groups into subordinate positions. Jarman was aware of the dangers of being depicted as an AIDS victim—notably that "the subjectivity of the person with AIDS disappears, while the body with AIDS remains visible."[34] Although he was attacked by the right-wing media, he escaped the worst of what Simon Watney has described as the spectacle of AIDS, a theater of ridicule and shame that evoked the

29. On queer martyrdom, see Janes (2015).
30. Garfield (1994), p. 3
31. Griffith (undated).
32. Janes (2009b), pp. 143–145.
33. Amato (1990), p. 67.
34. Lawrence (1997), p. 243; see also Watney (1987) and Crimp (2002).

actions of the eighteenth-century pillory in which the ill are exposed to ridicule before "the 'homosexual body' is 'disposed of' like so much rubbish, like the trash it was in life."[35] Richard Meyer, for instance, has explored the way in which *Life* magazine, in its edition of September 1985, juxtaposed publicity shots of Rock Hudson's muscular body from the 1950s with images of his wasted appearance when it was made public that he was dying of AIDS. Meyer comments that "what was absent from the prior images of Rock Hudson's body but what is now meant to be visible—to be visibly leaking out—is his homosexuality. With the economy of *Life*'s before and after circuit, the after image, the AIDS image, not only figures the physical signs of illness but proffers those signs as the evidence and horrific opening of Rock Hudson's closet."[36]

There was, therefore, at this time a concerned attempt in certain quarters not simply to emphasize the existence of the closet but to establish the appearance of unveiled homosexuality as a vision of horror.[37] I do not think it is a coincidence that it was also at this time that the old idea that Wilde had died of syphilis was given a fresh airing, most notoriously in Melissa Knox's study *Oscar Wilde: A Long and Lovely Suicide* (1994). The Wilde that emerges from this book is a syphilitic filled with self-hate for having passed the infection on to youths. The disease, she alleged, rotted him but did nothing to change his behavior: "for Wilde, who went back to boys the minute he was out of prison, resurrection was really re-erection; that is why he deemed himself unworthy of redemption."[38] While the right-wing media offered monstrosity as the truth of the closet, the liberal media in both Britain and the United States preferred picturesque victimhood as its spectacle. Thus, the film *Philadelphia* (1993), starring Tom Hanks, hinges upon the issue of whether his character has been wrongly fired for displaying the signs of danger and deviance in the form of the scarlet lesions of the AIDS-defining skin cancer Kaposi's sarcoma.[39]

In a radical attempt queerly to combine the sublime and the beautiful, and also to sidestep both depiction as monster or victim, Jarman visually absented himself altogether from his last film, *Blue* (1993). The underlying concept of the film was derived from the work of the artist famous for creating blue abstracts, Yves Klein, and had first come to Jarman as long ago as 1974.[40] He proposed a film in 1987 of 75 minutes duration with no images; however, various problems intervened. Klein was not known to have been personally interested in same-sex desire,

35. Watney (1987), p. 80; see also Seidman (1988), p. 189, and D. Campbell (2008), p. 31.
36. R. Meyer (1991), p. 275.
37. Herek and Capitano (1999), p. 1133.
38. Knox (1994), p. 135; on the ensuing row, see Holland (1996), and also note Gilman (1987), which compares the iconographies of syphilis and AIDS.
39. G. Griffin (2000), pp. 182–184.
40. Wymer (2005), p. 170.

nor had he had a particularly interesting life. The project failed to get off the ground. Nevertheless, Jarman wrote a series of poems on this subject in the course of the following year. For Klein, blue was the color that was the essence of freedom.[41] In the film, Jarman "contemplates the transience of all things, the melancholy which pervades all his films, even when they seem at their most "camp" and "outrageous.""[42] The voiceover ends like this:

> Dead good looking
> In beauty's summer
> His blue jeans
> Around his ankles . . .
> Our name will be forgotten
> In time
> No one will remember our work . . .

> I place a delphinium, Blue, upon your grave.

Rosalind Galt, in her book *Pretty: Film and the Decorative Image* (2011), has drawn attention to the importance of color in Jarman's work, a phenomenon that she sees as having powerfully queer potential when viewed against the backdrop of modernist concerns in film criticism, which focused on realism and structure. For her, *Blue* is, thus, "sensual, deep and joyful—not puritan at all."[43] She sets this work in the context of what she refers to as Jarman's interests in "the seductive qualities of bodily passivity and masochism [which] refute the dominance of masculinist line and instead propose a visual and erotic economy of engulfment."[44] Therefore, it is precisely Jarman's fascination with beauty—or, in the terms of her study, prettiness—which provide the essence of the transgressive aspects of his cultural production. Yet this film also stages his visual disappearance into a state of sublime obscurity and aestheticized pain. And if prettiness was a transgressive quality to many modernists, in popular culture it remained a mainstream and normative attribute that has long had a powerful influence on decisions concerning, for instance, house design. Jarman's aestheticization of aspects of suffering may have been rooted in a transgressive erotics that involved the creative embrace of suffering, but it also made some of his work, such as his garden, vulnerable to commercial re-appropriation as ascetic chic. William Pencak explains that the flower in the last line of *Blue* is a protest against the threat of erasure because "the delphinium stands for remembrance. . . . *Blue* is a challenge to its viewers to

41. Lawrence (1997), p. 256.
42. Wymer (2005), p. 180.
43. Galt (2011), p. 94; although compare the response of Hallas (2009), p. 235.
44. Galt (2011), pp. 85–86.

continue to construct history."[45] However, viewers are liable to undertake the work of construction that suits their own agenda, and that may include re-presenting Jarman as a producer of mere spectacle.

This chapter has looked at a range of commercial practices and their concerns and discourses, including those of architects, publishers, and journalists, which have acted to change both the built environment of Dungeness and the way it is talked about and economically valued. These materials do not necessarily tell us whether Jarman's work is or is not essentially transgressive, but they do document some of the ways in which transgressive elements have become erased in relation to the local landscape and its commercialization. None of this was based on Jarman's intentions, but rather derives from aspects of Jarman's aesthetic tastes, which have laid his artistic legacy open to popular cultural discourses and practices that, in distinction to those of strands of modernist artistic critique, regard beauty to be a normative (and salable) characteristic. The result has been the post-queer disappearance of many of Jarman's cherished countercultural values in the landscape of Dungeness.

When Jarman first bought Prospect Cottage, the West was gripped by fears of nuclear war, and no one who was not dying already wanted to live near a nuclear reactor such as that which loomed just along the coast. By contrast, today, the power station is staffed, according to the critic Matthew Collings, by thousands of people "mostly drinking tea it seems (how English), but in fact engaged in closing down the station. . . . Dungeness became trendy about 20 years ago. Previously it was off-putting because of the power-stations, but now the old scariness is a thrill in the mix of elements that attracts lovers of the area."[46] Is there not a whiff in this description of Burke's conservative fantasies of danger? Something similar can be said in relation to the presence of men who have sex with men in an age in which HAART drug treatment has, at least in the Western popular imagination, ended the threat of AIDS. Jarman wrote in a diary entry in 1990 that he could not abide "the values of this repression, its false houses, marriages, families, Church of England."[47] Today, he is left to enjoy his newfound respectability in his grave in a peaceful Anglican churchyard, but the tower not far from Jarman's resting place—unlike that appearing in his presentation of the death of Sebastian (Figure 10.4)—is no longer in ruins. The old Dungeness coastguard tower has been converted by a young couple, "Peter and Fiona," and now boasts American-oak floors, below which there is under-floor heating "which Fiona turns on remotely from their home in London." She has "lined up Richard Wilson, who created '20:50,' a tank of oil that was exhibited in the Saatchi Gallery,

45. Pencak (2002), p. 166.
46. Collings (2008), pp. 119–121.
47. Jarman (1992), p. 143.

to design a weatherproof sculpture for the site." According to the Conservative-supporting newspaper, *The Daily Telegraph*, which had once been one of Jarman's sharpest critics, the new owners bought the place so that they and their children could enjoy the "shingle life": and now, after the promiscuous, single queers have departed the scene, they can.[48]

The changes in the landscape of Dungeness over the last twenty years exemplify many of the wider, and not necessarily encouraging, developments in the evolving dynamic between politics, commerce, and expressions of sexual deviance. To read the British media today is to feel that some of the most queerly challenging aspects of Jarman's cultural stance have somehow been laid aside, forgotten, washed away by the tide. Dungeness has been reclaimed for conventional family life, centered on commercial expenditure, rather than on queer cultural and sexual experimentation. The radical poet Jeremy Reed has recently published a set of "Obsequies," in which Jarman "sits in a gold sequinned gown on the shore, blasted by toxic chemicals."[49] The collection in which the verse is published is called *This Is How You Disappear* (2007). If—and it is very much an if—we are now to look forward to an age in which the closet will have decreasing significance, we also need to come to terms with the fading from sight of its long-time companion, the spectacle of the closet, as the queer ironies of camp are dissolved into bland prettiness. For a long time the visual definition of that which is homosexual/gay/queer has been powerfully informed by the drama of concealment and revelation promised and effected by the closet and its spectacle. If the price of the end of persecution is the end of representation—which, of course, is also far from clear—then at least I think it is important to review the history of the closet and its spectacle as the source not simply of suffering, but also at times of pleasure and extraordinary resourcefulness and creativity.[50]

This book has charted the appearance in the eighteenth century of a gradual awareness of sodomy as being the vice of a particular sort of "effeminate" person. This was accompanied by the rise of what I have termed "sodomitical panic" that related to the fear of being, or of being suspected of being, *that* sort of person. Burke, in his separation of the sublime and the beautiful, plotted out a conceptual space in which sublime masculine encounters could take place in secret. Men such as Walpole and Beckford can then be seen to have begun to negotiate their position between the painfully erotic attractions of the sublime and the amusements of the beautiful. Certain Christian viewpoints, illustrated by a case study of some of the works of Holman Hunt that depicted sin as the burden of mankind that was borne for us by Christ,

48. Slade (2004).
49. J. Reed (2007), p. 46.
50. Walters (2001), p. 299.

elevated the importance of the role of the bearer of sexual shame, but also entrenched the horror with which such sin was viewed. The desire to contain that shameful secret of sodomitical desire within same-sex institutions such as public schools was contested by artists during and after the nineteenth century who were eager to express the truth of the human condition, or simply for amusement and personal pleasure. As medical and, subsequently, sociological discourse established homosexuality as an identity, the nature of that secret, not simply as a state of sodomitical temptation but also as a truth of the self, came to be entrenched. In the course of the twentieth century it became possible for artists to begin self-consciously to depict what they saw as the forms and practices of sublime, secret desire or to experiment empoweringly with the ornamental and theatrical diversions of the stereotypes of the spectacle of the closet. The disciplinary mechanisms of the state, such as the police, were, meanwhile, torn between their own desire to reinforce the closet through making examples of offenders and the need to avoid seeing or displaying the full contents of a closet that overlapped with their own homosocial environments. Gay liberation then gave a name to the state of concealment as "the closet" and proposed a model that understood it as a cruel state of repression of the self, from which escape was possible.

The results of the struggle for lesbian and gay rights, while extraordinary, have not always been quite what were expected. I do feel some fear that, as has been the case with Derek Jarman's Dungeness, heteronormativity might return by stealth, bearing in mind that the current fashion sometimes seems to lie in not wanting, culturally and economically, to be nonconformist or to stand out. And, thus, I have some sympathy with the comment of David Halperin in his book *How to Be Gay* (2012) that "as homosexuality has become increasingly public and dignified, the life of queer affect and feeling has become more and more demonized, more and more impossible to express openly, to explore, to celebrate. It has become an embarrassment . . . official post-Stonewall homosexuality is ashamed of our cultural practices and the distinctive pleasures they afford."[51] Yet Halperin's own shame at this latest cultural turn can also be viewed as another stage in the long history of queer disappointments. Rather than joining in such lamentation, might we not wish to engage with the cultural record of the past in all its pride and shame, in order to enrich our awareness of the full extent of queer possibility and achievement?[52] Of course, in many countries of the world there continue to be massive legal and cultural impediments to the open expression of same-sex desire. But even in places such as Britain, where there has been a powerful turn toward

51. Halperin (2012), p. 99.
52. Note the advantages of a recuperative approach to shameful or abject aspects of the queer past, as suggested in H. Love (2007) and Castiglia and Reed (2012).

the mainstreaming of lesbians and gay men, such changes may fore-shadow the reconfiguration rather than the disappearance of the closet in the context of new patterns of cultural and economic respectability. Halperin's elegiac talk may turn out, in fact, to represent an expression of that old but beloved gay cliché of the fate of a troubled youth as the closet matures in the twenty-first century.[53] Legal victories, in relation to such issues as same-sex marriage, may not, therefore, spell the end of a powerful and pervasive cultural tradition that seeks to separate the obvious spectacle of individual eccentricity from the queerly mysteri-ous essence of being human.

53. See Nunokawa (1991), p. 436, on the sentimentalization of the deaths of young men.

Acton, William, *The Functions and Disorders of the Reproductive Organs in Youth, in Adult Age, and in Advanced Life. Considered in their Physiological, Social and Psychological Relations* (London: John Churchill, 1857).

Adams, Byron, review, *Letters from a Life: Selected Letters and Diaries of Benjamin Britten*, ed. Donald Mitchell and Philip Reed, *Notes* 49.4 (1993), pp. 1406–1408.

Adams, James Eli, "Pater's muscular aestheticism," in Donald E. Hall, ed., *Muscular Christianity: Embodying the Victorian Age* (Cambridge: Cambridge University Press, 1994), pp. 215–238.

Adams, James Eli, *Dandies and Desert Saints: Styles of Victorian Manhood* (Ithaca, NY: Cornell University Press, 1995).

Allatini, Rose [writing as A. T. Fitzroy], *Despised and Rejected* (London: C. W. Daniel, 1918).

Ardut, Ari, "A theory of scandal: Victorians, homosexuality, and the fall of Oscar Wilde," *American Journal of Sociology* 111.1 (2005), pp. 213–248.

Agamben, Giorgio, *Homo Sacer: Sovereign Power and Bare Life* (Stanford, CA: Stanford University Press, 1998).

Aldrich, Robert, *Colonialism and Homosexuality* (London: Routledge, 2003).

Alexander, Peter F., "The process of composition of the libretto of Britten's *Gloriana*," *Music and Letters* 67.2 (1986), pp. 147–158.

Amato, Joseph A., *Victims and Values: A History and Theory of Suffering*, Contributions in Philosophy 42 (New York: Greenwood Press, 1990).

Annan, Noel, "The cult of homosexuality in England, 1850–1950," *Biography* 13.3 (1990), pp. 189–202.

Anon., "Black rubber beach house, Dungeness," *E-Architect* (undated): http://www.e-architect.co.uk/england/black_rubber_beach_house.htm, accessed September 11, 2011.

Anon., "Law report, July 26," *The Times*, July 27 (1910), p. 3.

Anon., "Olim Etoniensis," *English Journal of Education* (1882), p. 85.

Anon., *Our Public Schools* (London: Kegan Paul, 1881).

Anon., "Parsons and novels," *Saturday Review* 7 (1859), pp. 708–709.

Anon., "Picture exhibitions: *The Finding of the Saviour in the Temple*," *Art Journal* 6 (1860), p. 182.

Anon., *The Public Schools Year Book* (London: Swan Sonnenschein, 1889).

Anon., "Sweet thing in Christmas vestments," *Punch* 50 (1866), p. 11.

Armstrong, Elizabeth A., and Suzanna M. Crage, "Movements and memory: The making of the Stonewall myth," *American Sociological Review* 71 (2006), pp. 724–751.

Armstrong, Mark, "A room in Chelsea: Quentin Crisp at home," *Visual Culture in Britain* 12.2 (2011), pp. 155–169.

Armstrong, Mark, "The Quentin kind: Visual narrative and *The Naked Civil Servant*," PhD dissertation, University of Northumbria, 2012.

Arya, Rina, "Painting the Pope: An analysis of Francis Bacon's *Study after Velázquez's Portrait of Innocent X*," *Literature and Theology* 23.1 (2009a), pp. 33–50.

Arya, Rina, "Remaking the body: The cultural dimensions of Francis Bacon," *Journal for Cultural Research* 13.2 (2009b), pp. 143–158.

Arya, Rina, "Constructions of homosexuality in the art of Francis Bacon," *Journal for Cultural Research* 16.1 (2012), pp. 43–61.

Ashfield, Andrew, and Peter de Bolla, *The Sublime: A Reader in British Eighteenth-Century Aesthetic Theory* (Cambridge: Cambridge University Press, 1996).

Ashmolean Museum, "Extra-illustration (also known as 'Grangerization')" (2005): http://sutherland.ashmolean.museum/Grangerization.shtml, accessed November 20, 2012.

Avery, Gillian, "Written for children: Two eighteenth-century English fairy tales," *Marvels and Tales* 16.2 (2002), pp. 143–155.

Avery, Todd, " 'This intricate commerce of souls': The origins and some early expressions of Lytton Strachey's ethics," *Journal of the History of Sexuality* 13.2 (2004), pp. 183–207.

Avery, Todd, "The historian of the future: Lytton Strachey and modernist historiography between the two cultures," *English Literary History* 77.4 (2010), pp. 841–866.

Baillie, John, *An Essay on the Sublime*, Augustan Print Society Publication 43 (Los Angeles: Augustan Print Society, 1953).

Baker, Paul, "The construction of gay identity via Polari in the Julian and Sandy radio sketches," *Lesbian and Gay Psychology Review* 3.3 (2002), pp. 75–83.

Baldwin, Olive, and Thelma Wilson, "250 years of roast beef," *Musical Times* 126 (1985), pp. 203–207.

Bamford, T. W., *Rise of the Public Schools: A Study of Boys' Public Boarding Schools in England and Wales from 1837 to the Present Day* (London: Nelson, 1967).

Banks, Peter, ed., *Britten's "Gloriana": Essays and Sources* (Woodbridge: Boydell, 1993).

Barbauld, Anna, *The British Novelists*, 50 vols. (London: Rivington, 1810).

Barber, Fiona, "Disturbed ground: Francis Bacon, traumatic memory and the gothic," *Irish Review* 39 (2008), pp. 125–138.

Barber, Stephen M., and David L. Clark, *Regarding Sedgwick: Essays on Queer Culture and Critical Theory* (London: Routledge, 2002).

Barker, Charles, "Erotic martyrdom: Kingsley's sexuality beyond sex," *Victorian Studies* 44.3 (2002), pp. 465–488.

Barker-Benfield, *The Culture of Sensibility: Sex and Society in Eighteenth-Century Britain* (Chicago: University of Chicago Press, 1992).

Bartlett, Peter, "Sodomites in the pillory in eighteenth-century London," *Social and Legal Studies* 6.4 (1997), pp. 553–572.

Bartlett, Peter, "Silence and sodomy: The creation of homosexual identity in law," *Modern Law Review* 61.1 (1998), pp. 102–114.

Bartley, Paula, *Prostitution: Prevention and Reform in England, 1860–1914* (London: Routledge, 2000).

Bauer, Heike, "Richard von Krafft-Ebing's *Psychopathia Sexualis* as a sexual sourcebook for Radclyffe Hall's *The Well of Loneliness*," *Critical Survey* 15.3 (2003), pp. 23–38.

Baughman, Ernest W., "Public confession and *The Scarlet Letter*," *New England Quarterly* 40.4 (1967), pp. 532–550.

Beaton, Cecil, *My Royal Past*, 1st ed. (London: Batsford, 1939), 2nd ed. (London: Weidenfeld and Nicolson, 1960).

Beaton, Cecil, *The Strenuous Years: Diaries, 1948–55* (London: Weidenfeld and Nicolson, 1973).

Beaton, Cecil, *Theatre of War* (London: Jonathan Cape, 2012).

Beck, Alan, "You've got to hide your love away: Gay radio past and present," in Andrew Crisell, ed., *More Than a Music Box: Radio Cultures and Communities in a Multi-Media World* (New York: Berghahn, 2003), pp. 127–144.

Beck, Thomasina, "The jolly glitter of sequins," in *Norman Hartnell* (Brighton: Royal Pavilion, Art Gallery and Museums, 1985), pp. 71–78.

Beckford, William, *An Arabian Tale* [*A History of the Caliph Vathek*], trans. Samuel Henley, 3rd revised ed. (London: Johnson, 1786).

Beckford, William, *Vathek*, trans. H. B. Grimsditch (London: Nonesuch Press, 1929).

Belsey, Hugh, "Mann, Sir Horatio, first baronet (*bap.* 1706, *d.* 1786)," *Oxford Dictionary of National Biography* (Oxford: Oxford University Press; online ed., 2009): http://www.oxforddnb.com/view/article/17945, accessed March 9, 2011.

Bendall, Mark J., "Manhattan masquerade: Sexuality and spectacle in the world of Quentin Crisp," in Meriel D'Artrey, ed., *Cont_xts: Media, Representation and Society*, Issues in the Social Sciences 7 (Chester: Chester Academic Press, 2008), pp. 164–188.

Bendiner, Kenneth, "William Holman Hunt's *The Scapegoat*," *Pantheon* 45 (1987), pp. 124–128.

Bendiner, Kenneth, *Food in Painting from the Renaissance to the Present* (London: Reaktion, 2004).

Bengry, Justin, "Courting the pink pound: *Men Only* and the queer consumer, 1935–39," *History Workshop Journal* 68 (2009), pp. 123–148.

Bentman, Raymond, "Thomas Gray and the poetry of hopeless love," *Journal of the History of Sexuality* 3.2 (1992), pp. 203–222.

Bentman, Raymond, "Horace Walpole's forbidden passion," in Duberman (1997), pp. 276–289.

Bergeron, David M., *King James and Letters of Homoerotic Desire* (Iowa City: University of Iowa Press, 1999).

Bergman, David, ed., *Camp Grounds: Style and Homosexuality* (Amherst: University of Massachusetts Press, 1993).

Bernauer, James, and Jeremy Carrette, eds., *Michel Foucault and Theology: The Politics of Religious Experience* (Aldershot: Ashgate, 2004).

Berrett, Jesse, "Liberace: Behind the music," *Rethinking History* 4.1 (2000), pp. 77–79.

Bersani, Leo, "Is the rectum a grave?," *October* 43 (1987), pp. 197–222.

Bersani, Leo, *Homos* (Cambridge, MA: Harvard University Press, 1995).

Bertrand, Antoine, *Les curiosités esthétiques de Robert de Montesquiou*, 2 vols. (Geneva: Librairie Droz, 1996).

Betsky, Aaron, *Queer Space: Architecture and Same-Sex Desire* (New York: William Morrow, 1997).

Bindman, David, *The Shadow of the Guillotine: Britain and the French Revolution* (London: British Museum Press, 1989).

Binhammer, Katherine, "Accounting for the unaccountable: Lesbianism and the history of sexuality in eighteenth-century Britain," *Literature Compass* 6.6 (2010), pp. 1–15.

Blackwell, Mark, " 'It stood as an object of terror and delight': Sublime masculinity and the aesthetics of disproportion in John Cleland's *Memoirs of a Woman of Pleasure*," *Eighteenth-Century Novel* 3 (2003), pp. 39–64.

Bobker, Danielle, "Female favouritism, Orientalism, and the bathing closet in *Memoirs of Count Grammont*," *Eighteenth-Century Fiction* 24.1 (2011), pp. 1–30.

Boime, Albert, "William Holman Hunt's *The Scapegoat*: Rite of forgiveness/transference of blame," *Art Bulletin* 84.1 (2002), pp. 94–114.

Booth, Howard J., "Experience and homosexuality in the writing of Compton Mackenzie," *English Studies* 88.3 (2007), pp. 320–331.

Booth, Mark, "*Campe-toi!* On the origins and definitions of camp," in Cleto (1999), pp. 66–79.

Borwick, F., ed., *Clifton College Annals and Register, 1862–1925* (Bristol: J. W. Arrowsmith, 1925).

Bostridge, Mark, "Afterword," in Lytton Strachey, *Eminent Victorians: The Definitive Edition* (London: Continuum, 2002), pp. 171–180.

Boydell, Christine, *The Architect of Floors: Modernism, Art and Marion Dorn Designs* (Coggeshall: Schoeser, 1996).

Brady, Sean, *Masculinity and Male Homosexuality in Britain, 1861–1913* (Basingstoke: Palgrave, 2005).

Brake, Laurel, "'Gay discourse' and *The Artist and Journal of Home Culture*," in Laurel Brake, Bill Bell, and David Finkelstein, eds., *Nineteenth-Century Media and the Construction of Identities* (Basingstoke: Palgrave, 2000), pp. 271–294.

Brandenburg, Hugo, "The use of older elements in the architecture of fourth- and fifth-century Rome: A contribution to the evaluation of *spolia*," in Richard Brilliant and Dale Kinney, eds., *Reuse Value: "Spolia" and Appropriation in Art and Architecture from Constantine to Sherrie Levine* (Farnham: Ashgate, 2011), pp. 53–74.

Bray, Alan, "A traditional rite for blessing friendship," in Katherine O'Donnell and Michael O'Rourke, eds., *Love, Sex, Intimacy, and Friendship between Men, 1550–1800* (Basingstoke: Palgrave Macmillan, 2003a), pp. 87–98.

Bray, Alan, *The Friend* (Chicago: University of Chicago Press, 2003b).

Brett, Philip, *Music and Sexuality in Britten: Selected Essays*, ed. George Haggerty (Berkeley: University of California Press, 2006).

Brintnall, Kent L., *The Male-Body-in Pain: Ecce Homo as Redemptive Figure* (Chicago: University of Chicago Press, 2011).

Bristow, Joseph, "'Churlsgrace': Gerard Manley Hopkins and the working-class male body," *English Literary History* 59.3 (1992), pp. 693–711.

Bristow, Joseph, *Effeminate England: Homoerotic Writing after 1885* (Buckingham: Open University Press, 1995).

Bristow, Joseph, *Sexuality*, 2nd ed. (London: Routledge, 2011).

Broglio, Ron, "'The best machine for converting herbage into money': Romantic cattle culture," in Tamara S. Wagner and Narin Hassan, eds., *Consuming Culture in the Long Nineteenth Century: Narratives of Consumption, 1700–1900* (Lanham, MD: Lexington, 2007), pp. 35–48.

Bronkhurst, Judith, *William Holman Hunt: A Catalogue Raisonné*, 2 vols. (New Haven, CT: Yale University Press, 2006).

Brooks, Frederic, "A visit to Edward Carpenter," *Epoch* November (1915), pp. 325–331.

Brown, Gavin, Kath Browne, Michael Brown, et al., "Sedgwick's geographies: Touching space," *Progress in Human Geography* 35.1 (2011), pp. 121–131.

Brown, Laura, "Reading race and gender: Jonathan Swift," *Eighteenth-Century Studies* 23.4 (1990), pp. 425–443.

Brown, Michael P., *Closet Space: Geographies of Metaphor from the Body to the Globe* (London: Routledge, 2000).

Brown, Susanna, "Cecil Beaton and the iconography of the House of Windsor," *Photography and Culture* 4.3 (2011a), pp. 293–308.

Brown, Susanna, *Queen Elizabeth II: Portraits by Cecil Beaton* (London: Victoria and Albert Museum, 2011b).

Browne, Martin, *A Dream of Youth: An Etonian's Reply to "The Loom of Youth"* (London: Longmans, 1918).

Bruce, Susan, "'Rolling about from whore to whore': Rochester's satirico-sexual self and the art of conspicuous consumption," *Forum for Modern Language Studies* 30.4 (1994), pp. 305–315.

Bruns, Claudia, "*Masculinity, sexuality, and the German nation:* The Eulenburg scandals and Kaiser Wilhelm II in political cartoons," trans. Angela Davis, in Udo J. Hebel and Christoph Wagner, eds., *Pictorial Cultures and Political*

Iconographies: Approaches, Perspectives, Case Studies from Europe and America (Berlin: Walter de Gruyter, 2011), pp. 119–142.

Buckton, Oliver S., "'An unnatural state': Gender, 'perversion' and Newman's *Apologia pro Vita Sua*," *Victorian Studies* 35.4 (1992), pp. 359–383.

Buckton, Oliver S., *Secret Selves: Confession and Same-Sex Desire in Victorian Autobiography* (Chapel Hill: University of North Carolina Press, 1998).

Budziak, Anna, "Oscar Wilde's refutation of 'depth' in *The Picture of Dorian Gray*: A reading," *Brno Studies in English* 30 (2004), pp. 136–145.

Burke, Edmund, *A Philosophical Inquiry into the Origin of our Ideas of the Sublime and Beautiful*, ed. Adam Phillips (Oxford: Oxford University Press, 1998) [first published 1757].

Butler, Judith, *Precarious Life: The Powers of Mourning and Violence* (New York: Verso, 2004).

Butt, Trevor, and Paul Langdridge, "The construction of self: The public reach into the private sphere," *Sociology* 37.3 (2003), pp. 477–492.

Byron, John, "Byron and the Patagonian giants" [from *Journal of a Voyage around the World in the "Dolphin"* (London: M. Cooper, 1767)], in Jonathan Lamb, Vanessa Smith, and Nicholas Thomas, eds., *Exploration and Exchange: A South Seas Anthology, 1680–1900* (Chicago: University of Chicago Press, 2000), pp. 46–56.

Cady, Joseph, "'Masculine love': Renaissance writing and the 'new invention' of homosexuality," in Claude J. Summers, ed., *Homosexuality in Renaissance England: Literary Representations in Historical Context* (Binghampton: Haworth Press, 1992), pp. 9–40.

Campbell, David, *The Visual Economy of HIV/AIDS* (2008): http://www.david-campbell.org/visual-hivaids/contents/pdf/part2.pdf, accessed October 25, 2012.

Campbell, Jill, "'I am no giant': Horace Walpole, heterosexual incest, and love among men," *Eighteenth Century: Theory and Interpretation* 39.3 (1998), pp. 238–59.

Campbell, Michael J., *John Martin: Visionary Printmaker* (York: Campbell Fine Art, 1992).

Cannadine, David, "The context, performance and meaning of ritual: The British monarchy and the 'invention of tradition', c. 1820–1977," in Eric Hobsbawm and Terence Ranger, eds., *The Invention of Tradition* (Cambridge: Cambridge University Press, 1983), pp. 101–164.

Cantrell, Pamela, "Writing the picture: Fielding, Smollett, and Hogarthian pictorialism," *Studies in Eighteenth-Century Culture* 24 (1995), pp. 69–89.

Cappock, Margarita, *Francis Bacon's Studio* (London: Merrell, 2005).

Casarino, Cesare, "The sublime of the closet; or, Joseph Conrad's secret sharing," *Boundary 2* 24.2 (1997), pp. 199–243.

Castiglia, Christopher, and Christopher Reed, *If Memory Serves: Gay Men, AIDS and the Promise of the Queer Past* (Minneapolis: University of Minnesota Press, 2012).

Castle, Terry, *The Female Thermometer: Eighteenth-Century Culture and the Invention of the Uncanny* (Oxford: Oxford University Press, 1995).

Chandos, John, *Boys Together: English Public Schools, 1800–1864* (Oxford: Oxford University Press, 1985).

Châtel, Laurent, "The resistance of words and the challenge of images: Visual writing in late eighteenth-century Britain," *Interfaces* 32 (2011-12), pp. 49–64.

Chauncey, George, *Gay New York: Gender, Urban Culture, and the Making of the Gay Male World, 1890–1940* (New York: Basic Books, 1994).

Chitty, Susan, *The Beast and the Monk: A Life of Charles Kingsley* (New York: Mason/Charter, 1975).

Clark, Elizabeth A., "Foucault, the Fathers, and sex," *Journal of the American Academy of Religion* 56.4 (1988), pp. 619–641.

Claro, Daniel, "Historicizing masculine appearance: John Chute and the suits at The Vyne, 1740–76," *Fashion Theory: The Journal of Dress, Body and Culture* 9.2 (2005), pp. 147–174.

Cleland, John, *Memoirs of a Woman of Pleasure*, ed. Peter Sabor (Oxford: Oxford University Press, 1999) [1st ed. 1748–1749].

Cleto, Fabio, ed., *Camp: Queer Aesthetics and the Performing Subject: A Reader* (Edinburgh: Edinburgh University Press, 1999).

Coad, David, *The Metrosexual: Gender, Identity and Sport* (Albany: State University of New York Press, 2008).

Cocks, H. G., "Calamus in Bolton: Spirituality and homosexual desire in late Victorian England," *Gender and History* 13.2 (2001), pp. 191–223.

Cocks, H. G., "Making the sodomite speak: Voices of the accused in English sodomy trials, c. 1800–98," *Gender and History* 18.1 (2006a), pp. 87–107.

Cocks, H. G., "Safeguarding civility: Sodomy, class and moral reform in early nineteenth-century England," *Past and Present* 190 (2006b), pp. 121–146.

Cocks, H. G., "The discovery of Sodom, 1851," *Representations* 112.1 (2010), pp. 1–26.

Cohen, Ed, "Writing gone Wilde: Homoerotic desire in the closet of representation," *PMLA* 102.5 (1987), pp. 801–813.

Cohen, Michèle, "'Manners' make the man: Politeness, chivalry, and the construction of masculinity, 1750–1830," *Journal of British Studies* 44.2 (2005), pp. 312–329.

Cohler, Deborah, *Citizen, Invert, Queer: Lesbianism and War in Early Twentieth-Century Britain* (Minneapolis: University of Minnesota Press, 2010).

Cole, Sarah Rose, "The aristocrat in the mirror: Male vanity and bourgeois desire in William Makepeace Thackeray's *Vanity Fair*," *Nineteenth-Century Literature* 61.2 (2006), pp. 137–170.

Cole, Shaun, *"Don we now our Gay Apparel": Gay Men's Dress in the Twentieth Century* (Oxford: Berg, 2000).

Coleman, Simon, "From the sublime to the meticulous: Art, anthropology and Victorian pilgrimage to Palestine," *History and Anthropology* 13.4 (2002), pp. 275–290.

Colley, Linda, *Britons: Forging the Nation, 1707–1837* (New Haven, CT: Yale University Press, 1992).

Colligan, Colette, "'A race of born pederasts': Sir Richard Burton, homosexuality and the Arabs," *Nineteenth-Century Contexts* 25.1 (2003), pp. 1–20.

Collings, Matthew, "Beach house: Dungeness," *Blueprint* October (2008), pp. 116–124.

Connolly, Tristanne, *William Blake and the Body* (Basingstoke: Palgrave, 2002).

Cook, Matt, *London and the Culture of Homosexuality, 1885–1914* (Cambridge: Cambridge University Press, 2003).

Cook, Matt, ed., *A Gay History of Britain* (Greenwood: Oxford, 2007).

Cooper, Emmanuel, *The Sexual Perspective: Homosexuality and Art in the Last 100 Years in the West* (London: Routledge and Kegan Paul, 1986).

Corber, Robert J., "Representing the 'unspeakable': William Godwin and the politics of homophobia," *Journal of the History of Sexuality* 1.1 (1990), pp. 85–101.

Cosgrove, Peter, "Edmund Burke, Gilles Deleuze, and the subversive masochism of the image," *English Literary History* 66.2 (1999), pp. 405–437.

Crawford, Joseph, *Raising Milton's Ghost: John Milton and the Sublime of Terror in the Early Romantic Period* (London: Bloomsbury, 2011).

Crimp, Douglas, "Portraits of people with AIDS," in Crimp, ed., *Melancholia and Moralism: Essays on AIDS and Queer Politics* (Cambridge, MA: MIT Press, 2002), pp. 83–108.

Crisp, Quentin, *The Naked Civil Servant* (London: Fontana, 1977) [first published 1968].

Crown, Patricia, "Hogarth's working women: Commerce and consumption," in Bernadette Fort and Angela Rosenthal, eds., *The Other Hogarth: Aesthetics of Difference* (Princeton, NJ: Princeton University Press, 2001), pp. 224–239.

Crozier, Ivan D., "William Acton and the history of sexuality: The medical and professional context," *Journal of Victorian Culture* 5 (2000), pp. 1–27.

Crozier, Ivan D., "Nineteenth-century British psychiatric writing about homosexuality before Havelock Ellis: The missing story," *Journal of the History of Medicine and Allied Sciences* 63.1 (2008), pp. 65–102.

Cruickshank, Margaret, *The Gay and Lesbian Liberation Movement* (London: Routledge, 1992).

Custance, Roger, ed., *Winchester College: Sixth Centenary Essays* (Oxford: Oxford University Press, 1982).

D'Arch Smith, Timothy, *Love in Earnest: Some Notes on the Lives and Writings of English "Uranian" Poets from 1889 to 1930* (London: Routledge, 1970).

D'Emilio, John, "Foreword," in Jay and Young (1992), pp. xi–xxx.

Das, Santanu, "'Kiss me, Hardy': Intimacy, gender, and gesture in First World War trench literature," *Modernism/Modernity* 9.1 (2002), pp. 51–74.

Davies, Damian Walford, and Laurent Châtel, "'A mad hornet': Beckford's riposte to Hazlitt," *European Romantic Review* 10.1–4 (1999), pp. 452–479.

Davies, Hugh M., *Francis Bacon: The Papal Portraits of 1953* (San Diego: Museum of Contemporary Art, 2002).

Davis, Whitney, "The image in the middle: John Addington Symonds and homoerotic art criticism," in Elizabeth Prettejohn, ed., *After the Pre-Raphaelites: Art and Aestheticism in Victorian England* (Manchester: Manchester University Press, 1999), pp. 188–216.

Davis, Whitney, "The site of sexuality: William Beckford's Fonthill Abbey, 1780-1824," in Robert A. Schmidt and Barbara L. Voss, eds., *Archaeologies of Sexuality* (London: Routledge, 2000), pp. 104–13.

Davis, Whitney, "Queer family romance in collecting visual culture," *GLQ* 17.2–3 (2011), pp. 309–329.

Dawson, Christopher, *The Spirit of the Oxford Movement and Newman's Place in History* (London: Sheed and Ward, 1933).

Denisoff, Dennis, "Posing a threat: Queensbury, Wilde, and the portrayal of decadence," in Liz Constable, Dennis Denisoff, and Matthew Potolsky, eds., *Perennial Decay: On the Aesthetics and Politics of Decadence* (Philadelphia: University of Pennsylvania Press, 1999), pp. 83–100.

Dennis, John, *The Grounds of Criticism in Poetry* (London: Strachan and Lintott, 1704).

De Villiers, Nicholas, *Opacity and the Closet: Queer Tactics in Foucault, Barthes and Warhol* (Minneapolis: University of Minnesota Press, 2012).

Dobson, Michael, and Nicola J. Watson, *England's Elizabeth: An Afterlife in Fame and Fantasy* (Oxford: Oxford University Press, 2002).

Dolar, Mladen, "Introduction: The subject supposed to enjoy," in Grosrichard (1998), pp. ix–xxvii.

Donoghue, Emma, "Imagined more than women: Lesbians as hermaphrodites, 1671–1766," *Women's History Review* 2.2 (1993), pp. 199–216.

Douglas, Alfred, *Autobiography* (London: Martin Secker, 1929).

Douglas, Mary, *Purity and Danger: An Analysis of the Concepts of Pollution and Taboo* (London: Routledge, 1966).

Dowling, Linda, *Hellenism and Homosexuality in Victorian Oxford* (Ithaca, NY: Cornell University Press, 1994).

Duberman, Martin, *Stonewall* (New York: Plume, 1994).

Duberman, Martin, ed., *Queer Representations: Reading Lives, Reading Culture* (New York: New York University Press, 1997).

Durden, Michelle, "Not just a leg show: Gayness and male homoeroticism in burlesque, 1868 to 1877," *Third Space: A Journal of Feminist Theory and Culture* 3.2 (2004): http://www.thirdspace.ca/journal/article/viewArticle/durden/173, accessed March 10, 2013.

Durham, Martin, *Sex and Politics: The Family and Morality in the Thatcher Years* (London: Macmillan, 1991).

During, Simon, "Beckford in hell: An episode in the history of secular enchantment," *Huntingdon Library Quarterly* 70.2 (2007), pp. 269–288.

Dyer, Gary, "The arrest of Caleb Williams: Unnatural crime, constructive violence, and overwhelming terror in late eighteenth-century England," *Eighteenth Century Life* 36.3 (2012), pp. 31–56.

Dyer, Richard, "It's being so camp as keeps us going," in Cleto (1999), pp. 110–116.

Dyer, Richard, *Gay Icons* (London: National Portrait Gallery, 2009).

Edwards, Jason, *Eve Kosofsky Sedgwick* (London: Routledge, 2009).

Edwards, Tim, "Queer fears: Against the cultural turn," *Sexualities* 1.4 (1998), pp. 471–484.

Ehrman, Edwina, "The spirit of English style: Hardy Amies, royal dressmaker and international businessman," in Christopher Breward, Becky Conekin, and Caroline Cox, eds., *The Englishness of English Dress* (Berg: Oxford, 2002), pp. 133–146.

Elfenbein, Andrew, "Byronism and the work of homosexual performance in early Victorian England," *Modern Language Quarterly* 54.4 (1993), pp. 535–566.

Elfenbein, Andrew, *Romantic Genius: The Prehistory of a Homosexual Role* (New York: Columbia University Press, 1999).

Elias, Richard, "Political satire in *Sodom*," *Studies in English Literature, 1500–1900* 18 (1978), pp. 423–428.

Ellis, Edith, *Personal Impressions of Edward Carpenter* (Berkeley Heights: Free Spirit Press, 1922).

Ellis, Havelock [and John Addington Symonds], *Studies in the Psychology of Sex*, vol. 1, *Inversion* (London: Wilson and Macmillan, 1897).

Eribon, Didier, *Insult and the Making of the Gay Self*, trans. Michael Lucey (Durham, NC: Duke University Press, 2004).

Etherington-Smith, Meredith, "Obituary: Ian Thomas," *Independent*, June 5 (1993): http://www.independent.co.uk/news/people/obituary-ian-thomas-1489687.html, accessed February 28, 2014.

Faber, Geoffrey, *Oxford Apostles: A Character Study of the Oxford Movement* (London: Faber and Faber, 1933).

Farmer, Brett, "The fabulous sublimity of gay diva worship," *Camera Obscura* 20.2 (2005), pp. 165–194.

Farmer, Brett, "Julie Andrews made me gay," *Camera Obscura* 22.2 (2007), pp. 144–152.

Farson, Daniel, *The Gilded Gutter Life of Francis Bacon* (London: Vintage, 1994).

Fasick, Laura, "The failure of fatherhood: Maleness and its discontents in Charles Kingsley," *Children's Literature Association Quarterly* 18.3 (1993), pp. 106–111.

Fassler, Barbara, "Theories of homosexuality as sources of Bloomsbury's androgyny," *Signs* 5.2 (1979), pp. 237–251.

Faulks, Sebastian, *The Fatal Englishman: Three Short Lives* (London: Hutchinson, 1996).

Fausett, David, *Images of the Antipodes in the Eighteenth Century: A Study in Stereotyping* (Amsterdam: Rodopi, 1994).

Fielding, Henry, *Miscellanies*, vol. 3, *The Life of Mr. Jonathan Wild the Great*, 2nd ed. (London: Millar, 1743).

Fincher, Max, "Guessing the mould: Homosocial sins and identity in Horace Walpole's *The Castle of Otranto*," *Gothic Studies* 3.3 (2001), pp. 229–245.

Fincher, Max, *Queering the Gothic in the Romantic Age: The Penetrating Eye* (Basingstoke: Palgrave, 2007).

Fisher, Will, "The sexual politics of Victorian historiographical writing about the Renaissance," *GLQ* 14.1 (2008), pp. 41–67.

Fitch, Charles, *Come Out of Her My People* (Rochester, NY: J. V. Himes, 1843).

Fletcher, John, "The haunted closet: Henry James's queer spectrality," *Textual Practice* 14.1 (2000), pp. 53–80.

Fludernik, Monika, "William Godwin's *Caleb Williams*: The tarnishing of the sublime," *English Literary History* 68.4 (2001), pp. 857–996.

Foldy, Michael S., *The Trials of Oscar Wilde: Deviance, Morality, and Late-Victorian Society* (New Haven, CT: Yale University Press, 1997).

Forrest, Theodosius, *The Roast Beef of Old England: A Cantata* (London: Withy, ca. 1750–1759) [2nd ed. 1759].

Forster, E. M., *Maurice*, ed. P. N. Furbank (London: Penguin, 2005).

Fothergill, Brian, "The influence of landscape and architecture on the composition of *Vathek*," in Kenneth W. Graham, ed., *"Vathek" and the Escape from Time: Bicentenary Revaluations* (New York: AMS, 1990), pp. 33–47.

Foucault, Michel, *Religion and Culture*, ed. Jeremy Carrette (Manchester: Manchester University Press, 1999).

Francis, Martin, "Cecil Beaton's romantic Toryism and the symbolic economy of wartime Britain," *Journal of British Studies* 45.1 (2006), pp. 90–117.

Frank, Marcie, "Horace Walpole's family romances," *Modern Philology* 100.3 (2003), pp. 417–435.

Frantzen, Allen J., *Before the Closet: Same-Sex Love from "Beowulf" to "Angels in America"* (Chicago: University of Chicago Press, 1998).

Freccero, Carla, *Queer/Early/Modern* (Durham, NC: Duke University Press, 2006).

Frost, Lea Luecking, "'A kyng that ruled all by lust': Richard II in Elizabethan literature," *Literature Compass* 9 (2012), pp. 183–198.

Funke, Jana, "'We cannot be Greek now': Age difference, corruption of youth and the making of sexual inversion," *English Studies* 94.2 (2013), pp. 139–153.

Furniss, Tom, *Edmund Burke's Aesthetic Ideology: Language, Gender and Political Economy in Revolution* (Cambridge: Cambridge University Press, 1993).

Fussell, Paul, *The Great War and Modern Memory* (Oxford: Oxford University Press, 1975).

Galt, Rosalind, *Pretty: Film and the Decorative Image* (New York: Columbia University Press, 2011).

Garfield, Simon, "Gay icon whose courage was awesome," *Independent*, February 21 (1994), p. 3.

Garland, Rodney, *The Heart in Exile* (London: W. H. Allen, 1953).

Gathorne-Hardy, Jonathan, *The Public School Phenomenon, 597–1977* (London: Hodder and Stoughton, 1977).

Gay, Peter, *The Cultivation of Hatred* (London: Fontana, 1995).

Gentile, Kathy Justice, "Sublime drag: Supernatural masculinity in gothic fiction," *Gothic Studies* 11.1 (2009), pp. 16–32.

George, Laura, "The emergence of the dandy," *Literature Compass* 1.1 (2004), pp. 1–13.

Gessert, George, *Green Light: Towards an Art of Evolution* (Cambridge, MA: MIT Press, 2010).

Getsy, David J., "Recognizing the homoerotic: The uses of intersubjectivity in John Addington Symonds' 1887 essays on art," *Visual Culture in Britain* 8.1 (2007), pp. 37–57.

Ghaziani, Amin., "Post-gay collective identity construction," *Social Problems* 58.1 (2011), pp. 99–125.

Gibson, William T., "Homosexuality, class and the Church in nineteenth-century England: Two case studies," *Journal of Homosexuality* 21.4 (1991), pp. 45–56.

Giebelhausen, Michaela, *Painting the Bible: Representation and Belief in Mid-Victorian Britain* (Aldershot: Ashgate, 2006).

Gill, R. B., "The author in the novel: Creating Beckford in *Vathek*," *Eighteenth-Century Fiction* 15.2 (2003), pp. 241–254.

Gilman, Sander L., "AIDS and syphilis: The iconography of disease," *October* 43 (1987), pp. 87–107.

Girard, René: *The Scapegoat*, trans. Yvonne Freccero (London: Athlone, 1986).

Girouard Mark, *Life in the English Country House: A Social and Architectural History* (London: Penguin, 1980).

Glick, Elisa, "The dialectics of dandyism," *Cultural Critique* 48.1 (2001), pp. 129–163.

Goffman, Erving, "On the characteristics of total institutions: The inmate world," in Donald R. Cressey, ed., *The Prison: Studies in Institutional Organisation and Change* (New York: Holt, Rinehart and Winston, 1961), pp. 15–67.

Golding, William, *The Spire* (London: Faber and Faber, 1964).

Goldstein, Richard, *Homocons: The Rise of the Gay Right* (London: Verso, 2003).

Goring, Paul, *The Rhetoric of Sensibility in Eighteenth-Century Culture* (Cambridge: Cambridge University Press, 2005).

Graves, Robert, *Goodbye to All That* (London: Folio Society, 1981) [first published 1929].

Gray, Thomas, *Correspondence*, eds. Paget Toynbee and Leonard Whibley, 3 vols. (Oxford: Oxford University Press, 1971).

Gray, Thomas, "Elegy written in a country churchyard," in Alexander Huber, ed., *The Thomas Gray* Archive (2012): http://www.thomasgray.org/, accessed March 30, 2009.

Greene, Jody, "Public secrets: Sodomy and the pillory in the eighteenth century and beyond," *Eighteenth Century* 44.2-3 (2003), pp. 203–234.

Griffin, Gabriele, *Representations of HIV and AIDS: Visibility Blue/s* (Manchester: Manchester University Press, 2000).

Griffin, Randall C., "Thomas Eakins' construction of the male body, or 'men get to know each other across the space of time,'" *Oxford Art Journal* 18.2 (1995), pp. 70–80.

Griffith, Nicola, "Writing from the body" (undated): http://www.nicolagriffith.com/body.html, accessed March 9, 2010.

Grosrichard, Alain, *The Sultan's Court: European Fantasies of the East*, trans. Liz Heron (London: Verso, 1998).

Gross, Larry, *Contested Closets: The Politics and Ethics of Outing* (Minneapolis: University of Minnesota Press, 1993).

Gross, Robert F., "Consuming Hart: Sublimity and gay poetics in *Suddenly, Last Summer*," *Theatre Journal* 47.2 (1995), pp. 229–251.

Gundle, Stephen, "Mapping the origins of glamour: Giovanni Boldini, Paris and the Belle Epoque," *Journal of European Studies* 29 (1999), pp. 269–295.

Haggerty, George E., "'O lachrymarum fons': Tears, poetry, and desire in Gray," *Eighteenth-Century Studies* 30.1 (1996), pp. 81–95.

Haggerty, George E., "Desire and mourning: The ideology of the elegy," in David H. Richter, ed., *Ideology and Form in Eighteenth-Century Literature* (Lubbock: Texas Tech University Press, 1999), pp. 185–206.

Haggerty, George E., "Walpoliana," *Eighteenth-Century Studies* 34.2 (2001), pp. 227–249.

Haggerty, George E., "Keyhole testimony: Witnessing sodomy in the eighteenth-century," *Eighteenth Century* 44.2–3 (2003), pp. 167–182.

Haggerty, George E., "Love and loss: An elegy," *GLQ* 10.3 (2004), pp. 385–405.

Haggerty, George E., "'Dung, guts and blood': Sodomy, abjection and gothic fiction in the early nineteenth century," *Gothic Studies* 8.2 (2006a), pp. 35–51.

Haggerty, George E., *Queer Gothic* (Urbana: University of Illinois Press, 2006b).

Haggerty, George E., "Queering Horace Walpole," *Studies in English Literature* 46.3 (2006c), pp. 543–562.

Haggerty, George E., *Horace Walpole's Letters: Masculinity and Friendship in the Eighteenth Century* (Lanham, MD: Bucknell University Press, 2011).

Haggerty, George E., "Smollett's world of masculine desire in *The Adventures of Roderick Random*," *Eighteenth Century* 53.3 (2012), pp. 317–330.

Hall, Radclyffe, *The Well of Loneliness* (London: Virago, 1982) [first published 1928].

Hallas, Roger, *Reframing Bodies: AIDS, Bearing Witness, and the Queer Moving Image* (Durham, NC: Duke University Press, 2009).

Halperin, David M., *How to Be Gay* (Cambridge, MA: Harvard University Press, 2012).

Hamilton, Anthony, *Le Bélier* (Paris: Josse, 1730).

Hamilton, Anthony, *Tales and Romances*, trans M. Lewis, H. T. Hyde, and C. K. Kenney (London: Henry G. Bohn, 1849).

Hammer, Martin, "Francis Bacon: Painting after photography," *Art History* 35.2 (2012), pp. 354–371.

Hammer, Martin, and Chris Stephens, "'Seeing the story of one's time': Appropriations from Nazi photography in the work of Francis Bacon," *Visual Culture in Britain* 10.3 (2009), pp. 315–351.

Hanson, Ellis, *Decadence and Catholicism* (Cambridge, MA: Harvard University Press, 1997).

Hanson, Ellis, "Queer gothic," in Catherine Spooner and Emma McEvoy, eds., *The Routledge Companion to the Gothic* (London: Routledge, 2007), pp. 174–182.

Hardy, Keir, *The Queenie Gerald Case: A Public Scandal: White Slavery in a Piccadilly Flat* (Manchester: National Labour Press, 1913).

Harkin, Maureen, "Matthew Lewis's *Journal of a West India Proprietor*: Surveillance and space on the plantation," *Nineteenth-Century Contexts* 24.2 (2002), pp. 139–150.

Harrington, Henry R., "Charles Kingsley's fallen athlete," *Victorian Studies* 21.1 (1977), pp. 73–86.

Harris, Alexandra, "Seaside ceremonies: Coastal rites in twentieth-century art," in Lara Feigel and Alexandra Harris, eds., *Modernism on Sea: Art and Culture at the British Seaside* (Oxford: Peter Lang, 2009), pp. 227–244.

Harris, Bob, *Politics and the Nation: Britain in the Mid-Eighteenth Century* (Oxford: Oxford University Press, 2002).

Harris, Daniel, "The death of camp: Gay men and Hollywood diva worship, from reverence to ridicule," *Salmagundi* 112 Fall (1996), pp. 166–191.

Hartnell, Norman, *Silver and Gold* (London: Evans, 1955).

Harvey, A. D., "Homosexuality and the British Army during the First World War," *Journal of the Society for Army Historical Research* 79 (2001), pp. 313–319.

Harvey, Karen, *Reading Sex in the Eighteenth Century: Bodies and Gender in English Erotic Culture* (Cambridge: Cambridge University Press, 2004).

Hatch, John G., "Fatum as theme and method in the work of Francis Bacon," *Artibus et Historiae* 19.37 (1998), pp. 163–175.

Hatt, Michael, "Near and far: Homoeroticism, labour and Hamo Thornycroft's *Mower*," *Art History* 26.1 (2003), pp. 26–55.

Hattrick, Jane, "Collecting and displaying identity: Intimacy and memory in the staged interiors of the royal couturier Norman Hartnell," in Sandra H. Dudley et al., eds., *Narrating Objects, Collecting Stories: Essays in Honour of Professsor Susan M. Pearce* (London: Routledge, 2012), pp. 136–152.

Haydon, Colin, *Anti-Catholicism in Eighteenth-Century England, c. 1714–80: A Political and Social Study* (Manchester: Manchester University Press, 1993).

Herek, Gregory M., and John P. Capitano, "AIDS stigma and sexual prejudice," *American Behavioral Scientist* 42.7 (1999), pp. 1130–1147.

Herrmann, Anne, *Queering the Moderns: Poses/Portraits/Performances* (London: Palgrave, 2000).

Heward, Christine, *Making a Man of Him: Parents and their Sons' Education at an English Public School, 1929–50* (London: Routledge, 1988).

Hickson, Alisdaire, *The Poisoned Bowl: Sex, Repression and the Public School System* (London: Constable, 1995).

Hilliard, David, "UnEnglish and unmanly: Anglo-Catholicism and homosexuality," *Victorian Studies* 25.2 (1982), pp. 181–210.

Hoare, Philip, *Wilde's Last Stand: Decadence, Conspiracy and the First World War* (London: Duckworth, 1997).

Hobson, Christopher Z., *Blake and Homosexuality* (Palgrave: Basingstoke, 2000).

Holland, Merlin, "Comments on Susan Balée's review of *Oscar Wilde: A Long and Lovely Suicide*, by Melissa Knox," *Victorian Studies* 39.4 (1996), pp. 539–541.

Hollinghurst, Alan, *The Swimming Pool Library* (London: Chatto and Windus, 1988).

Holman Hunt, William, "Painting *The Scapegoat*," *Contemporary Review* 52 (1887), pp. 21–38.

Holroyd, Michael, *Lytton Strachey: A Critical Biography*, 2 vols. (London: Heinemann, 1967).

Holroyd, Michael, *Lytton Strachey* (London: Chatto and Windus, 1994).

Holt, Jenny, *Public School Literature, Civic Education and the Politics of Male Adolescence* (Aldershot: Ashgate, 2008).

Honey, J. R. de S., *Tom Brown's Universe: The Development of the Victorian Public School* (London: Millington, 1997).

Hood, Jack, *The Heart of a Schoolboy* (London: Longmans, 1919).

Hooker, Evelyn, "A preliminary analysis of group behavior of homosexuals," *Journal of Psychology* 42.2 (1956), pp. 217–25.

Hooker, Evelyn, "Reflections of a 40-year exploration: A scientific view on homosexuality," *American Psychologist* 48.4 (1993), pp. 450–453.

Hornsey, Richard, *The Spiv and the Architect: Unruly Life in Postwar London* (Minneapolis: University of Minnesota Press, 2010).

Horrocks, Jamie, "Asses and aesthetes: ritualism and aestheticism in Victorian periodical illustration," *Victorian Periodicals Review* 6.1 (2013), pp. 1–36.

Hotz-Davies, Ingrid, "Quentin Crisp, camp and the art of shamelessness," *Critical Studies* 34 (2010), pp. 165–184.

Houlbrook, Matt, *Queer London: Perils and Pleasures in the Sexual Metropolis, 1918–57* (Chicago: University of Chicago Press, 2005).

Houlbrook, Matt, "The man with the powder puff in interwar London," *Historical Journal* 50.1 (2007), pp. 145–171.

Houlbrook, Matt, and Chris Waters, "*The Heart in Exile*: Detachment and desire in 1950s London," *History Workshop Journal* 62.1 (2006), pp. 142–165.

Howard, Seymour, "William Blake: The antique, nudity, and nakedness: A study in idealism and regression," *Artibus et Historiae* 3.6 (1982), pp. 117–149.

Hughes, Thomas, *Tom Brown's Schooldays* (London: Penguin, 1994) [1st ed. 1857].

Humphreys, Laud, *Out of the Closets: The Sociology of Homosexual Liberation* (Englewood Cliffs, NJ: Prentice Hall, 1972).

Hunt, Alan, "The great masturbation panic and the discourses of moral regulation in nineteenth- and twentieth-century Britain," *Journal of the History of Sexuality* 8.4 (1998), pp. 575–615.

Hutson, Lorna, "Liking men: Ben Jonson's closet opened," *English Literary History* 71.4 (2004), pp. 1065–1096.

Huysmans, Joris-Karl, *Against Nature*, trans. Margaret Mauldon (Oxford: Oxford University Press, 1998) [first published 1884].

Hyam, Ronald, *Empire and Sexuality: The British Experience* (Manchester: Manchester University Press, 1990).

Imperial War Museum, *Press Release: Theatre of War Exhibition*, September 5, 2012: http://www.iwm.org.uk/sites/default/files/press-release/IWML_CecilBeaton_Aug2012.pdf, accessed February 6, 2013.

Ishii-Gonzalès, Sam, "Beyond the pale: Francis Bacon and the limits of portraiture," *GLQ* 6.4 (2000), pp. 631–639.

Jack, Sybil M., "No heavenly Jerusalem: The Anglican bishopric, 1841–83," *Journal of Religious History* 19.2 (1995), pp. 181–203.

Jacobi, Carol, *William Holman Hunt: Painter, Painting, Paint* (Manchester: Manchester University Press, 2006).

Jakobsen, Janet L., "Queers are like Jews, aren't they? Analogy and alliance politics," in Daniel Boyarin, Daniel Itzkovitz, and Ann Pellegrini, eds., *Queer Theory and the Jewish Question* (New York: Columbia University Press, 2003), pp. 64–89.

Janes, Dominic, "The rites of man: The British Museum and the sexual imagination in Victorian Britain," *Journal of the History of Collections* 20.1 (2008), pp. 101–112.

Janes, Dominic, "'Eternal master': Masochism and the sublime at the National Shrine of the Immaculate Conception, Washington, D.C.," *Theology and Sexuality* 15.2 (2009a), pp. 161–175.

Janes, Dominic, *Victorian Reformation: The Fight over Idolatry in the Church of England, 1840–1860* (Oxford: Oxford University Press, 2009b).

Janes, Dominic, "*The Catholic Florist*: Flowers and deviance in the mid-nineteenth-century Church of England," *Visual Culture in Britain* 12.1 (2011a), pp. 77–96.

Janes, Dominic, "Clarke and Kubrick's 2001: A queer odyssey," *Science Fiction Film and Television* 4.1 (2011b), pp. 57–78.

Janes, Dominic, "Frederick Rolfe's Christmas cards: Popular culture and the construction of queerness in late Victorian Britain," *Early Popular Visual Culture* 10.2 (2012a), pp. 105–124.

Janes, Dominic, "'One of us': The queer afterlife of Margaret Thatcher as a gay icon," *International Journal of Media and Cultural Politics* 8.2–3 (2012b), pp. 211–227.

Janes, Dominic, "Unnatural appetites: sodomitical panic in Hogarth's *The Gate of Calais, or O the Roast Beef of Old England (1748)*," *Oxford Art Journal* 35.1 (2012c), pp. 19–31.

Janes, Dominic, "Eminent Victorians, Bloomsbury queerness and John Maynard Keynes' *The Economic Consequences of the Peace* (1919)," *Literature and History* 23.1 (2014), pp. 19–32.

Janes, Dominic, *Visions of Queer Martyrdom from John Henry Newman to Derek Jarman* (Chicago: University of Chicago Press, 2015).

Janes, Dominic, "The Oxford Movement, asceticism and sexual desire," in Nicholas Groom, Joanne Parker, and Corinna Wagner, eds., *Oxford Handbook of Victorian Medievalism* (Oxford: Oxford University Press, forthcoming).

Jarman, Derek, *Dancing Ledge*, ed. Shaun Allen (London: Quartet Books, 1984).

Jarman, Derek, *Modern Nature: The Journals of Derek Jarman* (London: Vintage, 1992).

Jarman, Derek, *Derek Jarman's Garden, with Photographs by Howard Sooley* (London: Thames and Hudson, 1995).

Jarman, Derek, *Dancing Ledge*, reprint edition (Minneapolis: University of Minnesota Press, 2010).

Jarrett, Derek, *England in the Age of Hogarth* (London: Granada, 1976).

Jay, Karla, and Allen Young, eds., *Out of the Closets: Voices of Gay Liberation*, 1st ed. (Englewood Cliffs, NJ: Prentice Hall, 1972), new ed. (New York: Jove/HBJ, 1977), new ed. (London: GMP, 1992).

Jeffery-Poulter, Stephen, *Peers, Queers, and Commons: The Struggle for Gay Law Reform from 1950 to the Present* (Routledge: London, 1991).

Jerusalem Diocesan Fund, *A Reply to Two Pamphlets Concerning Jerusalem, Its Bishop, Missions, etc; Containing an Authorised Statement in Vindication of Bishop Gobat* (London: Seeley, Jackson and Halliday, 1858).

Johnson, Claudia L., " 'Let me make the novels of a country': Barbauld's *The British Novelists* (1810/1820)," *Novel: A Forum on Fiction* 34.2 (2001), pp. 163–179.

Johnson, Douglas H., "The death of Gordon: A Victorian myth," *Journal of Imperial and Commonwealth History* 10.3 (1982), pp. 285–310.

Jones, Paul Dafydd, "Jesus Christ and the transformation of English society: The 'subversive conservatism' of Frederick Denison Maurice," *Harvard Theological Review* 96.2 (2003), pp. 205–228.

Jones, Robert W., "Notes on the camp: Women, effeminacy and the military in late eighteenth-century literature," *Textual Practice* 11.3 (1997), pp. 463–476.

Jordan, Mark, *The Invention of Sodomy in Christian Theology* (Chicago: University of Chicago Press, 1997).

Joyce, Simon, "On or about 1901: The Bloomsbury Group looks back at the Victorians," *Victorian Studies* 46.4 (2004), pp. 631–654.

Kaplan, Morris B., *Sodom on the Thames: Sex, Love and Scandal in Wilde Times* (Ithaca, NY: Cornell University Press, 2005).

Katz, Jonathan Ned, *The Invention of Heterosexuality* (New York: Dutton Books, 1995).

Kelly, Jason M., "Riots, revelries, and rumor: Libertinism and masculine association in Enlightenment London," *Journal of British Studies* 45.4 (2006), pp. 759–795.

Kelly, Nigel, *Quentin Crisp: The Profession of Being* (Jefferson, NC: McFarland, 2011).

Kelsey, Sean, "Cary, Henry, first Viscount Falkland (c. 1575–1633)," *Oxford Dictionary of National Biography* (Oxford: Oxford University Press, 2004; online ed., January 2008): http://www.oxforddnb.com/view/article/4837, accessed March 14, 2013.

Kennedy, Dane, " 'Captain Burton's oriental muck heap': *The Book of the Thousand Nights* and the uses of orientalism," *Journal of British Studies* 39.3 (2000), pp. 317–339.

Keohane, Nannerl O., "Burke on his head and other postures," *Journal of Interdisciplinary History* 9.2 (1978), pp. 331–336.

King, Thomas A., *The Gendering of Men, 1600–1750*, vol. 2, *Queer Articulations* (Madison: University of Wisconsin Press, 2008).

Kingsley, Charles, *True Words for Brave Men* (London: Kegan Paul, 1878).

Kingsley, Charles, *Sanitary and Social Lectures and Essays* (London: Macmillan, 1880).

Kirschstein, Bette H., "The remasculinization of the artist and author in Ford Maddox Ford's life writing," *Biography* 21.2 (1998), pp. 153–174.

Klaver, J. M. I., *The Apostle of the Flesh: A Critical Life of Charles Kingsley*, Brill's Studies in Intellectual History 140 (Brill: Leiden, 2006).

Klein, Lawrence E., *Shaftesbury and the Culture of Politeness: Moral Discourse and Cultural Politics in Early Eighteenth-Century England* (Cambridge: Cambridge University Press, 1994).

Knox, Melissa, *Oscar Wilde: A Long and Lovely Suicide* (New Haven, CT: Yale University Press, 1994).

Kramnick, Isaac, *The Rage of Edmund Burke: Portrait of an Ambivalent Conservative* (New York: Basic Books, 1977).

Krysmanski, Bernd W., *Hogarth's Hidden Parts: Satiric Allusion, Erotic Wit, Blasphemous Bawdiness and Dark Humour in Eighteenth-Century English Art* (Hildesheim: Georg Olms, 2010).

Kubek, Elizabeth, "The man machine: horror and the phallus in *Memoirs of a Woman of Pleasure,*" in Patsy S. Fowler and Alan Jackson, eds., *Launching Fanny Hill: Essays on the Novel and Its Influences* (New York: AMS Press, 2003), pp. 173–198.

Kucich, John, *Imperial Masochism: British Fiction, Fantasy, and Social Class* (Princeton, NJ: Princeton University Press. 2007).

Kuefler, Matthew S., "Male friendship and the suspicion of sodomy in twelfth-century France," in Sharon A. Farmer and Carol Braun Pasternack, eds., *Gender and Difference in the Middle Ages* (Minneapolis: University of Minnesota Press, 2003), pp. 145–181.

Kuhn, William, *The Politics of Pleasure: A Portrait of Benjamin Disraeli* (London: Free Press, 2006).

Lake, Peter, "The significance of the Elizabethan identification of the Pope as Antichrist," *Journal of Ecclesiastical History* 31.2 (1980), pp. 161–178.

Lamarque, Peter, *Work and Object: Explorations in the Metaphysics of Art* (Oxford: Oxford University Press, 2010).

Landow, George P., *William Holman Hunt and Typological Symbolism* (New Haven, CT: Yale University Press, 1979).

Langford, Paul, "The uses of eighteenth-century politeness," *Transactions of the Royal Historical Society* 12 (2002), pp. 311–331.

Laqueur, Thomas, *Solitary Sex: A Cultural History of Masturbation* (New York: Zone, 2003).

Lawrence, Tim, "AIDS, the problem of representation, and plurality in Derek Jarman's *Blue,*" *Social Text* 52/53 (1997), pp. 241–264.

Lehmann, Rosamond, *The Echoing Grove* (London: Collins, 1953).

Leigh, Maxwell Studdy, *Winchester College, 1884–1934: A Register* (Winchester: P. and G. Wells, 1940).

Lepper, Larry, "The Rhetorical Consequences of Mr. Keynes: Intellectuals and the Communication of Economic Ideas," PhD dissertation, Victoria University of Wellington, 2010.

Levin, Gail, *Hopper's Places,* 2nd ed. (Berkeley: University of California Press, 1998).

Lewis, C. S., *Surprised by Joy: The Shape of My Early Life* (London: Geoffrey Bles, 1955).

Lewis, Wilmarth Sheldon, *Horace Walpole's Library* (Cambridge: Cambridge University Press, 1958).

Lipsedge, Karen, "Representations of the domestic parlour in Samuel Richardson's *Clarissa,* 1747–48," *Eighteenth-Century Fiction* 17.3 (2005), pp. 391–423.

Lipsedge, Karen, " 'Enter into thy closet': Women, closet culture, and the eighteenth-century," in John Styles and Amanda Vickery, eds., *Gender, Taste, and Material Culture in Britain and North America, 1700–1830* (New Haven, CT: Yale Center for British Art, 2006), pp. 107–122.

Lindsay, Suzanne G., "Emblematic aspects of Fuseli's *Artist in Despair,*" *Art Bulletin* 68.3 (1986), pp. 483–484.

Lock, F. P., *Edmund Burke,* 2 vols. (Oxford: Oxford University Press, 2006).

Lord, Catherine, "Inside the body politic: 1980–present," in Lord and Meyer (2013), pp. 29–48.

Lord, Catherine, and Richard Meyer, *Art and Queer Culture* (London: Phaidon, 2013).

Love, Heather, *Feeling Backward: Loss and the Politics of Queer History* (Cambridge, MA: Harvard University Press, 2007).

Love, Walter D., "Edmund Burke and an Irish historiographical controversy," *History and Theory* 2.2 (1962), pp. 180–198.

Lubenow, William, *The Cambridge Apostles, 1820–1914: Liberalism, Imagination, and Friendship in British Intellectual and Professional Life* (Cambridge: Cambridge University Press, 1998).

Lubenow, William, "Lytton Strachey's *Eminent Victorians*: The rise and fall of an intellectual aristocracy," in Miles Taylor and Michael Woolff, eds., *The Victorians since 1901: Histories, Representations and Revisions* (Manchester: Manchester University Press, 2004), pp. 17–28.

Lucas, Ian, *Impertinent Decorum: Gay Theatrical Manoeuvres* (Cassell: London, 1994).

Lucey, Michael, *Never Say I: Sexuality and the First Person in Colette, Gide and Proust* (Durham, NC: Duke University Press, 2006).

Lunn, Arnold, *The Harrovians* (London: Methuen, 1913).

Mack, Edward C., *Public Schools and British Opinion since 1860: The Relationship between Contemporary Ideas and the Evolution of an English Institution* (New York: Greenwood, 1941).

Mackenzie, Compton, *Sinister Street* (London: Penguin Books, 1960) [first published 1913–1914].

Mahood, Linda, and Barbara Littlewood, "The 'vicious' girl and the 'street-corner' boy: Sexuality and the gendered delinquent in the Scottish child-saving movement, 1850–1940," *Journal of the History of Sexuality* 4.4 (1994), pp. 549–578.

Maidment, Brian, "Ludlow, Henry Stephen (1861–1925)," in Laurel Brake and Marysa Demoor, eds., *Dictionary of Nineteenth-Century Journalism in Great Britain and Ireland* (London: Academia Press/British Library, 2009), p. 383.

Mallalieu, Ben, "Avant garden," *Guardian*, March 13 (2004): http://www.guardian.co.uk/travel/2004/mar/13/unitedkingdom.guardiansaturdaytravelsection, accessed October 7, 2011.

Markley, A. A., " 'The success of gentleness': Homosocial desire and the homosexual personality in the novels of William Godwin," *Queer Romanticism* 36–37 (2004–2005): http://www.erudit.org/revue/RON/2004/v/n36/011139ar.html, accessed June 1, 2013.

Marshall, Douglas A., "Temptation, tradition, and taboo: a theory of sacralization," *Sociological Theory* 28.1 (2010), pp. 64–90.

Martin, Maureen M., " 'Boys who will be men': Desire in *Tom Brown's Schooldays*," *Victorian Literature and Culture* 30 (2002), pp. 483–502.

Maskovsky, Jeff, "Do we all 'reek of the commodity'? Consumption and the erasure of poverty in lesbian and gay studies," in Ellen Lewin and William L. Leap, eds., *Out in Theory: The Emergence of Lesbian and Gay Anthropology* (Chicago: University of Illinois Press, 2002), pp. 264–286.

Maxwell, Catherine, *The Female Sublime from Milton to Swinburne: Bearing Blindness* (Manchester: Manchester University Press, 2001).

Maynard, John, *Victorian Discourses on Sexuality and Religion* (Cambridge: Cambridge University Press, 1993).

McCalman, Iain, "The virtual infernal: Philippe de Loutherbourg, William Beckford and the spectacle of the sublime," *Romanticism on the Net* 46 (2007): http://www.erudit.org/revue/ron/2007/v/n46/016129ar.html, accessed November 24, 2012.

McClive, Cathy, "Masculinity on trial: Penises, hermaphrodites and the uncertain male body in early modern France," *History Workshop Journal* 68.1 (2009), pp. 45–68.

McCuskey, Brian, "Fetishizing the flunkey: Thackeray and the uses of deviance," *Novel: A Forum on Fiction* 32.3 (1999), pp. 384–400.

McDiarmid, Lucy, "Oscar Wilde's speech from the dock," *Textual Practice* 15.3 (2001), pp. 447–466.

McDowell, Colin, "Royal clothes," in *Norman Hartnell* (Brighton: Royal Pavilion, Art Gallery and Museums, 1985), pp. 61–70.

McGuirk, Justin, "Simon Conder's rubber house," *Icon*, May 12 (2004): http://www.iconeye.com/read-previous-issues/icon-012-l-may-2004/simon-conder-s-rubber-house-l-icon-012-l-may-2004, accessed October 7, 2011.

McKay, George, *Radical Gardening: Politics, Idealism and Rebellion in the Garden* (London: Frances Lincoln, 2011).

McKenna, Neil, *The Secret Life of Oscar Wilde: An Intimate Biography* (London: Century, 2003).

McKenna, Neil, *Fanny and Stella: The Young Men Who Shocked Victorian England* (London: Faber and Faber, 2013).

McNeil, Peter, "'That doubtful gender': Macaroni dress and male sexualities," *Fashion Theory: The Journal of Dress, Body and Culture* 3.4 (1999), pp. 411–447.

McNeil, Peter, "Macaroni masculinities," *Fashion Theory: The Journal of Dress, Body and Culture* 4.4 (2000), pp. 373–404.

McNeil, Peter, "Dissipation and extravagance: Ageing fops" (Sydney: UTS E-Press, 2007): http://epress.lib.uts.edu.au/research/handle/10453/3030, accessed May 1, 2013.

Medhurst, Andy, *Victim*: Text as context', *Screen* 25.4–5 (1984), pp. 22–35.

Medhurst, Andy, *A National Joke: Popular Comedy and English Cultural Identities* (Abingdon: Routledge, 2007).

Medhurst, Andy, "One queen and his screen: Lesbian and gay television," in Glyn Davis and Gary Needham, eds., *Queer TV: Theories, Histories, Politics* (London: Routledge, 2009), pp. 79–97.

Meller, Horst, "The parricidal imagination: Schiller, Blake, Fuseli and the romantic revolt against the father," in Frederick Burwick and Jürgen Klein, eds., *The Romantic Imagination: Literature and Art in England and Germany* (Amsterdam: Rodopi, 1996), pp. 76–94.

Mellor, Leo, *Reading the Ruins: Modernism, Bombsites and British Culture* (Cambridge: Cambridge University Press, 2011).

Meyer, Moe, "Under the sign of Wilde: An archaeology of posing," in Meyer, ed., *The Politics and Poetics of Camp* (London: Routledge, 1994), pp. 75–109.

Meyer, Moe, "The signifying invert: Camp and the performance of nineteenth-century sexology," *Text and Performance Quarterly* 15.4 (1995), pp. 265–281.

Meyer, Richard, "Rock Hudson's body," in Diana Fuss, ed., *Inside/Out: Lesbian Theories, Gay Theories* (London: Routledge, 1991), pp. 259–288.

Meyer, Richard, "Nature revers'd: Satire and homosexual difference in Hogarth's London," in Bernadette Fort and Angela Rosenthal, eds., *The Other Hogarth: Aesthetics of Difference* (Princeton, NJ: Princeton University Press, 2001), pp. 162–173.

Meyer, Richard, *Outlaw Representation: Censorship and Homosexuality in Twentieth-Century American Art* (Boston: Beacon Press, 2002).

Meyer, Richard, "Gay power circa 1970: Visual strategies for sexual revolution," *GLQ* 12.3 (2006), pp. 441–464.

Millar, Oliver, *The Victorian Pictures in the Collection of Her Majesty the Queen: Text* (Cambridge: Cambridge University Press, 1992).

Miller, D. A., "Secret subjects, open secrets," *Dickens Studies Annual* 14 (1985), pp. 17–38.

Miller, D. A., *The Novel and the Police* (Berkeley: University of California Press, 1988).

Miller, James, *The Passion of Michel Foucault* (New York: Simon and Schuster, 1993).

Miller, William Ian, *The Anatomy of Disgust* (Cambridge, MA: Harvard University Press, 1997).

Milton, John, *Paradise Lost*, ed. John Leonard (London: Penguin, 2000).

Mishra, Vijay, *The Gothic Sublime* (Albany: State University of New York Press, 1994).

Mitchell, Donald, with John Evans, *Benjamin Britten, 1913–1976: Pictures from a Life* (London: Faber and Faber, 1978).

Modern House Company (undated): http://www.expertagent.co.uk, accessed October 7, 2011.

Mohr, Richard D., *Gay Ideas: Outing and other Controversies* (Boston: Beacon Press, 1992).

Moore, Alison, "Rethinking gendered perversion and degeneration in visions of sadism and masochism, 1886–1930," *Journal of the History of Sexuality* 18.1 (2009), pp. 138–157.

Moran, Leslie J., *The Homosexual(ity) of Law* (London: Routledge, 1996).

Moran, Leslie J., "Dangerous words and dead letters: Encounters with law and 'The love that dares to speak its name,'" *Liverpool Law Review* 23 (2001a), pp. 153–165.

Moran, Leslie J., "Gothic law," *Griffith Law Review* 10.2 (2001b), pp. 75–100.

Moran, Leslie J., and Derek McGhee, "Perverting London: The cartographic practices of law," *Law and Critique* 9.2 (1998), pp. 207–224.

Mowl, Timothy, *Horace Walpole: The Great Outsider* (London: John Murray, 1996).

Mowl, Timothy, *William Beckford: Composing for Mozart* (London: John Murray, 1998).

Muirhead, J. A. O., ed., *Clifton College Register, 1862–1947* (Bristol: Old Cliftonian Society, 1948).

Mulvey-Roberts, Marie, "Hogarth on the square: Framing the Freemasons," *Journal for Eighteenth-Century Studies* 26 (2003), pp. 251–270.

Munhall, Edgar, *Whistler and Montesquiou: The Butterfly and the Bat* (New York: Frick, 1995).

Munt, Sally, *Queer Attachments: The Cultural Politics of Shame* (Aldershot: Ashgate, 2007).

Murray, Martin G., "'Pete the Great': A biography of Peter Doyle," *Walt Whitman Quarterly Review* 12 Summer (1994), pp. 1–51.

Museum of Modern Art, New York, "Francis Bacon, *Painting* (1946)": http://www.moma.org/collection/object.php?object_id=79204, accessed November 6, 2011.

Muybridge, Eadweard, *Animal Locomotion: An Electro-Photographic Investigation of Connective Phases of Animal Movements* (Philadelphia: University of Pennsylvania, 1887).

Myrone, Martin, *Bodybuilding: Reforming Masculinities in British Art, 1750–1810* (New Haven, CT: Yale University Press, 2005).

Myrone, Martin, *Gothic Nightmares: Fuseli, Blake and the Romantic Reputation* (London: Tate, 2006).

Nealon, Christopher, *Foundlings: Lesbian and Gay Historical Emotion before Stonewall* (Durham, NC: Duke University Press, 2001).

Neff, David Sprague, "Bitches, mollies, and tommies: Byron, masculinity, and the history of sexualities," *Journal of the History of Sexuality* 11.3 (2002), pp. 395–438.

Nichols, John, *Biographical Anecdotes of William Hogarth* (London: Nichols, 1782).

Nichols, John Bowyer, *Anecdotes of William Hogarth [and] a Catalogue of his Prints* (London: J. B. Nichols and Son, 1833).

Nicolson, Marjorie Hope, *Mountain Gloom and Mountain Glory: The Development of the Aesthetics of the Infinite* (Seattle: University of Washington Press, 1997).

Nochlin, Linda, *The Politics of Vision: Essays on Nineteenth-Century Art and Society* (London: Thames and Hudson, 1991).

Noel, E. B., *Winchester College Cricket* (London: Williams and Norgate, 1926).

Norton, Rictor, *Mother Clap's Molly House: The Gay Subculture in England, 1700–1830* (London: GMP, 1992).

Norton, Rictor, "Lord Strutwell, 1748," *Homosexuality in Eighteenth-Century England: A Sourcebook*, February 22 (2003): http://rictornorton.co.uk/eighteen/strutwel.htm, accessed November 19, 2012.

Norton, Rictor, "The macaroni club: Homosexual scandals in 1772," in Norton, *Homosexuality in Eighteenth-Century England: A Sourcebook*, June 11 (2005): http://rictornorton.co.uk/eighteen/macaroni.htm, accessed March 10 2013.

Norton, Rictor, review, Haggerty, "Queer gothic," *Eighteenth Century Life* 32.1 (2008), pp. 96–98.

Noyes, John K., *The Mastery of Submission: Inventions of Masochism* (Ithaca, NY: Cornell University Press, 1997).

Nunokawa, Jeff, "*In Memoriam* and the extinction of the homosexual," *English Literary History* 58.2 (1991), pp. 427–438.

Nussbaum, Felicity, *The Limits of the Human: Fictions of Anomaly, Race, and Gender in the Long Eighteenth Century* (Cambridge: Cambridge University Press, 2003).

O'Brien, Henry, *The Round Towers of Ireland; or, the History of the Tuath-de-Danaans*, 2nd ed. (London: Whittaker, 1834).

O'Brien, J. R., "Photography and crime," *Metropolitan Police College Journal* (1937), pp. 225–229.

O'Donnell, Katherine, "'Dear Dicky,' 'dear Dick,' 'dear friend,' 'dear Shackleton': Edmund Burke's love for Richard Shackleton," *Studies in English Literature 1500–1900* 46.3 (2006), pp. 619–640.

Ofield, Simon, "Wrestling with Francis Bacon," *Oxford Art Journal* 24.1 (2001), pp. 113–130.

Ofield, Simon, "Cruising the archive," *Journal of Visual Culture* 4.3 (2005), pp. 351–364.

Ofield, Simon, "Cecil Beaton: designs on Francis Bacon," *Visual Culture in Britain* 7.1 (2006), pp. 21–38.

Ohi, Kevin, "Devouring creation: Cannibalism, sodomy, and the scene of analysis in *Suddenly, Last Summer*," *Cinema Journal* 38.3 (1999), pp. 27–49.

O'Neill, Alistair, *London: After a Fashion* (London: Reaktion, 2007).

O'Neill, Alistair, "Available in an array of colours," *Visual Culture in Britain* 10.3 (2009), pp. 271–291.

O'Rourke, Michael, and David Collings, "Introduction: Queer romanticisms: Past, present, and future," *Romanticism on the Net* 36–37 (2004–2005): http://www.erudit.org/revue/ron/2004/v/n36-37/011132ar.html, accessed November 20, 2012.

Palmer, Charles, "More about Queenie Gerald," *John Bull*, May 8 (1920), p. 6.

Parker, Wendy, "The reasonable person: A gendered concept," *Victoria University of Wellington Law Review* 23 (1993), pp. 105–112.

Patrick, Adele, "Queening it: Women's taste for jewelry excesses in post-war Britain," *Women and Performance* 15.2 (2005), pp. 119–146.

Paulson, Ronald, "Smollett and Hogarth: The identity of Pallet," *Studies in English Literature, 1500–1900* 4.3 (1964), pp. 351–359.

Paulson, Ronald, *Hogarth*, vol. 2, *High Art and Low, 1732–1750* (Cambridge: Lutterworth Press, 1992).

Peake, Tony, *Derek Jarman: A Biography* (London: Little Brown, 1999).

Pearman, Hugh, "The amoebic house: Simon Conder returns to Dungeness," *Gabion: Retained Writing on Architecture* (2009): http://www.hughpearman.com/2009/10.html, accessed October 7, 2011.

Pencak, William, *The Films of Derek Jarman* (Jefferson, NC: McFarland. 2002).

Peppiatt, Michael, *Francis Bacon in the 1950s* (Norwich: Sainsbury Centre for the Visual Arts, 2006).

Perriam, Chris, "Queer borders: Derek Jarman, *The Garden*," in Isabel Santaolalla, ed., *"New Exoticism": Changing Patterns in the Construction of Otherness*, Postmodern Studies 29 (Amsterdam: Rodopi, 2000), pp. 115–125.

Phillips, Kim M., and Barry Reay, *Sex before Sexuality: A Premodern History* (Cambridge: Polity Press, 2011).

Pick, Daniel, *Faces of Degeneration: A European Disorder, c. 1848–1918* (Cambridge: Cambridge University Press, 1989).

Pick, Michael, *Be Dazzled!: Norman Hartnell: Sixty Years of Glamour and Fashion* (New York: Pointed Leaf Press, 2007).

Pick, Michael, *Hardy Amies* (Woodbridge: ACC, 2012).

Piggford, George, "Camp sites: Forster and the biographies of queer Bloomsbury," in Robert K. Martin and George Piggford, eds., *Queer Forster* (Chicago: University of Chicago Press, 1997), pp. 89–112.

Pittock, Murray, "Lionel Johnson's letters to Charles Sayle," *English Literature in Transition, 1880–1920* 30.3 (1987), pp. 263–278.

Pointon, Marcia R., *Milton and English Art* (Manchester: Manchester University Press, 1970).

Prettejohn, Elizabeth, *Art for Art's Sake: Aestheticism in Victorian Painting* (New Haven, CT: Yale University Press, 2007).

Puccio, Paul M., "At the heart of *Tom Brown's Schooldays*: Thomas Arnold and Christian friendship," *Modern Language Studies* 25 (1995), pp. 57–74.

Rambuss, Richard, *Closet Devotions* (Durham, NC: Duke University Press, 1998).

Rauser, Amelia, "Hair, authenticity, and the self-made macaroni," *Eighteenth-Century Studies* 38.1 (2004), pp. 101–117.

Rawson, Claude, "I could eat you up: The life and adventures of a metaphor," *Yale Review* 97.1 (2009), pp. 82–112.

Rayne, Edward, "Hartnell, Sir Norman Bishop (1901–1979)," rev. Amy de la Haye, *Oxford Dictionary of National Biography* (Oxford: Oxford University Press, 2004; online ed., May 2008): http://www.oxforddnb.com/view/article/31209, accessed December 29, 2013.

Reed, Christopher, "Imminent domain: Queer space in the built environment," *Art Journal* 55.4 (1996), pp. 64–70.

Reed, Christopher, *Art and Homosexuality* (Oxford: Oxford University Press, 2011).

Reed, Jeremy, *This Is How You Disappear* (London: Enitharmon, 2007).

Reeve, Matthew, "Dickie Bateman and the gothicisation of Old Windsor: Gothic architecture and sexuality in the circle of Horace Walpole," *Architectural History* (2013a), pp. 99–133.

Reeve, Matthew, "Gothic architecture, sexuality and license at Horace Walpole's Strawberry Hill," *Art Bulletin* 95.3 (2013b), pp. 411–439.

Reinhold, Susan, "Through the Parliamentary looking glass: 'Real' and 'pretend' families in contemporary British politics," *Feminist Review* 48 (1994), pp. 61–79.

Rendell, Jane, "'Serpentine allurements,' disorderly bodies/disorderly spaces," in Iain Borden and Jane Rendell, eds., *Intersections: Architectural Histories and Critical Theories* (London: Routledge, 2000), pp. 247–268.

Reynolds, Nigel, "Tracey Emin enters her blue beach hut period," *Daily Telegraph*, September 13 (2000): http://www.telegraph.co.uk/news/uknews/1355181/ Tracey-Emin-enters-her-blue-beach-hut-period.html, accessed October 7, 2011.

Richards, Jeffrey, "'Passing the love of women': Manly love and Victorian society," in J. A. Mangan and James Walvin, eds., *Manliness and Morality: Middle-Class Masculinity in Britain and America, 1800–1940* (Manchester: Manchester University Press, 1987), pp. 92–122.

Richards, Jeffrey, *Happiest Days: The Public Schools in English Fiction* (Manchester: Manchester University Press, 1988).

Richardson, Niall, *The Queer Cinema of Derek Jarman* (London: I. B. Taurus, 2009).

Richlin, Amy, *The Garden of Priapus: Sexuality and Aggression in Roman Humor* (Oxford: Oxford University Press, 1992).

Richter, Anne Nellis, "Spectacle, exoticism, and display in the gentleman's house: The Fonthill auction of 1822," *Eighteenth-Century Studies* 41.4 (2008), pp. 543–563.

Robb, Graham, *Strangers: Homosexual Love in the Nineteenth Century* (London: Picador, 2003).

Roberton, Michael, *Worshipping Walt: The Whitman Disciples* (Princeton, NJ: Princeton University Press, 2008).

Robertson, D. H., review, Keynes, *"The Economic Consequences of the Peace," Economic Journal* 30.117 (1920), pp. 77–84.

Robinson, David M., *Closeted Writing and Lesbian and Gay Literature: Classical, Early Modern, Eighteenth-Century* (Aldershot: Ashgate, 2006).

Robinson, Keith, "The passion and the pleasure: Foucault's art of not being oneself," *Theory, Culture and Society* 20.2 (2003), pp. 119–144.

Robinson, Lucy, *Gay Men and the Left in Post-War Britain: How the Personal got Political* (Manchester: Manchester University Press, 2007).

Rogers, Ben, *Beef and Liberty: Roast Beef, John Bull and the English Nation* (London: Chatto and Windus, 2003).

Rogers, Pat, "Getting Horace Walpole straight," *Times Literary Supplement*, October 4 (1996), p. 33.

Rosenbaum, S. P., "Strachey, (Giles) Lytton (1880–1932)," *Oxford Dictionary of National Biography* (Oxford: Oxford University Press, online ed. 2008): http:// www.oxforddnb.com/view/article/36338, accessed April 17, 2012.

Rousseau, George, *Perilous Enlightenment: Pre- and Post-Modern Discourses—Sexual, Historical* (Manchester: Manchester University Press, 1991).

Rousseau, George, ed., *Children and Sexuality from the Greeks to the Great War* (Basingstoke: Palgrave Macmillan, 2007).

Rowbotham, Sheila, *Edward Carpenter: A Life of Liberty and Love* (London: Verso, 2008).

Ruffolo, David V., *Post-Queer Politics* (Farnham: Ashgate, 2009).

Rugoff, Ralph, with Anthony Vidler and Peter Wollen, *Scene of the Crime* (Cambridge, MA: MIT Press, 1997).

Sacher-Masoch, Leopold von, *Venus in Furs*, in *Masochism* (New York: Zone Books, 1991), pp. 143–293 [first published 1870].

Sacks, Peter, *The English Elegy: Studies in the Genre from Spenser to Yeats* (Baltimore, MD: Johns Hopkins University Press, 1985).

Samson, John, "Politics gothicized: The Conway incident and *The Castle of Otranto*," *Eighteenth Century Life* 10.3 (1986), pp. 145–158.

Santesso, Aaron, "William Hogarth and the tradition of the sexual scissors," *SEL: Studies in English Literature* 39.3 (1999), pp. 499–521.

Saslow, James M., *Pictures and Passions: A History of Homosexuality in the Visual Arts* (New York: Viking, 1999).

Savran, David, "The sadomasochist in the closet," *Contemporary Theatre Review* 8.3 (1998), pp. 79–91.

Schaffer, Talia, "Fashioning aestheticism by aestheticizing fashion: Wilde, Beerbohm, and the male aesthetes' sartorial codes," *Victorian Literature and Culture* 28.1 (2000), pp. 39–54.

Schmid, Marion, "Ideology and discourse in Proust: The making of 'M. de Charlus pendant la guerre'," *Modern Language Review* 94.4 (1999), pp. 961–977.

Schultz, David, "Redressing Oscar: Performance and the trials of Oscar Wilde," *TDR: The Drama Review* 40.2 (1996), pp. 37–59.

Sedgwick, Eve Kosofsky, *Between Men: English Literature and Male Homosocial Desire* (New York: Columbia University Press, 1985).

Sedgwick, Eve Kosofsky, *Tendencies* (Durham, NC: Duke University Press, 1993).

Sedgwick, Eve Kosofsky, *Epistemology of the Closet* (Berkeley: University of California Press, 2008) [1st ed. 1990].

Seidman, Steven, "Transfiguring sexual identity: AIDS and the contemporary construction of homosexuality," *Social Text* 19/20 (1988), pp. 187–205.

Seidman, Steven, *Beyond the Closet: The Transformation of Gay and Lesbian Life* (London: Routledge, 2002).

Seitler, Dana, "Queer physiognomies; or, how many ways can we do the history of sexuality?" *Criticism* 46.1 (2004), pp. 71–102.

Sekula, Allan, "The body and the archive," *October* 39 (1986), pp. 3–64.

Senelick, Laurence, "Mollies or men of mode? Sodomy and the eighteenth-century London stage," *Journal of the History of Sexuality* 1.1 (1990), pp. 33–67.

Shapiro, S. C., "'Yon plumed dandebrat': Male effeminacy in English satire and criticism," *Review of English Studies* 39 (1988), pp. 400–412.

Shaw, Philip, *The Sublime* (Abingdon: Routledge, 2006).

Shepard, Benjamin H., "The queer/gay assimilationist split: the suits vs. the sluts," *Monthly Review* 53.1 (2001): http://www.monthlyreview.org/0501shepard.htm, accessed March 11, 2008.

Shirland, Jonathan, "'Embryonic phantoms': Materiality, marginality and modernity in Whistler's black portraits," *Art History* 34.1 (2011), pp. 80–101.

Siegel, Jonah, *Desire and Excess: The Nineteenth-Century Culture of Art* (Princeton, NJ: Princeton University Press, 2000).

Silver, Sean R., "Visiting Strawberry Hill: Horace Walpole's gothic historiography," *Eighteenth Century Fiction* 21.4 (2009), pp. 535–564.

Simon Conder Associates, "Kent beach house 1" (undated a): http://www.simonconder.co.uk/res_dung.html, accessed October 7, 2011.

Simon Conder Associates, "Kent beach house 2" (undated b): http://www.simonconder.co.uk/res_elray.html, accessed October 7, 2011.

Simon, Robin, *Hogarth, France and British Art: The Rise of the Arts in Eighteenth-Century Britain* (London: Paul Holberton/Hogarth Arts, 2007).

Simpson, Mark, *Male Impersonators: Men Performing Masculinity* (London: Cassell, 1994).

Simpson, Mark, *Anti-Gay* (London: Cassell, 1999).

Sinfield, Alan, *The Wilde Century: Effeminacy, Oscar Wilde and the Queer Moment* (London: Cassell, 1994).

Sinfield, Alan, "The challenge of transgender, the moment of Stonewall, and Neil Bartlett," *GLQ* 10.3 (2004), pp. 267–272.

Skura, Meredith, "Elizabeth Cary and Edward II: What do women want to write?" *Renaissance Drama* 27 (1996), pp. 79–104.

Slade, Jane, "In search of the shingle life," *Daily Telegraph*, April 21 (2004): http://www.telegraph.co.uk/property/3323896/In-search-of-the-shingle-life.html, accessed October 7, 2011.

Smith, Leonard V., "Paul Fussell's *The Great War and Modern Memory*: Twenty-five years later," *History and Theory* 40.2 (2001), pp. 241–260.

Smith, W. H., *Originals Abroad* (New Haven, CT: Yale University Press, 1952).

Smollett, Tobias, *The Adventures of Roderick Random*, 2 vols. (London: J. Osborn, 1748).

Smollett, Tobias, *The Adventures of Peregrine Pickle*, 4 vols. (London: Wilson, 1751).

Snodin, Michael ed., *Horace Walpole's Strawberry Hill* (New Haven, CT: Yale University Press, 2009).

Spurr, Barry, "Camp mandarin: The prose style of Lytton Strachey," *English Literature in Transition 1880–1920* 33.1 (1990), pp. 31–45.

Spurr, Barry, *A Literary-Critical Analysis of the Complete Prose Works of Lytton Strachey (1880–1932): A Reassessment of His Work and Career,* Studies in British Literature 19 (New York: Edwin Mellen Press, 1995).

Stanworth. Karen, "Picturing a personal history: The case of Edward Onslow," *Art History* 16.3 (1993), pp. 408–423.

Steakley, James D., "Iconography of a scandal: Political cartoons and the Eulenburg affair," *Studies in Visual Communication* 9.2 (1983), pp. 20–51.

Stephen, Lauren Craig, " 'Preternatural pollutions': Nature, culture, and same-sex desire in Edward Ward's *Of the Mollies Club*," *Lumen* 24 (2005), pp. 105–120.

Stephens, F. G., *William Holman Hunt and His Works: A Memoir of the Artist's Life, with a Description of his Pictures* (London: James Nisbet, 1860).

Stephenson, Andrew, "Precarious poses: The problem of artistic visibility and its homosocial performances in late-nineteenth-century London," *Visual Culture in Britain* 8.1 (2007), pp. 71–103.

Stevenson, Warren, *Romanticism and the Androgynous Sublime* (Madison, NJ: Fairleigh Dickinson University Press, 1996).

Stewart, Allan, "The early modern closet discovered," *Representations* 50 (1995), pp. 76–100.

Stewart, Allan, *Close Readers: Humanism and Sodomy in Early Modern England* (Princeton, NJ: Princeton University Press, 1997).

Strachey, Lytton, *Eminent Victorians* (London: Chatto and Windus, 1918).

Strachey, Lytton, *Queen Victoria* (London: Chatto and Windus, 1921).

Strachey, Lytton, *Elizabeth and Essex: A Tragic History* (London: Chatto and Windus, 1928).

Stray, Christopher, "Schoolboys and gentlemen: Classical pedagogy and authority in the English public school," in Yun Lee Too and Niall Livingstone, eds., *Pedagogy and Power: Rhetorics of Classical Learning* (Cambridge: Cambridge University Press, 1998), pp. 29–46.

Street Offences Committee, *Report* (London: HMSO, 1928).

Sutherland, John, "Introduction," in Lytton Strachey, *Eminent Victorians*, ed. Sutherland (Oxford: Oxford University Press, 2003), pp. vii–xviii.

Swift, Jonathan, *A Treatise on Polite Conversation (A Compleat Collection of Genteel and Ingenious Conversation)* (Dublin: Faulkner, 1738).

Sylvester, David, "Bacon's course," in Achille Bonito Oliva, ed., *Figurabile: Francis Bacon* (Milan: Electa, 1993a), pp. 19–86.

Sylvester, David, *Interviews with Francis Bacon*, 3rd ed. (London: Thames and Hudson, 1993b).

Symonds, John Addington, *Memoirs*, ed. Phyllis Grosskurth (London: Hutchinson, 1984).

Taddeo, Julie, "Plato's Apostles: Edwardian Cambridge and the new style of love," *Journal of the History of Sexuality* 8.2 (1997), pp. 196–228.

Taddeo, Julie, *Lytton Strachey and the Search for Modern Sexual Identity: The Last Eminent Victorian* (New York: Harrington Park, 2002).

Tagg, John, *The Burden of Representation: Essays on Photographies and Histories* (Basingstoke: Macmillan, 1998).

Tamagne, Florence, *A History of Homosexuality in Europe: Berlin, London, Paris, 1919–1939* (New York: Algora Publishing. 2004).

Tambling, Jeremy, *Confession: Sexuality, Sin and the Subject* (Manchester: Manchester University Press, 1990).

Tate Online, "Study of a dog 1952" (London: Tate Gallery, undated): http://www.tate.org.uk, accessed November 24, 2011.

Thackeray, William Makepeace, *Vanity Fair: A Novel Without a Hero* (New York: Harper, 1848).

Thomas, Bernard, ed., *Repton, 1557 to 1957* (London: B. T. Batsford, 1957).

Thomas, Philip A., "The nuclear family, ideology and AIDS in the Thatcher years," *Feminist Legal Studies* 1.1 (1993), pp. 23–44.

Tindall, Gillian, *Rosamond Lehmann: An Appreciation* (London: Chatto and Windus, 1985).

Toda, Ángeles, "The construction of male-male relationships in the Edwardian age: E. M. Forster's *Maurice*, H. A. Vachell's *The Hill*, and public school ideology," *Atlantis* 23.2 (2001), pp. 133–145.

Todd, Dennis, *Imagining Monsters: Miscreations of the Self in Eighteenth-Century England* (Chicago: University of Chicago Press, 1995).

Townsend, Dale, "'Love in a convent': or, gothic and the perverse father of queer enjoyment," in William Hughes and Andrew Smith, eds., *Queering the Gothic* (Manchester: Manchester University Press, 2009), pp. 11–35.

Traub, Valerie, "Friendship's loss: Alan Bray's making of history," *GLQ* 10.3 (2004), pp. 339–365.

Tromans, Nicholas, "Palestine: Picture of prophecy," in Katherine Lochnan and Carol Jacobi, eds., *Holman Hunt and the Pre-Raphaelite Vision* (Toronto: Art Gallery of Ontario, 2008), pp. 135–160.

Troy, Frederick S., "Edmund Burke and the break with tradition: History vs psychohistory," *Massachusetts Review* 22.1 (1981), pp. 93–132.

Trumbach, Randolph, *Sex and the Gender Revolution*, vol. 1, *Heterosexuality and the Third Gender in Enlightenment London* (Chicago: University of Chicago Press, 1998).

Trumbach, Randolph, "Blackmail for sodomy in eighteenth-century London," *Historical Reflections/Réflexions Historiques* 33.1 (2007a), pp. 23–39.

Trumbach, Randolph, "Renaissance sodomy, 1500–1700" and "Modern sodomy: The origins of homosexuality, 1700–1800," in Matt Cook, ed., *A Gay History of Britain* (Oxford: Greenwood, 2007b), pp. 45–105.

Trumbach, Randolph, "The transformation of sodomy from the Renaissance to the modern world and its general sexual consequences," *Signs* 37.4 (2012), pp. 832–847.

Tuite, Clara, "Cloistered closets: Enlightenment pornography, the confessional state, homosexual persecution and *The Monk*," *Romanticism on the Net* 8 (1997): http://www.erudit.org/revue/ron/1997/v/n8/005766ar.html, accessed October 25, 2012.

Turner, James, "The libertine sublime: Love and death in Restoration England," *Studies in Eighteenth-Century Culture* 19 (1989), pp. 99–116.

Upchurch, Charles, *Before Wilde: Sex Between Men in Britain's Age of Reform* (Berkeley: University of California Press, 2009).

Urbach, Henry, "Closets, clothes, disclosure," *Assemblage* 30 (1996), pp. 62–73.

Valeri, Valerio, *The Forest of Taboos: Morality, Hunting and Identity among the Huaulu of the Moluccas* (Madison: University of Wisconsin Press, 1999).

Vallancey, Charles, *A Vindication of the Ancient History of Ireland* (Dublin: Luke White, 1786).

Vassal, Gabrielle, "Annam I: Its quaint folk, civilized and savage," in J. A. Hammerton, ed., *Peoples of all Nations: Their Life Today and Story of their Past*, vol. 1 [of 7] (London: Fleetway House, 1922–1924), pp. 121–166.

Vicinus, Martha, "'The gift of love': Nineteenth-century religion and lesbian passion," *Nineteenth-Century Contexts* 23 (2001), pp. 241–264.

Vickers, Hugo, *Cecil Beaton: The Authorised Biography* (London: Weidenfeld and Nicolson, 1985).

Vickers, Hugo, "Beaton, Sir Cecil Walter Hardy (1904–1980)," *Oxford Dictionary of National Biography* (Oxford: Oxford University Press, 2004; online ed., 2008): http://www.oxforddnb.com/view/article/30801, accessed February 7, 2013.

Volke-Birke, Sabine, "Questions of taste: The critic as connoisseur and the hungry reader," in Marion Gymnich and Norbert Lennartz, eds., *The Pleasures and Horrors of Eating* (Bonn: Bonn University Press, 2010), pp. 165–186.

Wade, Alex, "The £100,000 beach hut: The humble beach hut has grown into a luxury bolthole," *The Times*, October 10 (2008): http://property.timesonline.co.uk/tol/life_and_style/property/buying_and_selling/article4912355.ece, accessed October 7, 2011.

Wagner, Peter, *Eros Revived: Erotica of the Enlightenment in England and America* (London: Paladin, 1990).

Wagner, Peter, "The artistic framing of English nationalism in Hogarth's *The Gate of Calais, or The Roast Beef of Old* England," in Frédéric Ogée, ed., *"Better in France?": The Circulation of Ideas across the Channel in the Eighteenth Century* (Lewisburg: Bucknell University Press, 2005), pp. 71–87.

Wainewright, John Bannerman, ed., *Winchester College, 1836–1906: A Register* (Winchester: P. and G. Wells, 1907).

Waites, Matthew, "Homosexuality and the new right: The legacy of the 1980s for new delineations of homophobia," *Sociological Research Online* 5.1 (2000): http://www.socresonline.org.uk/5/1/waites.html, accessed March 20, 2012.

Wall, Cynthia, "*The Castle of Otranto*: A Shakespeareo-political satire?" in Lorna Clymer and Robert Mayer, eds., *Historical Boundaries, Narrative Forms: Essays on British Literature in the Long Eighteenth-Century in Honor of Everett Zimmerman* (Cranbury, NJ: Associated University Presses, 2007), pp. 184–198.

Walpole, Horace, *An Account of the Giants Lately Discovered* (London: F. Noble, 1766).

Walpole, Horace, *A Description of the Villa of Mr. Horace Walpole* (Strawberry Hill: Thomas Kirkgate, 1784).

Walpole, Horace, *The Correspondence*, 48 vols, ed. W. S. Lewis (New Haven, CT: Yale University Press, 1937–1983).

Walpole, Horace, *The Castle of Otranto*, eds. W. S. Lewis and E. J. Clery (Oxford: Oxford University Press, 1998) [1st ed. 1764].

Walters, Suzanna Danuta, *All the Rage: The Story of Gay Visibility in America* (Chicago: University of Chicago Press, 2001).

Watney, Simon, "The spectacle of AIDS," *October* 43 (1987), pp. 71–86.

Watson, Nicola J., "Gloriana Victoriana: Victoria and the cultural memory of Elizabeth I," in Margaret Homans and Adrienne Munich, eds., *Remaking Queen Victoria* (Cambridge: Cambridge University Press, 1997), pp. 79–104.

Waugh, Alec, *The Loom of Youth* (London: Grant Richards, 1917).

Waugh, Alec, *Public School Life: Boys, Parents, Masters* (London: W. Collins, 1922).

Waugh, Auberon, "Waugh, Alexander Raban (1898–1981)," *Oxford Dictionary of National Biography* (Oxford: Oxford University Press, online ed., 2011): http://www.oxforddnb.com/view/article/31813, accessed April 13, 2012.

Waugh, Thomas, "Films by gays for gays," *Jump Cut* 16 (1977), pp. 14–18.

Weeks, Jeffrey, "Inverts, perverts and Mary-Annes: Male prostitution and the regulation of homosexuality in England in the nineteenth and early twentieth centuries," *Journal of Homosexuality* 6.1–2 (1980–1981), pp. 113–134.

Weeks, Jeffrey, *The Languages of Sexuality* (London: Routledge, 2011).

West, Shearer, "The Darly macaroni prints and the politics of 'private man,'" *Eighteenth Century Life* 25.2 (2001), pp. 170–182.

White, Rob, "Homosexuality and *The Third Man*," BFI Screen-Online (undated): http://www.screenonline.org.uk/film/id/591536, accessed November 1, 2011.

Widdicombe, Gillian, "The good companions," *Observer, Review Section*, March 30 (1980), p. 33.

Wiebe, Heather, "'Now and England': Britten's *Gloriana* and the 'New Elizabethans,'" *Cambridge Opera Journal* 17.2 (2005), pp. 141–172.

Wilde, Oscar, *The Picture of Dorian Gray*, ed. Robert Mighall (London: Penguin, 2003).

Williams, Anne, *Art of Darkness: A Poetics of Gothic* (Chicago: University of Chicago Press, 1995).

Williams, Anne, "Horace in Italy: Discovering a gothic imagination," *Gothic Studies* 8.1 (2006), pp. 22–35.

Williams, Gordon, *A Dictionary of Sexual Language and Imagery in Shakespearean and Stuart Literature* (London: Athlone Press, 1994).

Williams, Kenneth, *The Kenneth Williams Diaries*, ed. Russell Davies (London: HarperCollins, 1993).

Wilper, James, "Sexology, homosexual history, and Walt Whitman: The "Uranian" identity in *Imre: A Memorandum*," *Critical Survey* 22.3 (2010), pp. 52–68.

Wymer, Rowland, *Derek Jarman* (Manchester: Manchester University Press, 2005).

Young, Allen, "Out of the closets, into the streets," in Jay and Young (1992), pp. 6–31.

Zoberman, Pierre, "Queer(ing) pleasure: Having a gay old time in the culture of early-modern France," in Paul Allen Miller and Greg Forter, eds., *The Desire of the Analysts* (Albany: State University of New York Press, 2008), pp. 225–252.

Žižek, Slavoj, "What Rumsfeld doesn't know that he knows about Abu Ghraib," *In these Times*, May 24 (2004): http://http://www.inthesetimes.com/article/747, accessed November 20, 2012.

Britten, Benjamin, 24, 137, 173, 176, **177**
Britten, Benjamin, *Death in Venice*, 177
Britten, Benjamin, *Gloriana*, 137
Britten, Benjamin, *Peter Grimes*, 177
Brooks, Frederic, 104
Browne, Martin, *A Dream of Youth*, 124
Browning, Oscar, 119
Bull, Richard, 58
Burke, Edmund, 20, 41–52, 55, 60, 62, 66, 71, 73, 77, 81, 89, 97, 100, 161, 189–190
Burke, Edmund, personal life of, 45–47
Burke, Edmund, and masochism, 49
Burke, Edmund, and sodomy, 46–47
Burke, Edmund, *A Philosophical Enquiry*, 20, 44–48, 51–52
Burke, William, 46–47
Burnet, Thomas, 42–43
Burnet, Thomas, *Telluris Theoria Sacra*, 42
Burton, Richard Francis, *Arabian Nights*, 89
Byron, John, 56, 57
Byron, John, *An Account of the Giants*, 56

Cairo, 88
Calais, 31, 36, 38
Cambridge, 98, 108, 111
Camp, 10, 16, 19 n71, 27, 105, 163, 169, 188
Carpenter, Edward, 103, **104**, 105
Carr, Joseph Comyns, 109
Carter, John, 57
Cary, Henry, 66
Cather, John, 64
Catholicism, Roman, 15–16, 42, 45, 98, 110, 113
Celibacy, 99
Charles II, king of England, 27, 57
Chartres, 111
Cheltenham College, 126
Chesterfield, 104
Children, 92–93, 114–115, 119–135
Christ, Jesus, 5, 15, 61, 90, 103, 190
Christian socialism, 97
civil rights movement, 45. *See also* lesbian and gay liberation
Clap, Mother [Margaret], 1, 29
class, 96–105
Cleland, John, *Memoirs of a Woman of Pleasure*, 33, 60
Clifton College, 126, 128, 129–31
Clondalkin, **75**
closet, as physical space, 13, 19, 54, 63, 169–170
closet, come out of, 13, 17, 24, 170–173, **174**, 175
closet, definition of, 12
closet, origins of, 12–13
closet, spectacle of the, 5–9, 67, 77–79, 100–103, 107, 117, 135, 141, 163–169, 191
clubs, queer, 23, 151–154, 157–159
Cole, William, 57
coming out, origins of the term, 16–17
Conder, Simon, 181, **182**
confession, 15
Conservative Party, 179
Constantine the Great, Roman emperor, 67
consumerism, 19, 31, 169, 184
Conway, Henry Seymour, 63–64

Coronation, of Elizabeth II, 23, 137–138, **165, 166**
Cory, William Johnson, 119
Cosmetics, 140, 153–155
Courtenay, William, 73
courtiers, 14, 23, 164–169
Cozens, John Robert, *Satan Summoning His Legions*, **72**
Crimean War, 113
Criminal Law Amendment Act (1912), 155
Crisp, Quentin, 10–12, 140
Crisp, Quentin, *The Naked Civil Servant*, 10–11
Cromwell, Oliver, 57
cross-dressing. *See* drag
crucifix, 33
cruising, 1

D'Éon, Chevalier, 60
Damietta, 88
Dandyism, 5, 7, 82–83, 101, 108
Dashwood, Francis, 33
Dead Sea, 89
Deakin, John, 152
De Charlus, Baron, character in Proust, *Remembrance of Things Past*, 5–6, 8–9, 101, 153
De Gandarillas, Antonio, 166, **167**
De Hegedus, Adam. *See* Garland, Rodney
De Montesquiou-Fezensac, Robert, 6–9, 18, 105
Deism, 42
Dennis, John, 43–44
depression, 51
De Saulcy, Louis, 87
Dilettanti, Society of, 33
discourse, 13
disgust, 160
Disorderly Houses Act (1751), 142–143, 159
Disraeli, Benjamin, 114
diva worship, 168–169
Dorn, Marion, 76–77, **78**
Douglas, Alfred, 122, 128, 132–133
Douglas, Alfred, *Autobiography*, 122
Douglas, John Sholto, 87
Dover, 38
Doyle, Peter, 97
drag, 7, 10, 30, 37, 145–146, 166–167, 173
Duff, Charles Michael, 166–167
Dungeness, 24, 180–181, **182**, 184–185, 189–190

Eblis, character in Beckford, *Vathek*, 70–72
Edward VIII, king of England, 157
Effeminacy, 10–12, 14, 18, 20–21, 23, 25, 63–64, 67, 77, 99–100, 111, 135, 145, 155
Elizabeth I, queen of England, 114, 137
Elizabeth II, queen of England, 23, **164, 165**
Ellesmere College, 120
Ellis, Edith, *Personal Impressions of Edward Carpenter*, 103–104
Ellis, Havelock, 103, 121–122, 133
Emin, Tracey, 182–183
Enlightenment, 20, 25, 27, 33
Epicurus, 42
Eton College, 119, 120, 124, 134
Eulenberg affair, 5–6

eyes, 70–71, 77–78
expulsion, from public schools, 120–135

Faber, Geoffrey, 110
fashion, 39–40, 164–168
Fearon, William, 131–132
Fielding, Henry, 31, 33–34
Fielding, Henry, *The Grub Street Opera,* 31–32
Fielding, Henry, *The Life and Death of Jonathan Wild,* 34
Firbank, Ronald, 9
Fitch, Charles, 16
Florence, city in Italy, 36
Fonthill, Wiltshire, 72–75, **76**
Fops, 14
Forrest, Theodosius, 34
Forster, Edward Morgan, 97–98, 102–103
Forster, Edward Morgan, *Maurice,* 102–103
Foucault, Michel, 13, 15, 50
Fra Angelico, 111
France, 4, 20, 27, 30–40, 42, 59
France, Philippe de, 27
freemasonry, 70
Freud, Sigmund. *See* psychoanalysis
Friars, 33, 38
friendship, 46–47, 55, 124
Froude, Richard Hurrell, 112
Fuseli, Henry, 67–69
Fuseli, Henry, *Drawing of a Figure,* 67

Ganymede, 15, 33
Garland, Rodney, *The Heart in Exile,* 139–141
Garrick, David, 14
gay and lesbian liberation, 3, 11, 13, 17, 20, 24,
    171–173, 191
gay, origin of the term, 2
Gerald, Queenie, 153
Germany, 16
Gérôme, Jean-Léon, 92–93
Gérôme, Jean-Léon, *The Snake Charmer,* **93**
giants, 55–56, 65
glasses, 85
Glorious Revolution, 27
Gobat, Samuel, bishop of Jerusalem, 90
God, 3, 15, 42–44, 54, 97
Gold, Jack, 10
Golding, William, 74, 75 n95
Gothic, 6, 37, 59, 60, 67, 74 n91
Gordon, Charles George, 110, 114–115
Goursat, Georges, 7–8
Goursat, Georges, *Robert de Montesquiou,* **8**
Grand Tour, 53, 62
Graves, Robert, *Goodbye to All That,* 133
Gray, Thomas, 36, 53–55, 60, 111
Gray, Thomas, "Elegy Written in a Country Churchyard," 61
Greatheed, Bertie, 67–69
Greatheed, Bertie, *Manfred's Servants Frightened,* **68**
Greatheed, Bertie, *The Destruction of the Castle,* **69**
Greece, ancient, 122
Greene, Graham, 120
Guthrie, William, 63–65

Hadrian, Roman emperor, 33
Hall, Radclyffe, 113
Hallward, Basil, character in Wilde, *Dorian Gray,* 6
Hamilton, Anthony, 59–60
Hamilton, Anthony, "Le Bélier," 59
Hammerton, John Alexander, *Peoples of All Nations,*
    150, 151
Hardy, Keir, 152
Haring, Keith, **170**, 171
Harrow School, 119, 122, 124–125
Hartnell, Norman, 167, **168**
Hazlitt, William, 76
Herculaneum, 68
hermaphrodites, 40, 59, 65
Hill, Fanny, character in Cleland, *Memoirs of a Woman of
    Pleasure,* 3, 60
HIV, 185. *See also* AIDS
Hogarth, William, 20, 31–40, 42
Hogarth, William, and Francophobia, 31–32, 37
Hogarth, William, and sodomy, 32–33, 35–38
Hogarth, William, *The Analysis of Beauty,* 33
Hogarth, William, *An Election,* 35
Hogarth, William, *Gate of Calais,* 20, 31–33, **37**
Hogarth, William, *Marriage à-la-Mode,* 32
Hogarth, William, *The Marriage Contract,* 33
Hogarth, William, *The Rake's Progress,* 34
Hogarth, William, *The Shrimp Girl,* 36
Hogarth, William, *Sir Francis Dashwood at his Devotions,* 33
Hollinghurst, Alan, *The Swimming Pool Library,* 9
Homo sacer, 95
homophobia, 14, 38, 76, 163
homosexual, origin of term, 2
homosexual panic. *See* panic, homosexual
homosociality, 20–25, 27, 35, 81, 96–97
Hood, Jack, *The Heart of a Schoolboy,* 124
Hooker, Evelyn, 17
Hopkins, Gerard Manley, 98
Hopper, Edward, *South Carolina Morning,* 181, **182**
Horton v. Mead, 154
Housman, Alfred Edward, 97
Hudson, Rock, 186
Hughes, Thomas, 98–99
Hunt, William Holman, 23, 87, **88**, 91–94, 190
Hunt, William Holman, and sodomy, 87–94
Hunt, William Holman, and orientalism, 87–94
Hunt, William Holman, *The Finding of the Saviour in the
    Temple,* 91, **92**, 93–94
Hunt, William Holman, *The Scapegoat,* **89**, 91–92
Hurt, John, 10

impersonation, male, 100
incest, 65
institutions, introduction to culture of, 81–83
inversion, 87, 121–122, 133, 140
Ireland, 45, 59, 74–75
Islam, 89
Italy, 69

Jacobites, 30
Jamaica, 73

Otranto. *See* Walpole, Horace, *The Castle of Otranto*
outing, 21, 63–64, 73, 170–171
Oxford, 85–86, 111, 122
Oxford Movement, 99, 110–112

Pallet, character in Smollett, *Peregrine Pickle*, 37
panic, homosexual, 3, 20, 37, 49
panic, sodomitical, 12, 20, 37, 49
papacy, 16, 157
Paris, 7, 155
Park, Frederick, 82
Parliament (United Kingdom), 42, 46
patriarchy, 51, 100
Patriotism, British, 23, 32, 164–166
Pears, Peter, 173, 176, **177**
pedophilia, 92–93, 114–115, 119, 135
Pelham-Clinton, Henry, 62
penetration, 43, 48, 185
perversion, 11, 49, 99
phallicism, 54, 60, 72, 74
Philadelphia, dir. Jonathan Demme, 187
Pillory, 41–42, 49
Pine, John, 36
Plomer, William, 137
Police, Metropolitan, 23, 141–143, 145–148, 153–155, 157–159, 161
politeness, 78
pollution, anthropological concept of, 94–95, 159
pose, 7–9, 85
post-gay, 13, 191
postmodernism, 19
post-queer, 13, 191
power, 3, 9, 23, 44, 49–52, 56, 161
prayer, 15
priest, 15, 38, 110–112
prison, 17
promiscuity, 50, 190
Prospect Cottage, Dungeness, 180–181, 189
prostitution, 23, 33–34, 124, 142, 153–154
Protestantism, 15–16, 20, 45
Proust, Marcel, 4–8, 12, 83, 87, 101
Proust, Marcel, *Remembrance of Things Past*, 5–8
psychoanalysis, 16, 45–46, 49, 94, 119, 137
public schools. *See* schools, public
Punch, 99

quaens. *See* queens
queens, 10, **11**, 140–141, 167
Queensbury, Lord. *See* Douglas, John Sholto
queer, definition of, 2, 47, 108

Radley College, 125
rakes, 15, 20, 35, 38
rape, male, 43
reasonable man, legal test, 144
Reed, Jeremy, 190
Reformation, 15–16
Renaissance, 14–15

Repton School, 126–128
respectability, 21
Revelation, biblical book of, 16
Rex v. Billie Joyce and Others, 155
Rex v. Britt and Others, 145–151
Rex v. Neave and Others, 153, 157–159
Rex v. Rosenz and Others, 141–142
rhetoric, classical, 43
Richard II, king of England, 66
Richardson, Samuel, *Clarissa*, 63
Rochester, Lord. *See* Wilmot, John
Roman Catholicism. *See* Catholicism, Roman
Rome, ancient, 67–70, 95
Ross, Robert, 128
Round the Horne, radio series, 163
Round towers, Irish, 75–76
Rugby School, 115–117
Rumsfeld, Donald, 24
Rutter, John, 75–76
Rutter, John, *View of Fonthill*, **76**

Saatchi, Charles, 183
Sacher-Masoch, Leopold von, 49, 52
Sacher-Masoch, Leopold von, *Venus in Furs*, 52
sadomasochism, 49–52, 100, 152–153
sadomasochism, and the sublime, 49–52, 161
Satan, 71–72
scapegoat, 9, 41, 89–91, 94–96, 101, 134
scapegoat, in the Old Testament, 89–91, 94–96
scatology, 56
scent, 148, 157–158
schools, public, 22–23, 115–117, 119–138
sculpture, Roman, 67–68
secrecy, 12–13, 15, 18
secretary, 13
Sedgwick, Eve Kosofsky, 3–7, 12–14, 18–21, 27, 37, 87, 101, 171
Sedgwick, Eve Kosofsky, and the 1980s, 3, 13, 171
Selznick, David O., 120
Sem. *See* Goursat, Georges
Seventh-day Adventists, 16
Sexual Offences Act (1967), 18
Shackleton, Richard, 46–47, 55, 62
Shakespeare, William, 66
shame, gay, 17, 48, 151, 191
Sheffield, 103
sin, 3, 23, 71, 190
slavery, 73
Smollett, Tobias, 29, 35–37
Smollett, Tobias, *The Adventures of Peregrine Pickle*, 37
Smollett, Tobias, *The Adventures of Roderick Random*, 29, 35
Society of Dilettanti, 33
Sodom, biblical city of, 3, 33, 43, 87–89
sodomitical panic. *See* panic, sodomitical
sodomy, English law, 41
sodomy, origins of term, 2
Solomon, Simeon, 82
Sontag, Susan, 12